*Seurat and the Science of Painting*

# Seurat and the Science of Painting

*by William Innes Homer*

The M.I.T. Press
Massachusetts Institute of Technology
Cambridge, Massachusetts

Second printing, February, 1970
First MIT Press paperback edition, September 1978

ISBN 0 262 08018 4 (hardcover)
ISBN 0 262 58036 5 (paperback)
Library of Congress Catalog Card number: 64-15751

*To Virginia*

# Preface

FORTUNATELY, MUCH IS ALREADY known about the life and work of Georges Seurat (1859–1891), one of the leading French painters of the nineteenth century and instigator of the Neo-Impressionist movement. Through the collective efforts of art historians and critics, there have been studies of various aspects of his style, several reliable biographies, and two catalogues of his work. However, in publications on the artist, relatively little attention has been devoted to his theories of painting and their sources — particularly in nineteenth-century scientific thought. It is well known, for example, that he carefully studied the principles of light and color promulgated by such scientists as Chevreul, Maxwell, and Rood, and that under the influence of Charles Henry he became acquainted with psychological laws governing the expressive value of color, tone, and line. In addition, he hoped to find in the work of earlier painters and in the writings of academic art theorists further solutions to the problems that confronted him. But, with a few exceptions, historians of art have not delved very deeply into the complexities of Seurat's theories and

their application in his paintings, preferring merely to list the sources
he is known to have consulted. After surveying existing writings on
the subject, it became apparent to me that his theories of color and expression still required considerable explanation and that their basis in
nineteenth-century science and art remained to be probed in depth.

Because Seurat was strongly influenced by a number of major
discoveries in physics, optics, and experimental psychology, I tried
to explore as thoroughly as possible the range of his scientific
knowledge and to show how it contributed to his theory, technique, and method. This study, too, involved detailed analysis of
the application of scientific principles in a group of his paintings.
As a result, one may receive the impression, incorrectly, that
Seurat was nothing more than a scientist working in a laboratory,
oblivious to the intuitive elements that enter into the creation of
significant works of art. I have tried to counteract this impression
by pointing out in the last chapter that his scientific and psychological theories were not infallible rules to be followed mechani-
cally, but, rather, comprised an "exact and demonstrated basis,"
as one of his friends put it, which served to guide his vision and
the expressive content of his paintings.

To some readers such a careful examination of a narrowly
demarcated area in the history of art may seem too restricted in
scope. But in writing this book, I followed a personal conviction,
reinforced by the counsel of my former professor and adviser,
Dr. Frederick B. Deknatel, that nineteenth-century scholarship
today requires not so much the broad, synthetic survey but,
rather, a solid foundation in more specialized studies on the basis
of which (if we are fortunate) meaningful surveys may one day
be written. Therefore, it is hoped that the conclusions reached in
the following pages will bring about a better comprehension of
Seurat's art and theory and will contribute to an understanding
of his position in the history of modern painting.

In the course of writing this book, I enjoyed the generous cooperation of numerous individuals and organizations. First I

PREFACE

should like to express my debt to Richard F. Brown, whose graduate seminar on color theory, given at Harvard University, provided the initial impetus for this study. In the early stages of writing, I profited from discussions and correspondence with Frederick B. Deknatel, Henri Dorra, John Rewald, and Meyer Schapiro. As the work progressed, I had occasion to consult several other art historians who made suggestions that were particularly valuable: André Chastel, Sir Kenneth Clark, Donald Drew Egbert, Lee Johnson, S. Rees Jones, Benedict Nicolson, Robert Rosenblum, Mark Roskill, and William C. Seitz; in addition, Charles Gillispie's recommendations about sources in the history of science proved to be quite useful.

To those who were kind enough to read and criticize parts of the manuscript I owe a great debt of gratitude: Charles Dempsey, Donald Drew Egbert, George Mras, Richard E. Quandt, A. Schroeder, and Dr. Jean Sutter.

A number of museum officials and librarians who facilitated my research deserve special mention here: Jean Adhémar, Ronald Alley, Mme. Jacqueline Bouchot-Saupique, Mme. W. Bouleau-Rabaud, Germain Calmette, Mme. Geneviève Homolle, Mme. Andrée Jaillant, Daniel Catton Rich, and Ian Robertson.

I also received the cooperation of a group of private collectors and art dealers who kindly made works by Seurat and his circle available for study: the late Stephen C. Clark, Miss Patricia Davis, Samuel Josefowitz, S. Kramarsky, Henry P. McIlhenny, Mr. and Mrs. Hugo Perls, Jacques Rodrigues-Henriques, M. R. Schweitzer, and the late Georges Wildenstein; also, the Hammer Galleries, Marlborough Fine Art, Ltd., and Parke-Bernet Galleries.

This book could not have been written without the assistance of Mme. Ginette Signac, Paul Signac's daughter, and César M. de Hauke, friend of the late Félix Fénéon. Both gave me access to important documents relating to Seurat and the Neo-Impressionist movement, and patiently answered many of my queries. Pierre Angrand, Mme. Françoise Cachin, Miss Orovida C. Pissarro, Guy Pogu, and Dr. Jean Sutter also provided much helpful information.

The translations of French texts quoted in this book were made by Myron Newman, whose skill and perseverance deserve more recognition than this brief mention. I also wish to thank Edward Fry for research assistance in Paris and for taking the photographs for Figures 44 and 45.

A Sachs Traveling Research Fellowship, Harvard University, and grants from the Spears Research Fund and from the Committee on Research in the Humanities and Social Sciences, Princeton University, enabled me to travel to Europe for work on this project in 1957 and 1962. I am particularly indebted to the Spears Fund for subsidizing my photographic expenses. The book was completed in 1962–1963 under a Junior Fellowship of the Council of the Humanities, Princeton University.

The costs of manufacturing and printing the color plates were covered by generous grants from the Department of Art and Archaeology Publication Fund, Princeton University, and from the Wildenstein Foundation, New York.

Lastly, I wish to acknowledge the very real help of my wife, an artist in her own right, who followed the progress of the book with unflagging interest and made many valuable suggestions.

WILLIAM INNES HOMER

*Department of Art and Archaeology*
*Princeton University*
*June 1, 1963*

NOTES ON THE SECOND PRINTING

Rereading this book after six years, it still seems to me valid; there is little that I would change. Several factual errors and misprints have been corrected in the second printing, and a list of selected publications that appeared between 1964 and 1970 has been added to the bibliography. Art historians have shown much interest in the book, but I am gratified, too, by the fact that painters have also found it useful.

W. I. H.

# Contents

Preface

Contents

List of Illustrations       xiii

1   Introduction       1

2   *Une Baignade* and the Origins of Neo–Impressionism       13
     SEURAT'S EARLY CAREER       13
     SCIENTIFIC AND THEORETICAL SOURCES       20
     STYLISTIC SOURCES       48
     *UNE BAIGNADE:* STYLISTIC AND THEORETICAL SOURCES       54
     THE ROLE OF THE PREPARATORY DRAWINGS FOR
     *UNE BAIGNADE*       101

3   The Theory, Technique, and Methods of
    Chromo-luminarism (1884–1887)       112
     THE PREPARATORY STUDIES FOR *LA GRANDE JATTE*       115
     *UN DIMANCHE À LA GRANDE JATTE* (1884–1886)       131
     ASPECTS OF SEURAT'S CHROMO-LUMINARIST TECHNIQUE
     AND METHOD: *LES POSEUSES* AND *LA PARADE*       164

4   Seurat's Theories of Expression,
    Their Sources and Application (1887–1891)       180
     THE CHANGE IN SEURAT'S INTERESTS AFTER 1886       180
     CHARLES HENRY AND SEURAT'S LATER THEORY OF ART       188
     THE THEORETICAL BASIS OF SEURAT'S LATER PAINTINGS       217

5   Seurat and Science       235

    Epilogue       250

    Notes       259

    Selected Bibliography       305

    Index       319

# List of Illustrations

*(All paintings and drawings are by Seurat unless otherwise noted.)*

*Figure*

1 Chromatic Circle (from Arthur Pope, *The Language of Drawing and Painting*). 7

2 Tone Solid (from Pope, *op. cit.*). 7

3 Diagram of Values and Hues (from Pope, *op. cit.*). 7

4 Subtractive Mixture Diagram. 9

5 Additive Mixture Diagram. 10

6 *Une Baignade, Asnières*, Tate Gallery, London (on deposit in the National Gallery, London). 16

7 Chromatic Circle (from M.-E. Chevreul, *De la loi du contraste simultané des couleurs*). 22

8*A* Harmony of Analogous Hues on the Same Scale. (Based on Chevreul.) 23

8*B* Harmony of Analogous Hues on Neighboring Scales. 23

8*C* Harmony of Contrasting Hues on the Same Scale. 25

8*D* Harmony of Contrasting Hues on Neighboring Scales. 25

8*E* Harmonies of Hues on Complementary Scales. 26

9 Chromatic Diagram (from Charles Blanc, *Grammaire des arts du dessin*). 31

10 Diagram Illustrating Optical Mixture (from Blanc, *op. cit.*). 32

11 Diagrams Illustrating Methods of Optical Mixture (from Blanc, *op. cit.*). 33

12 Color-Mixing Apparatus with Maxwell's Discs (from Amédée Guillemin, *La Lumière et les couleurs*). 37

13 Color Triangle (from O. N. Rood, *Students' Text-Book of Color, or Modern Chromatics*). 38

14 Contrast-Diagram (from Rood, *op. cit.*). 40

15 Contrast-Diagram (from Rood, *Théorie scientifique des couleurs*). 41

16 Seurat's Copy of Rood's Contrast-Diagram, Mme. Ginette Signac Collection, Paris. 41

17 Chromatic Diagram (from David Sutter, *Philosophie des beaux-arts*). 44

LIST OF ILLUSTRATIONS

*Figure*

18  Eugène Delacroix, *La Lutte de Jacob et de l'ange*, Chapelle des Saints-Anges, Saint-Sulpice, Paris. (Photo Bulloz.)  52

19  Delacroix, *Héliodore chassé du Temple*, Chapelle des Saints-Anges, Saint-Sulpice, Paris. (Photo Bulloz.)  53

20  *Étude finale pour "Une Baignade,"* The Art Institute of Chicago, Bequest of Mrs. David Levy.  58

21  *Vêtements, étude pour "Une Baignade,"* Tate Gallery, London.  59

22  Camille Pissarro, *Paysannes au repos*, Toledo Museum of Art, Gift of Edward Drummond Libbey, 1935.  61

23  Pierre-Auguste Renoir, *Rocky Crags, L'Estaque* [detail], Museum of Fine Arts, Boston.  62

24  Claude Monet, *River Scene, Vétheuil*, The Metropolitan Museum of Art, New York, Bequest of William Church Osborn, 1951.  63

25  Pierre-Auguste Renoir, *Boating Party at Châtou*, National Gallery of Art, Washington. Gift of Sam A. Lewisohn.  71

26  Paolo Veronese, *Il Calvario*, Louvre, Paris. (Photo Archives Photographiques, Paris.)  81

27  Plate Illustrating Value Contrast (from Chevreul, *op. cit.*).  82

28  Plate Illustrating Simultaneous Contrast of Color (from Chevreul, *op. cit.*).  84

29  Diagram of Color Relationships in *Une Baignade*.  92

30  *Écho, étude pour "Une Baignade"* (conté crayon drawing), Edith Wetmore Collection, New York.  102

31  *Homme étendu, étude pour "Une Baignade"* (conté crayon drawing), Ernst Beyeler Collection, Basle.  104

32  *Un Dimanche à la Grande Jatte*, The Art Institute of Chicago, Helen Birch Bartlett Memorial Collection.  113

33  *Vue du fond avec quelques personnages, étude pour "La Grande Jatte,"* Mr. and Mrs. Robert Lehman Collection, New York.  117

34  *Vue du fond avec quelques personnages, étude pour "La Grande Jatte,"* Wertheim Collection, Fogg Museum of Art, Harvard University, Cambridge, Mass.  121

35  *Étude finale pour la composition de "La Grande Jatte,"* Metropolitan Museum of Art, New York. Bequest of Sam A. Lewisohn, 1951. (Photo Giraudon.)  124

36  *Vieille femme et nourrice, étude pour "La Grande Jatte"* (conté crayon drawing), General A. Conger Goodyear Collection, Old Westbury, Long Island, New York.  126

# LIST OF ILLUSTRATIONS

*Figure*

37   *Trois femmes, étude pour "La Grande Jatte"* (conté crayon drawing), Smith College Museum of Art, Northampton, Mass.      127

38   Bartolomé Esteban Murillo, *La Naissance de la Vierge* [detail], Louvre, Paris. (Photo Giraudon.)      146

39   Eugène Delacroix, *Scène du massacre de Scio* [detail], Louvre, Paris.      147

40   Claude Monet, *La Chasse*, Louvre, Paris. (Photo Bulloz.)      148

41   Diagram of Seurat's Palette, Mme. Ginette Signac Collection, Paris.      149

42   Prismatic Spectrum (from Rood, *Text-Book*).      149

43   Chromatic Circle (from Rood, *Text-Book*).      150

44   Signac's Palette, drawn by the artist (from a letter in the Amédée Ozenfant Collection, Cannes).      151

45   Diagram of Color Mixture drawn by Signac (from a letter in the Amédée Ozenfant Collection, Cannes).      152

46   Diagram of Color Relationships in *La Grande Jatte*.      155

47   *Honfleur, un soir, embouchure de la Seine*, Collection, The Museum of Modern Art, New York, Gift of Mrs. David Levy.      166

48   *Les Poseuses* (small version), Henry P. McIlhenny Collection, Philadelphia. (Photo Giraudon.)      168

49   *La Parade de cirque*, The Metropolitan Museum of Art, New York, Bequest of Stephen C. Clark, 1960.      176

50   Diagram of Color Relationships in *La Parade de cirque*.      178

51   Esthetic Protractor (from Charles Henry, *Rapporteur esthétique*).      193

52   Illustration of Chromatic Circle (from Henry, *Cercle chromatique*).      195

53   Screen Marked Off in Harmonious Intervals.      197

54   Diagrams of Linear Directions (from Humbert de Superville, *Essai sur les signes inconditionnels dans l'art*).      200

55   Diagram of Linear Directions (from Humbert de Superville, *op. cit.*).      201

56   Drawings of the Human Face (from Humbert de Superville, *op. cit.*).      201

57   Synoptic Table (from Humbert de Superville, *op. cit.*).      203

58   Diagrams of Linear Directions (from Seurat's Letter to Maurice Beaubourg, August 28, 1890).      204

59   Diagram Illustrating Charles Henry's Theory of Expression.      206

LIST OF ILLUSTRATIONS

*Figure*

60   Diagram Illustrating Seurat's Theory of Expression.          207
61   Diagram of Linear Directions (from Blanc, *op. cit.*).       208
62   Pierre Puvis de Chavannes, *Le Pauvre pêcheur*, Louvre, Paris.
     (Photo Giraudon.)                                            213
63   Diagram Illustrating Correlation of Colors and Linear
     Directions in *Les Poseuses*.                                218
64   *Le Chahut*, Rijksmuseum Kröller-Müller, Otterlo.            221
65   *Le Cirque*, Louvre, Paris. (Photo Giraudon.)                222
66   Diagram of Color Relationships in *Le Chahut*.               224
67   Linear Structure of *Le Chahut*.                             225
68   Angular Measurements in *Le Chahut*.                         227
69   Diagram of Color Relationships in *Le Cirque*.               229
70   Linear Structure of *Le Cirque*.                             231
71   Angular Measurements in *Le Cirque*.                         233


*Color Plates*                                                 *Facing*

A   *Une Baignade, Asnières* [detail center].                     78
B   *Une Baignade, Asnières* [detail right].                      78
C   Eugène Delacroix, *La Lutte de Jacob et de l'ange*, Chapelle des
    Saints-Anges, Saint-Sulpice, Paris [detail].                  134
D   *Un Dimanche à la Grande Jatte* [detail].                     134

*Seurat and the Science of Painting*

# I

# Introduction

THIS STUDY WAS UNDERTAKEN
as a result of the writer's desire to re-evaluate the book that has
served to the present day as the primary source of information
about the theory and practice of Neo-Impressionism: Paul Signac's
*D'Eugène Delacroix au néo-impressionnisme* (Paris, 1899).[1] Because
it was written by a member of the Neo-Impressionist group and a
close friend of Georges Seurat, it has been accepted almost without question as the definitive work on the subject. But after
careful study, a number of major shortcomings in this volume
became apparent. In the first place, Signac did not delve very
deeply into the intricacies of Neo-Impressionist theory, preferring
instead to discuss this subject in general, oversimplified language.
Also, many questions relating to Neo-Impressionist practice that
arise when one examines closely the paintings of Seurat and his
friends simply were not brought up in this book. And because
Signac omitted considerable material relating to the history of
Neo-Impressionism — particularly to Seurat's early career — his
book must be considered an incomplete, and consequently a somewhat distorted, account of the subject.

Why did Signac, who knew Seurat and his friends well, present a historically inaccurate picture of the Neo-Impressionist

movement? There are several reasons for his position. He did not design the book as an art-historical account, but rather as a defense of the traditional aspects of Neo-Impressionism and as a comprehensible exposition of its methods. In 1898, the year in which it was completed, Signac stood almost alone in fighting the battle for Neo-Impressionism; Seurat had died seven years before, and during the 1890s many former members of the group defected to other movements in painting. *D'Eugène Delacroix au néo-impressionnisme* was Signac's attempt to demonstrate the positive virtues of Neo-Impressionism and to clarify its fundamental tenets once and for all. In so doing, he simplified his case, undoubtedly because he was competing with other manifestoes, such as those of the Symbolists and the Neo-Traditionalists, that appeared in the late 1880s and 1890s. Also, the Neo-Impressionists had been attacked by these groups, as well as by the Impressionists, for their excessively dogmatic approach. As a result, Signac felt obliged to point out that much of the artistic language of Neo-Impressionism had been foreshadowed by the work of Delacroix and the Impressionists and that the science used by Seurat and his friends was simple and general in nature and could be learned by anyone. In presenting his arguments, Signac was not interested in tracing objectively the historical development of the movement but rather in using all of the available evidence in defending the Neo-Impressionists' artistic program.

His reduction of the importance of science may be explained partially by the fact that his own aims in painting had changed considerably from the period between 1884 and 1891, when he was close to Seurat, and 1898, the year in which his book was completed. In Signac's diary[2] these changes in his art and theory are clearly echoed: he began to regard the period before Seurat's death as a time of experimentation and trial, and only in the 1890s, he implied, did Neo-Impressionism reach its full stride. During this decade, Signac showed an increasing concern with greater brilliance of color and a higher degree of pictorial abstraction at the expense of verisimilitude, without relying on highly involved theories of color and expression. Thus his book was biased not only through being a propagandistic effort, but because it reflected a genuine change in the author's artistic outlook, which, unfortunately, colored his explanation of Seurat's aims and theories.[3]

There are additional reasons why the writer felt that this study should be undertaken. Partly as a result of unreservedly accepting Signac's *D'Eugène Delacroix au néo-impressionnisme*, many writers, both scholarly and popular, have circulated a series of myths and half-truths about Seurat's "science," his theories, and his technique. It is not surprising that such misconceptions should occur, since few art historians have attempted to evaluate Signac's book critically or to utilize fully the wealth of material on the subject published before 1898, much of which will be found to contradict Signac's highly personal account. Therefore we believe that a historical study made in the light of the available evidence will contribute positively to an understanding of Seurat's art and theory and can do much to counteract the myths that have grown up about the subject.[4]

Our procedure will be to analyze carefully Seurat's major paintings, along with some of their preparatory studies, in an effort to trace the evolution of his Neo-Impressionist theory, technique, and method in relation to the pictorial sources and the scientific and theoretical writings he is known to have studied. The contents of the books and articles he consulted will be examined with care, both in themselves and in relation to his paintings, with the aim of assessing the degree to which he relied on them. Also, we shall have occasion to explain Seurat's theories by analyzing them in relation to his paintings and, at times reversing this procedure, to study the paintings with the intention of discovering the degree to which they were governed by his theories. It is hoped that this approach will shed more light on the nature of his theories and their application, and provide some answers to the question of how completely his art was determined by them.

In addition to examining paintings and theoretical texts, the

writer also consulted a large group of articles and critical reviews
published during Seurat's lifetime. These sources, which have not
been utilized sufficiently by art historians, have yielded many
valuable insights about Seurat's theories, aims, and methods. In
view of the fact that he wrote little about his own art, these texts
assume special importance in reflecting his thoughts, since many
of them were written by friends who knew him well and had
consulted him about his ideas on painting. Moreover, these
sources echo the year-by-year changes in the Neo-Impressionists'
esthetic theories and avoid the excessive partiality that is so
evident in Signac's book.

Previous writings that have dealt with these problems may be
grouped in two classes: those that depend uncritically on Signac's
book, which are of little scholarly value, and art-historical studies
that rely on primary sources other than Signac and/or on a
rigorous examination of Seurat's paintings. Of the second type,
Rey's essay on Seurat[5] is one of the most valuable discussions of
the sources of Seurat's theories and of the ways in which they
were applied in his paintings. However, in this writer's opinion,
Rey's account is unbalanced in its tendency to favor the mathematical and geometrical side of Seurat's thought at the expense of
other equally important aspects of his theory. And while Rey
drew upon many primary sources not used previously by art
historians, many relevant writings were left untouched. Moreover, the brevity of his essay seriously limits its value.

Of special interest, too, is a study by Dorra[6] in which some of
Seurat's paintings were examined in relation to the writings of
Charles Henry, a contemporary esthetician and scientist, who
influenced his theories of expression and composition. Dorra is one
of the first art historians to analyze carefully the structure and
method used in specific paintings in relation to the theoretical
sources the artist is known to have studied. But, like Rey's essay,
his remarks are relatively brief and concentrate on the latter part
of Seurat's career; little is said about the theoretical basis of his
"chromo-luminarist" phase of 1884–1887.

While Rey's and Dorra's studies represent significant attempts to relate Seurat's paintings to his theories — and to trace the sources of these theories — several other art historians have discovered valuable material of a biographical-historical nature that is ultimately necessary for the type of study to be undertaken here. Rewald, more than any other writer, has established a solid factual foundation for the subject in a series of books and articles,[7] one of which was checked for accuracy by Seurat's close friend Félix Fénéon.[8] Rewald has also provided comprehensive bibliographies of writings by and about the Neo-Impressionist painters,[9] which were indispensable to the present writer.

Herbert,[10] too, has discussed some questions close to the subject of this book, and like Rewald has carefully established the biographical and historical framework necessary to the understanding of Seurat's art and theory. He has also brought to light some important documents that apparently were not discovered by other scholars and which will be referred to in this study. Although he has discussed Seurat's theory of painting and identified some of the artist's sources, none of Herbert's publications analyzes at length the nature of the application of these sources.

In addition to the art-historical studies cited thus far, there is another class of writings by such authors as Roland Rood,[11] Previati,[12] Fer,[13] and Keller and MacLeod[14] that have succeeded in demonstrating ways in which laws of physics and optics may be applied to the representation of light and color in painting. Their writings have contributed significantly to our understanding of the scientific laws governing this medium, but their approach is not historical, nor are they ultimately concerned with the analysis of specific paintings by specific artists. Rather, their interest is in establishing close connections between physical and optical principles and painting in general.

There are, however, several art historians who have utilized a knowledge of the science of color in their approach to problems in late nineteenth-century painting: Brown,[15] Badt,[16] and Webster.[17] Although they have dealt, respectively, with Pissarro, Van Gogh, and Impressionism — rather than Neo-Impressionism — these three writers have analyzed closely, in a historical context, specific paintings in relation to the theories that governed them. This method, needless to say, reduces the possibility of misconceptions that are likely to arise when either the paintings or theories are studied in isolation, and it has been followed by the present writer in the second and third chapters of this book.

In discussing hue and value relationships in Seurat's paintings and drawings, it was necessary to adopt a uniform system of color notation and terminology that would bridge the gap between the language used by painters and that used by the scientists whose writings they studied. Brown[18] has pointed out the difficulties involved in employing systems of absolute color identification, such as those devised by Richter[19] and Grautoff,[20] as well as systems that depend on identification by letter or number, such as Ostwald's.[21] The value of both types is limited because neither is well suited to the notation of color-value relationships as they actually occur in painting and drawing. In Brown's opinion, the method, terminology, and means of representing color relationships devised by Pope[22] (Figures 1 to 3) is the most workable system for the art historian in discussing specific color phenomena in paintings because it corresponds to visual experience.

Pope eliminated numerical equivalents and physical samples in favor of a three-dimensional, cylindrical color diagram, which permits the main characteristics of color and their relationships to be visualized immediately (Figure 2). While Pope's method of diagramming colors will be used here only occasionally, it will be assumed as the implicit basis of our discussion of the phenomena of color and value in Seurat's paintings. And, significantly, it corresponds closely to Seurat's and Signac's mode of visualizing color relationships.

The three main "dimensions" of color, according to Pope, are *value* ("the degree of lightness or darkness"), *hue* ("the quality due to the predominance of some one of the wave lengths which

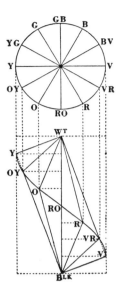

Figure 1. Chromatic Circle (from Arthur Pope, *The Language of Drawing and Painting*).

Figure 2. Tone Solid (from Pope, *op. cit.*).

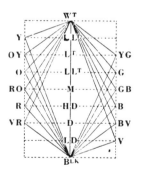

Figure 3. Diagram of Values and Hues (from Pope, *op. cit.*).

make up white light"), and *intensity* ("the strength of the hue as distinguished from neutrality"). These he diagrammed on a nearly cylindrical "tone solid" (Figure 2), the central axis of which is used to represent a graduated range of values from black (at the bottom) to white (at the top). Twelve hues at full intensity are distributed around the circumference of the cylinder, and varying degrees of their intensity may be plotted on a line moving from each color to the central, or neutral, black-to-white axis of the tone solid.[23] With Pope's system it is possible to represent not only the coordinates of single colors but combinations of colors as well; thus the tone solid serves as a convenient abstraction which will permit one to discuss color relationships with some degree of consistency and uniformity.

Although valuable as a three-dimensional device, Pope's tone solid must be fragmented in order to represent the elements of color on a two-dimensional surface. If the cylinder is viewed from one side and is flattened out (Figure 3), it may be used to represent the relative positions of *value* (on the center axis) and *hue* (on the left and right, corresponding to the outer borders of the cylinder). It should be noted that the hues in question fall at different levels on this diagram because, when represented at full intensity, as they are here, their intrinsic values seen solely on a light-dark scale will vary from near-white to near-black. Hue and intensity, on the other hand, may be plotted on a circular diagram (Figure 1). As we have seen, hues at full intensity are grouped around the perimeter of the color circle; their intensity varies according to their closeness to the center of the circle, which represents the point of least intensity, that is, a neutral.

Pope's system of notation is based on the principles of subtractive mixture of pigments. Because we are concerned here with a group of artists who relied heavily on the additive mixture of color, the hue circles used as illustrations in this book will be revised to read according to the principles of additive mixture.[24] In this system the primary colors are not only different from the subtractive primaries, but the hues derived from their combination also fall in different positions on the color circle. The distinction between additive and subtractive mixture will be of considerable importance in this book and therefore requires a brief explanation here.[25]

By subtractive mixture[26] is meant that method of combining different *pigments* physically; in painting, this usually occurs on the artist's palette, although it sometimes takes place accidentally on the surface of the picture. The primary colors in the subtractive process are red, yellow, and blue. According to this system, the mixture of red and yellow produces orange; yellow and blue together produce green; and blue and red produce violet. (These primaries and their mixtures have been diagrammed in Figure 4.) If the three primaries are mixed with each other, the result will be a desaturated, almost black neutral tone. The same result will be obtained if any pair of complementaries (hues that are opposite each other on the chromatic circle) are mixed in equal proportions.

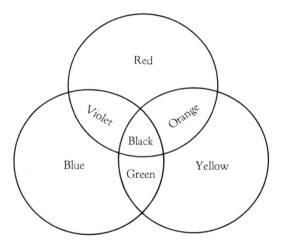

Figure 4. Subtractive Mixture Diagram.

Additive mixture,[27] on the other hand, involves the combination of colored *lights*, not pigments. In this system, several different techniques may be used to effect mixture, the most usual being superimposition of beams of light projected through colored filters, or rotating discs of variously colored sectors at high speeds. The additive primaries (which are different from the subtractive ones) are most frequently defined as red, green, and blue-violet.[28] Their mixture yields results that are quite different from the subtractive primaries: red and green produce yellow or yellow-orange; green and blue-violet produce blue-green or cyan-blue;

and red and blue-violet produce purple.[29] When all three primaries are mixed, the result is white light; similarly, the mixture of any pair of complementaries also yields white light.[30] (These relationships have been diagrammed in Figure 5.)[31]

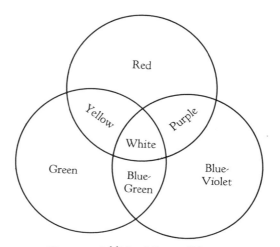

Figure 5. Additive Mixture Diagram.

Returning to the possible methods of mixing light additively, it is significant that, according to modern physicists and color-technicians, a third type of mixture may be employed — a method that is relevant to painting in general and to Neo-Impressionism in particular: this involves the application of a number of very small spots or bands of color of uniform size to a two-dimensional surface.[32] When such a technique is used, additive mixture of the component colors will take place.[33] The applied pigments, however, are not combined physically (that is, subtractively) but are juxtaposed and thus reflect colored light.[34]

Naturally, in order to bring about additive mixture from small spots or bands of color, the observer must move some distance away from the object so painted. If one steps back far enough, the individual component colors will in fact fuse into a third, or resultant, hue generated from the additive mixture of the two (or more) original components. The process involved in this mixture, or fusion "in the eye," is referred to by most color scientists as "optical mixture" or "optical fusion."[35] (It should be reiterated that, though the materials in question are, in fact, pigments, they reflect colored light; thus their combination will be guided by the principles of additive, not subtractive, mixture.)

Before embarking on a discussion of Seurat's art and theory in Chapter 2, we shall present a brief account of his early career. Then his first major painting, *Une Baignade*, will be analyzed with the aims of discovering its roots in earlier, as well as contemporary, art and theory; of assessing the relative weight of pictorial and theoretical sources in its conception; and of considering the degree to which this painting foretells the appearance of the Neo-Impressionist style as seen in *Un Dimanche à la Grande Jatte*.

The emergence of the first stage of Neo-Impressionism (perhaps better termed "chromo-luminarism"), as exemplified by *La Grande Jatte*, will be examined in some detail in Chapter 3. As with *Une Baignade*, an effort will be made to trace Seurat's sources in theoretical and scientific writings and to examine the nature of his esthetic aims, as of 1884–1886, in relation to the synthesis achieved in *Une Baignade* and in relation to Impressionism. At the end of this chapter, several special aspects of his fully developed "chromo-luminarist" technique will be explored.

In Chapters 2 and 3, we shall consider primarily the following elements in four of Seurat's major paintings: color-value relationships, technique, method, "mode of operation," and the relationship of the representational language of the paintings to the world of nature. These elements were of very special interest to Seurat and his friends, particularly between 1884 and 1888, as witnessed by writings of the painters and their critics. Most of the Neo-Impressionists' conscious concern at this time was not primarily with figure style, composition, or spatial rendering — which they felt should be handled according to personal judgment — but with the means of achieving intensity, luminosity, and harmony of color. For this reason we intend to devote most of our attention in the second and third chapters to the pictorial elements enumerated at the beginning of this paragraph, realizing, at the same time, that to emphasize these selected aspects of Seurat's style at the expense of others is likely to destroy the balance of formal elements evident in his work.

Following a change in Seurat's interests and theories, our attention will shift in Chapter 4 from color technique to his use, between about 1887 and 1891, of hue, value, and line in combinations that produce predictable emotional responses in the beholder. Very little has been published about these later theories, their origins, and the way in which they influenced his paintings. Yet we have in Seurat's well-known letter to Maurice Beaubourg,[36] where his later ideas on esthetics and techniques are outlined, a concise statement of his aims in painting, as of August 28, 1890. This statement will be related both to the major paintings he executed between 1886 and 1891 and to the scientific and theoretical writings he is known to have studied at this time. Finally, an effort will be made in Chapter 5 to comprehend the nature of Seurat's "science" and to determine the extent to which it dominated his art.

# 2

# *Une Baignade*
# and the Origins of
# Neo-Impressionism

## SEURAT'S EARLY CAREER

GEORGES SEURAT[1] WAS BORN ON December 2, 1859, in Paris, where, except for summer trips and a year's military service at Brest, he spent his entire life. We know that he grew up in a bourgeois, commercial district of the city and attended *collège* until the age of sixteen.[2] In 1875, he enrolled in a neighborhood municipal art school where, under the tutelage of Justin Lequien, he drew from plaster casts and copied lithographs.[3] For the young artist the main function of this training was to prepare him for the École des Beaux-Arts, which he entered shortly before February, 1878.[4]

At the École, he was enrolled in the *atelier* of one of Ingres' best pupils, Heinrich Lehmann, an academic artist who commanded a certain amount of respect in his day.[5] From Seurat's early drawings and paintings, as well as from witness accounts, it is evident that in his school days he shared his teacher's admiration for Ingres.[6] Unfortunately, few of the paintings he did at the École have survived; but we know that he followed the traditional academic practice of making numerous drawings from the model and from plaster casts.[7]

As a student at the École, Seurat studied the work of earlier artists at the Louvre and in the library of the school.[8] The Louvre, of course, contained an outstanding array of paintings, sculpture, and drawings, while the library of the École housed an extensive collection of books on the art of the past, as well as on art theory; in addition, Seurat could have found at the library several hundred thousand drawings, prints, and photographs of works of art.[9] He was also undoubtedly acquainted with the collection of plaster casts, paintings, sculpture, and copies on display at the École des Beaux-Arts.

From recollections of his friends, we learn that he gradually became dissatisfied with the routine academic character of Lehmann's classes and turned increasingly to the fundamental artistic principles to be found in the art of the old masters.[10] And in conjunction with two fellow students in Lehmann's *atelier*, Ernest Laurent and Edmond Aman-Jean, he was soon drawn to an even more radical source of inspiration: the art of the Impressionists. Moved by a visit they paid to an exhibition of Impressionist paintings, these three resolved to withdraw from the school to form a small independent group devoted to the creation of a free art.[11]

Seurat's connection with the École was permanently severed as a result of joining the army in November, 1879.[12] After his year's military service at Brest, he returned to Paris and rented a studio not far from his parents' apartment on the Boulevard Magenta. From 1881 to 1884, as far as we know, he worked independently at painting and drawing without affiliating himself with any school or group, except, of course, his friends Laurent and Aman-Jean. Like most young artists, Seurat required a period of germination; these years served as a bridge between traditional academic training and his emergence as a progressive painter and leader of the Neo-Impressionist group.

In 1883, Seurat undertook his first major painting, *Une Baignade, Asnières* (Figure 6), the site being a popular bathing place on the banks of the Seine. The canvas was completed in 1884 and was submitted to the jury of the official Salon in that year, but for reasons that are unknown it was rejected. Soon afterward, however, the picture was accepted and shown under the auspices of the Groupe des Artistes Indépendants, an organization comprised of artists who would not, or could not, exhibit their work at the Salon. It was here, incidentally, that he met the painter Paul Signac, four years his junior, who was to become his close friend and ally, and eventually the leading propagandist for the Neo-Impressionists.[13]

From 1876, when he first began to paint, to 1884, Seurat experimented with a variety of different styles, ranging from that of Ingres to the Barbizon School and Impressionism. Some of his early essays were undoubtedly blind alleys; but toward the end of this formative period Seurat began to turn for inspiration to nineteenth-century painters working in the coloristic tradition. Although he received his initial training at a citadel of artistic conservatism, the École des Beaux-Arts, he was gradually drawn to the work of Delacroix, Monet, Pissarro, and Renoir by a desire to probe their secrets and, later, to perfect their methods of representing light and color. In different ways, these painters had attempted to discover new pictorial techniques through which artist's pigments could be made to appear more intense and vibrant, and in the case of the Impressionists, to capture the scintillating quality of sunlight.

We know that in 1881 Seurat studied a group of paintings by Delacroix because some of the dated notes he took from them have survived.[14] In addition, he spent considerable time analyzing one of Delacroix's great decorative schemes: the frescoes in the Chapelle des Saints-Anges at Saint-Sulpice, in Paris.[15] And judging from the style of some of the paintings he executed in

Figure 6. *Une Baignade, Asnières*, Tate Gallery, London (on deposit in the National Gallery, London).

1881–1884, we may be certain that he looked carefully at the work of the Barbizon School and the Impressionists.[16] He could have seen Impressionist paintings not only at their annual exhibitions in the late seventies and early eighties but also at a series of important one-man shows held in 1883 by Durand-Ruel which were devoted to the works of Monet, Renoir, Pissarro, and Sisley.[17] We know, too, that Seurat admired Puvis de Chavannes at this time, and there is even a possibility that he may have visited the artist.[18] His unmistakable influence on Seurat's early work suggests that the young artist examined his paintings with care.[19]

During his formative period, he also turned for advice to a group of scientific and theoretical writings on the subject of luminosity, intensity, and harmony of color, a knowledge of which enabled him to "reform" the artistic language of Delacroix and the Impressionists. Fortunately, from a letter Seurat wrote to Félix Fénéon, and from witness accounts by the artist's friends, we have considerable information about which texts he consulted between 1876 and 1884. As to his sources, he wrote the following:

> Having read Charles Blanc in school and being acquainted with Chevreul's laws and Delacroix's precepts for this reason;
> Having read the studies of the same Charles Blanc on the same painter [Delacroix] (*Gazette des beaux-arts*, volume XVI, if I remember correctly);
> Being acquainted with Corot's ideas (copy of a private letter of October 28, 1875) on the subject of tone, and the precepts of Couture on the *finesse* of colors (at the time of his exhibition);
> Having been struck by the intuition of Monet and Pissarro;
> Agreeing with certain of Sutter's ideas on classical Greek art, which I pondered at Brest (in the magazine *L'Art*) March and February 1880;
> Rood having been brought to my attention by an article by Philippe Gille, *Le Figaro*, 1881.[20]

The book by Charles Blanc that Seurat read in school was the *Grammaire des arts du dessin* (Paris, 1867).[21] Written by an eminent critic and art historian, this volume included a résumé of Michel-Eugène Chevreul's theories and an analysis of Delacroix's views about color. Seurat also indicated that he had read Blanc's study of

Delacroix in the *Gazette des beaux-arts*; this was a two-part article published in the issues of January and February, 1864, and later reprinted in *Artistes de mon temps* (Paris, 1876). Blanc had known Delacroix personally, and on at least one occasion had persuaded him to explain his color theory and technique.[22] Partly on the basis of this interview, he wrote informatively about the artist in both of these works. Although he did not mention the fact in the list cited earlier, Seurat also studied and took notes on one of the most influential treatises on color written during the nineteenth century: Chevreul's *De la loi du contraste simultané des couleurs* (Paris, 1839).[23] In addition, he was acquainted with some of Delacroix's writings, excerpts from which were found among his effects.[24]

Seurat also acknowledged his familiarity with Corot's ideas on the subject of tone in painting, as expressed in notes from conversations between Mme. J. Aviat and Corot, entitled *Extrait des souvenirs de mes bonnes et intéressantes causeries avec M. Corot, année 1869, à Méry-sur-Seine*.[25] In writing that he became acquainted with Thomas Couture's precepts on the *finesse* of color at the time of his exhibition, he was probably referring to the large Couture show held in Paris at the Palais de l'Industrie in September, 1880. Although we cannot be certain which of the academic master's writings Seurat knew, it was probably his well-known *Méthode et entretiens d'atelier* (Paris, 1868), in which methods of obtaining delicate color effects were described in some detail.[26]

The articles in *L'Art* to which the artist referred were published in six installments (January 18–March 14, 1880) entitled "Les Phénomènes de la vision," and were written by David Sutter, a Swiss esthetician and art theorist active in Parisian academic circles.[27] Finally, Seurat pointed out that his attention had been called to Rood by an article in *Le Figaro*. The article in question appeared in the issue of January 26, 1881, and was, in fact, a brief review of a book entitled *Théorie scientifique des couleurs* (Paris, 1881), a French translation of the American physicist Ogden N.

Rood's *Modern Chromatics* (New York, 1879; also issued in 1881 as *Students' Text-Book of Color*). This text, which was to be of the utmost importance for Seurat, came into his hands immediately after reading Gille's review of it in *Le Figaro*.[28]

From Seurat's letter to Fénéon (and drafts for it) we know that between 1876 and 1884 he consciously sought a formula for what he called "*peinture optique*," a term that he seems to have preferred to the more popular appellation "*néo-impressionnisme*." It is evident from the letter quoted earlier that he turned methodically to every source, whether textual or pictorial, that might contribute to his discovery of "a formula for optical painting" — to use his own words.[29] What did Seurat draw from these sources, and how were they used in formulating his Neo-Impressionist technique, theory, and method? Our aim in the present chapter will be to answer this question as completely as possible.

Rather than trace his progress step by step from his roots in the academic tradition to the realization of his "*peinture optique*," we shall begin with a major work dating from the end of his formative period — *Une Baignade, Asnières* (1883–1884; Figure 6), in which Seurat already had synthesized a number of influential stylistic and theoretical sources. This painting will also serve as a significant point of departure because in it he both summarized his early search for a style and foreshadowed his mature Neo-Impressionist idiom. Before proceeding to a discussion of *Une Baignade*, we shall summarize the contents of the relevant parts of five of the more important texts, enumerated previously, that Seurat studied before 1884. The writer feels that, while some of the ideas contained in them may not be as significant for *Une Baignade* as they are for later paintings, it would still be better to present a brief résumé of their contents at one time, instead of citing excerpts from them at random without a comprehensive view of the texts as a whole. Subsequently, we shall consider the value for Seurat of two major pictorial sources: Delacroix and Impressionism.

## SCIENTIFIC AND THEORETICAL SOURCES

*Chevreul's* De la loi du contraste simultané des couleurs

Michel-Eugène Chevreul's[30] interest in color stemmed from his position in the dyeing department of the tapestry workshops of Les Gobelins, in Paris, where he had been called upon to work on the problem of color intensity in wools. In the course of his researches, he discovered that the apparent intensity of color did not depend as much on the inherent pigmentation of the material used as it did on the hue of the neighboring fabric.[31] This kind of practical observation set the stage for Chevreul's more involved research on the principles governing, and specific applications of, the law of simultaneous contrast of color. At first, he explored earlier writings to see whether contrast phenomena had been discussed systematically: he found that some previous investigators had been aware of the effects of contrast but had not derived any general principles governing their behavior.[32] Chevreul then attempted to formulate his own observations as a law. It is this law, its experimental basis, and its practical application that constitute the main body of his *De la loi du contraste simultané des couleurs* (Paris, 1839).

After conducting numerous experiments on value and color contrast, he formulated the law of simultaneous contrast in the following terms: "In the case where the eye sees at the same time two contiguous colours, they will appear as dissimilar as possible, both in their optical composition and in the height of their tone. We have then, *at the same time*, simultaneous contrast of colour properly so called, and contrast of tone."[33] In the second part of his book, Chevreul turned to the practical application of this law to various problems of color in architecture, painting, and the decorative arts. At the outset, however, he provided precise definitions of his terms, which are essential to an understanding not only of his principles of harmony, but also of Seurat's art and theory:

The word *tones* [*tons*] of a colour will be exclusively employed to designate the different modifications which that colour, taken at its maximum intensity, is capable of receiving from the addition of white, which weakens its *tone*, and black, which deepens it.

The word *scale* [*gamme*] is applied to the collection of tones of the same colour thus modified. . . .

The word *hues* [*nuances*] of a colour will be exclusively applied to the modifications which that colour receives by the addition of a small quantity of another colour.[34]

Chevreul diagrammed these variables of tone and hue on a chromatic circle (Figure 7) divided by twelve equidistant radii, each of which represents a single color; those included on the circle are the three primaries (red, yellow, and blue), three secondary colors (orange, green, and violet), and six intermediate colors (orange-red, orange-yellow, yellow-green, green-blue, blue-violet, violet-red). Each radius is divided into twenty equal parts, which represent the full scale of "tones" of any given color. According to Chevreul, this circle will be valuable to the painter and dyer because it represents every possible modification of color, and because one can readily locate the complementary colors opposite each other on any diameter.

Having established a workable set of terms and a chromatic circle that denotes the chief variables of color, Chevreul set out to enunciate several principles of harmony. These are of two main types: harmonies of analogous colors and harmonies of contrast. He summarized them as follows (the color relationships described by Chevreul have been diagrammed in Figure 8*A* to *E*):

Ist Kind

*Harmonies of Analogous Colours*

1. The *harmony of scale*, produced by the simultaneous view of different tones of a single scale, more or less approximating (Figure 8*A*).
2. The *harmony of hues*, produced by the simultaneous view of tones of the same height, or nearly so, belonging to scales more or less approximating (Figure 8*B*).

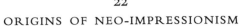

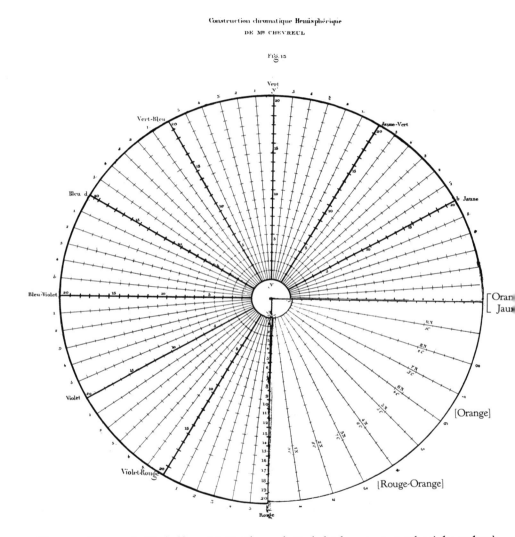

Figure 7. Chromatic Circle (from M.-E. Chevreul, *De la loi du contraste simultané des couleurs*).

SCIENTIFIC AND THEORETICAL SOURCES

Figure 8*A*. Harmony of Analogous Hues on the Same
Scale. (Based on Chevreul.)

[Red]           [Red-Orange]

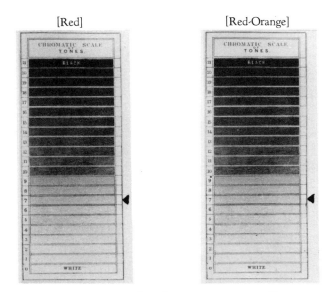

Figure 8*B*. Harmony of Analogous Hues on Neighboring
Scales.

3. The *harmony of a dominant coloured light*, produced by the simultaneous view of different colours assorted conformably to the law of contrast, but one of them predominating, as would result from seeing these colours through a slightly stained glass.

IInd Kind

*Harmonies of Contrasts*

1. The *harmony of contrast of scale*, produced by the simultaneous view of two tones of the same scale, very distant from each other (Figure 8C).
2. The *harmony of contrast of hues*, produced by the simultaneous view of tones of different height, each belonging to contiguous scales (Figure 8D).
3. The *harmony of contrast of colours*, produced by the simultaneous view of colours belonging to scales very far asunder, assorted according to the law of contrast: the difference in height of juxtaposed tones may also augment the contrast of colours (Figure 8E).[35]

After establishing these principles and providing numerous examples of their application, Chevreul turned to the question of chiaroscuro and color in painting. First, he recommended that the artist study the ways in which the apparent hue of objects might be modified by lights of different color falling upon them. Aware that the local color of things can be varied in this fashion, he discussed a variety of such modifications that depend on the color of light and the position of the object.[36] Chevreul wanted painters to follow the principle of "true or absolute coloring," by which he meant "the faithful reproduction in painting of the modifications which light enables us to perceive in the objects which the painter selects for his models."[37] In other words, he recommended not only that the local colors in nature be depicted accurately but that all of the external factors of light, color, and atmosphere that modify them also be taken into account.

At the same time, he cited several cases in which the painter may arbitrarily exaggerate nature's hues for esthetic effect, since, even though the colors of nature might be copied accurately in a painting, the result will not necessarily be harmonious. In this context, Chevreul described the perfect colorist in the following way:

SCIENTIFIC AND THEORETICAL SOURCES

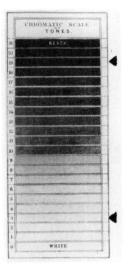

Figure 8*C*. Harmony of Contrasting Hues on the Same Scale.

[R~d]                    [Red-Orange]

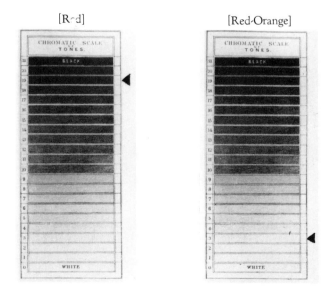

Figure 8*D*. Harmony of Contrasting Hues on Neighboring Scales.

[Red]  [Green]

[Red]  [Green]

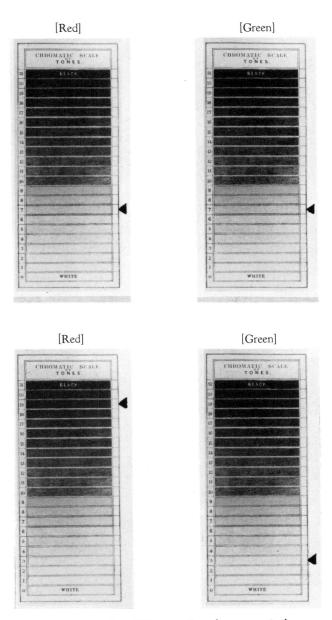

Figure 8E. Harmonies of Hues on Complementary Scales.

He must not only imitate the model by reproducing the image faithfully, in respect to aerial perspective relative to the variously coloured light, but also, the harmony of tints must be found in the local colours, and in the colours of the different objects imitated; and this is the place to remark, that if in every composition there are colours inherent to the model which the painter cannot change without being unfaithful to nature, there are others at his disposal which must be chosen so as to harmonize with the first.[38]

It will readily be seen from this excerpt that, while he favors naturalistic representation, Chevreul is willing to have the artist make arbitrary adjustments in order to achieve pictorial harmony — a point of view later shared by Seurat and his friends.

One of the more important sections of the book for our purposes is the chapter on "The Utility of the Law of Simultaneous Contrast of Colours in the Science of Colouring," which deals with the application of the contrast principle to painting. According to Chevreul, this law offers advantages to the artist when perceiving and imitating the effects of light on the model and allows him to harmonize the colors of a composition. He insisted that "the painter must know and especially *see*, the modifications of white light, shade, and colours which the model presents to him in the circumstances under which he would reproduce it."[39] The law of simultaneous contrast of colors can guide him in viewing objects in nature: it states that when two colored objects are scrutinized together, the color of each will be influenced by the complementary of its neighbor. This principle applies equally to value: when two objects of different value are juxtaposed, the lighter one will become lighter and the darker even more dark in appearance.

Chevreul also applied this law to the harmony of color in pictorial compositions. He distinguished between colors that the painter was obliged to use in a picture (such as those representing the local colors of the model) and those that could be chosen freely because they were not inherent in the model. On this subject he wrote as follows:

In a landscape, the colours are given by the subject, yet not so arbitrarily but we can substitute for the true colour the colour of a neighbouring scale; the artist can choose the colour of the sky, imagine numerous accidental effects, introduce into his composition animals, draped figures, carriages, etc., the form and colour of which may be selected in such manner as to produce the best possible effect with the objects peculiar to the scene.[40]

In this excerpt Chevreul once again opens the way for the use of arbitrarily chosen colors as agents of pictorial harmony, the chief type being harmony of contrasts ("The law of simultaneous contrast indicates the means by which the pure colours may be made to impart value to each other."),[41] although the "harmony of scale" and the "harmony of hues" are also recommended as alternatives.

The remainder of the second part of the book deals with problems of color in tapestries, carpets, wallpaper, and the like, and concerns us only in respect to his discussion of optical mixture. Chevreul found that, as a rule, threads of two complementary colors woven together resulted in gray, when seen at a distance, and that if the quantity of one or the other was emphasized, the gray would appear to be tinted with the hue of whichever set of threads dominated the mixture.[42]

In the third and last part of the book, Chevreul proposed two important sets of rules governing harmonious relationships of color. The first set concerns the association of complementary colors and the other relates to the association of noncomplementary colors. He summarized these rules in a single sentence: "The greater the difference between the colours, the more they mutually beautify each other; and inversely, the less difference there is, the more they will tend to injure one another."[43]

Most of Chevreul's book deals, as we have seen, with the principles and laws of color. But in the closing paragraphs he introduced a discussion of contrast phenomena on all levels in the visual arts and drew interesting analogies between vision and the other senses. His final conclusion was that in all of the senses "two different objects, placed side by side, appear by the comparison more different than they really are."[44] Chevreul closed with a plea for the human capacity of reasoning: man, he believed, is distinguished from animals by the faculty of abstraction, which permits him to discover the relationships between the phenomena that surround him and to communicate these discoveries to his fellows. He concluded with the warning that man should "not . . . pass beyond the limits traced by rigorous reasoning."[45]

*Charles Blanc's* Grammaire des arts du dessin *and Essay on Delacroix*

Blanc's[46] *Grammaire des arts du dessin* (Paris, 1867) was conceived, in the author's words, as a "lucid résumé of all accepted ideas touching the arts of design" — these arts being painting, engraving, sculpture, and architecture.[47] He wrote it for those who had finished their scholastic studies but because of the lack of public instruction in matters of art had an inadequate knowledge of the subject. Although the whole book undoubtedly interested Seurat, only the chapter on color will occupy us for the present.

Blanc thought that color and chiaroscuro were both essential in painting, though color was more intimately associated with sentiment than was chiaroscuro. The role of color, he wrote, "is to tell us what agitates the heart, while drawing shows us what passes in the mind. . . ."[48] For Blanc, color plays an important part as the vehicle of mobile, intangible feelings, while form, as described by chiaroscuro, is precise and palpable. But one cannot exist without the other. While insisting that color is the feminine element in painting, guided more by instinct than intellect, he believed, paradoxically, that it obeyed "certain and invariable" principles that could be learned by artists: "Not only can color, which is under fixed laws, be taught like music, but it is easier to learn than drawing, whose absolute principles cannot be taught."[49]

According to Blanc, there are six major colors, of which three — yellow, red, and blue — are primitive or primary, and three — violet, green, and orange — are composite, or binary;

the latter are produced by mixing each of the primary colors with its neighbor. Blanc conceived of the world as containing an infinite variety of colors — the primaries, binaries, and all of the intermediate shades that fall between them: "Separated, these colors and these shades enable us to distinguish and recognize all the objects of creation. Reunited they give us the idea of white. White light is the union of all colors, all are contained and latent in it."[50]

Blanc also summarized Charles Bourgeois' statement that white light contains three generative colors, yellow, red, and blue.[51] Although later physicists demonstrated that this proposition was incorrect (because the primaries of light are red, green, and blue-violet), it sufficed for discussing pigmentary complementaries used in painting. Bourgeois also described the conventional pairs of complementaries common to nineteenth-century color theory: red-green, yellow-violet, and blue-orange. To this statement of complementaries, Blanc added a brief résumé of Chevreul's law of simultaneous contrast of colors, which in its simplest form stated that complementaries, when juxtaposed, mutually intensify each other; when mixed, however, they destroy one another. This destruction of color by the mixture of complementaries Blanc called "achromatism" — which also occurs if one mixes equal quantities of the three primaries, red, yellow, and blue. Blanc diagrammed these relationships on a color circle based on two overlapping triangles, one upright, for the primaries, and the other inverted for the secondary colors. An additional set of six intermediate tones was derived from the mixture of each of the six primary and secondary colors with its neighbor (see Figure 9).[52]

Chevreul's discovery of complementary haloes or aureoles that appear around areas of strong color was also summarized by Blanc, who felt that a knowledge of such phenomena would help the artist obtain greater brilliance of color in his paintings. Blanc also pointed out that Delacroix, even before being influenced by Chevreul, had observed this principle when, as the story goes, he discovered that the yellow cabs of Paris produced violet shadows.

# SCIENTIFIC AND THEORETICAL SOURCES

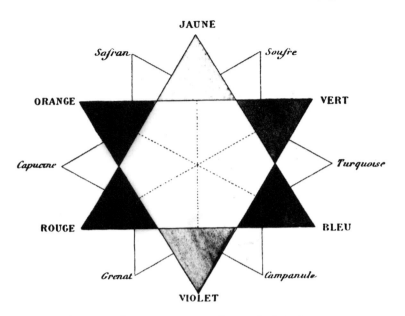

Figure 9. Chromatic Diagram (from Charles Blanc,
*Grammaire des arts du dessin*).

In his text Blanc revealed his awareness of the laws promulgated by Chevreul — which have already been discussed — by summarizing the scientist's method of producing colored grays through the optical mixture of juxtaposed complementaries. Similarly, Blanc reviewed Chevreul's system of obtaining harmony through contrast and analogy. In summary, his advice to the painter was as follows:

> The moment colors are not to be employed in equal quantities, nor of equal intensity, the artist is free, but within the limits of infallible laws. He must try his *doses*, must distribute to his tints their places and roles, calculate the extent he will give them, and make, as it were, a secret rehearsal of the drama his coloring will form. He must employ the resources of white and black, foresee the optical mixture, know the vibration of colors, and finally take care of the effect the diversely colored light is to produce, according as it is of the morning or the evening, from the North or the South.[53]

Blanc then explained each of these recommendations in greater detail. On the subject of optical mixture, he drew illustrations from Delacroix's work and, indirectly, reflected a knowledge of Chevreul's theories. Selecting an example from the central cupola of the library of the Luxembourg Palace, he pointed out that Delacroix had achieved remarkable delicacy, freshness, and transparency in the flesh tones of one of the half-nude female figures. The body, Blanc discovered, was slashed with strokes of green, which partially neutralized its complementary, pink (the local color of the flesh), thus producing a tone of unusual freshness that was discernible only at a distance. This new color, not evident at the close view, he called a "resultant," arising from the application of the laws of optical mixture.

Like Chevreul, Blanc noticed that new, or third, colors could be generated by optical mixture of two tones applied side by side if the observer moved sufficiently far away from the painting in question. To illustrate this phenomenon, Blanc devised a colored diagram composed of equal-sized parallel bands of red and green (Figure 10); when viewed at a distance, the red and green no

Figure 10. Diagram Illustrating Optical Mixture (from Blanc, *op. cit.*).

longer function as individual hues but destroy each other, as it were, appearing gray and colorless. However, if the proportions of red and green are made unequal, the result will be a delicate reddish-gray or a greenish-gray, depending on which of the two colors predominates. At the same time Blanc suggested a method of mixing colors optically through small spots or stars of pigment, which undoubtedly served as a source of inspiration for Seurat's pointillist technique (see Figure 11).

Figure 11. Diagrams Illustrating Methods
of Optical Mixture (from Blanc, *op. cit.*).

In discussing the laws governing the vibration of color, Blanc
recommended that, in order to avoid flat, monotonous tones,
color be made to vibrate "by putting tone upon tone in a pure
state, blue upon blue, yellow upon yellow, red upon red." In this
way, Blanc pointed out, the orientals "obtain harmony in their
stuffs, carpets, or vases, even when they have employed but a
single tint, because they have varied its values from light to dark."[54]
Delacroix, he said, was a master of this device; by such gradation,
or laying tone upon tone, he made the colors of his paintings
appear to vibrate.

Finally, Blanc maintained that the color of the light should be
considered carefully by the painter because it has a pronounced
influence upon objects in nature. Its influence, in turn, should be
recorded by the artist in his picture. Blanc confines his examples to
two: the effect of the cold light from the north and the orange-
colored light of the sun. These two types of light, respectively,
can intensify or neutralize the objects they illuminate. What is
important here, as before, is that the painter have an absolute
knowledge of the natural phenomena in question; otherwise, he
will not be able to represent them effectively.

The rules Blanc insisted the artist take advantage of — those of
optical mixture, the vibration of colors, and the effects of diversely
colored lights — were, however, not to be employed just for the
sake of optical beauty. The main purpose of color, as he stated
earlier in the chapter, was to express emotion, thought, and moral
character. Blanc chastised such painters as Veronese and Rubens,
who, he said, used the same color harmonies for all of their

pictures, even though their subjects were quite different from each other. Delacroix avoided this error; he is to be praised because he "never fails to tune his lyre to the tone of his thought, so that the first aspect of his picture shall be the prelude to his melody, grave or gay, melancholy or triumphant, sweet or tragic."[55] Blanc closed his chapter on color with the warning that painters should not be carried away by the beauty of color. If the artist is not careful, he will fall into excessive colorism while sacrificing drawing; or he may begin to use color for its own sake, without keeping in mind the thought, or sentiment, it should express.

Blanc referred frequently to the work of Delacroix to illustrate the precepts on color in his *Grammaire des arts du dessin*. Indeed, this book might well serve as an introduction to Delacroix's theories because, as we noted earlier, its author had personally interviewed the artist. But another of Blanc's writings, which is similar in content to parts of the *Grammaire*, went even more deeply into the matter of Delacroix's color: this is his article, "Eugène Delacroix," published in the *Gazette des beaux-arts*, January and February, 1864. Here Seurat found a complete explanation, through Blanc's eyes, of Delacroix's color technique, which played an important part in the formation of the Neo-Impressionist style.

In this essay Blanc proposed the idea that Delacroix's art and theory were based on "the mathematical rules of color."[56] Indeed, Blanc himself believed, as we saw, that "coloring is learned like music"[57] and that the "orientals" worked with fixed laws governing color that were passed on from generation to generation. And according to Blanc,[58] the scientific laws of color developed by two modern *savants*, Bourgeois and Chevreul, were studied carefully by Delacroix.[59] Although these so-called scientific principles correspond in many respects to those discussed two years later in the *Grammaire*, it would be well to enumerate them here, giving special attention to points not fully elucidated in that book.

In his article on Delacroix, as in the *Grammaire*, Blanc showed that color could be "exalted," or intensified, by placing two complementaries side by side, and that if they were mixed, the result would be gray. However, colorful grays could be produced if these complementaries were mixed in unequal proportions. Harmonies of analogy and contrast were then described, but in greater detail than in the *Grammaire*:

> New contrasts could be born of the juxtaposition of two complementaries, of which one is pure and the other modified. The struggle being unequal, one of the two colors triumphs, and the intensity of the dominant one does not hinder the harmony of the pair. Now if one brings two similar colors together in their pure state, but at different degrees of energy, for example, dark blue and light blue, one will obtain another effect, in which there will be contrast through difference of intensity, and harmony through similarity of the colors. In short, if two similar colors are juxtaposed, one in a pure state and the other modified, for example, blue with blue-gray, another kind of contrast, tempered by analogy, will be the result.[60]

However, these "mathematical" and "infallible" means of obtaining harmony — which were clearly inspired by Chevreul — require delicate sensitivities and experience on the part of the artist; Delacroix is cited again as one who combines both delicacy of artistic vision and a calculated theory.

Delacroix's means of obtaining harmony through contrast were also explained further: not only did he realize which colors mutually harmonized each other by contrast, but he also knew how to spread them effectively throughout the canvas: "He pursued unity in the interpenetration of opposites. Bringing together all the facets of green, all the variants of red, he modified them, mixed them together, provided them with weakened echoes or redoublings of force, and composed of them a harmony mordant for the mind, caressing for the eyes."[61] Such harmonies, according to Blanc, are to be found in *Les Femmes d'Alger*, the color scheme of which he analyzed in a long passage[62] that, incidentally, appears to have served as the basis for Signac's laudatory remarks on the picture in *D'Eugène Delacroix au néo-impressionnisme*.[63] Gradation and optical mixture were likewise discussed in Blanc's article, and once more Delacroix's discoveries are singled out for praise. And of special importance for Seurat was Blanc's analysis of Delacroix's highly rationalized procedure, which was, contrary to popular opinion, slow and deliberate in nature.[64]

Blanc's writings thus served as an effective introduction to Chevreul's principles and to Delacroix's methods. His remarks were undoubtedly of particular value to Seurat because he explained specifically how the science of color could be applied in painting and illustrated his points with appropriate references to Delacroix's work. It was but a short step for Seurat to turn from these writings to a firsthand study of Delacroix's paintings and to Chevreul's *De la loi du contraste simultané des couleurs*.

### *Rood's* Modern Chromatics (Students' Text-Book of Color)

Though trained as a physicist, Ogden N. Rood's[65] activities as an amateur painter undoubtedly made him sympathetic to artists' problems. In the book that was to influence Seurat and his friends, *Modern Chromatics (Students' Text-Book of Color)* (New York, 1879), he addressed his remarks to artists, rather than to scientists, and avoided overly difficult technical terminology; indeed, most of the latter half of the book is couched in painters' language, not in scientific terms. At the same time, the *Text-Book* contains a thoroughgoing explanation of physical phenomena relevant to the problems of painting. For Seurat the chapters on the mixture of colors, complementary colors, contrast, gradation, and color combinations were of particular interest.

Let us begin with the chapter entitled "On the Mixture of Colours," where Rood explained the difference between mixing *light* of different colors and mixing *pigments* — a distinction that was to be of paramount importance for Neo-Impressionist theory — and insisted that the artist be aware that these two kinds of mixture are not governed by the same laws. He demonstrated that the mixture of light could be effected either by projecting beams of colored light on a screen or by rotating sets of Maxwell's discs at high speed. (An illustration of a color-mixing apparatus with Maxwell's discs has been reproduced as Figure 12.) For experimental purposes, Rood preferred the latter method because it facilitated the measurement of the proportions of color involved in the mixtures. While on this subject, he described several other techniques of mixing colored light, including one contrived by Mile that was to be of special interest to Seurat and his friends: according to Mile, small dots of color placed next to each other, when viewed at a distance, yield the same effects as mixtures obtained by rotating discs or from projected beams of colored light.[66]

Rood also observed that mixtures of colored light took place constantly in nature, and pointed out that this kind of mixture was quite distinct from that achieved through the combination of pigments, to which artists were accustomed. He summed up the difference as follows:

Figure 12. Color-Mixing Apparatus with Maxwell's Discs (from Amédée Guillemin, *La Lumière et les couleurs*).

It is evident that by *mingling two pigments* we obtain the resultant effect of two acts of absorption due to the two pigments: white light is twice subjected to the process of subtraction, and what remains over is the coloured light which finally emerges from the painted surface. On the other hand, the process of *mixing coloured light* is essentially one of addition; and, this being so, we find it quite natural that the results given by these two methods should never be identical, and often should differ widely.[67]

Then he suggested that the artist study the important differences between additive mixture of light and subtractive mixture of pigments,[68] and demonstrated through numerous experiments with Maxwell's discs that superior luminosity could be obtained by mixing color additively. Rood's conclusion was that the mixture of pigments on the painter's palette, as opposed to "the true mixture of the colours" (that is, additive mixture), tends toward black.[69] To simplify the artist's task of predicting mixtures, he published a color triangle (Figure 13) based on Maxwell's

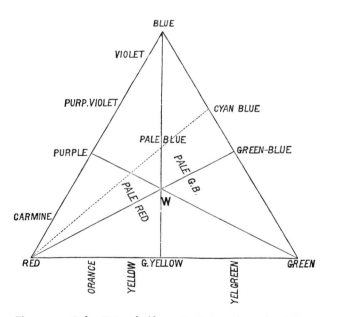

Figure 13. Color Triangle (from O. N. Rood, *Students' Text-Book of Color, or Modern Chromatics*).

researches, which showed the results of mixing the primaries and complementaries with each other.

He also studied the influence of colored lights on objects and found that additive mixture was an important factor here, too:

> In calculating for the effects produced by illuminating coloured surfaces by coloured light, we must be guided mainly by the laws which govern mixtures of coloured lights, rather than by those which can be deduced from experience with pigments; they are certainly useful in teaching us, when studying from nature, fearlessly to follow even the most evanescent indications of the eye, utterly regardless of the fact that they disobey laws which we have learned from the palette.[70]

In his chapter, "On the Duration of the Impression on the Retina," Rood provided an explanation of the theoretical basis of additive mixture of color through the use of Maxwell's discs. He pointed out that Helmholtz had conducted experiments on this subject and had concluded that the hues of the rapidly rotating discs mixed "in the eye" because the initial impression of light on the retina lasted "with undiminished strength about one forty-eighth of a second."[71] The duration of the sensation of light on the retina, or "positive after-image," had a definite function, according to Rood, in permitting one to mix masses of light in varying proportions by using Maxwell's discs. However, he gave no specific recommendations about how the laws governing this phenomenon should be applied to painting.[72]

The problem of color contrast, too, occupied Rood, as it did Chevreul; but the former took a more rigorous scientific approach to the matter. While Chevreul gained most of his experience in a tapestry workshop and did not rely on accurate physical measurements, Rood presented as evidence for his conclusions the results of his own and others' laboratory experiments. Among his contributions, on the subject of contrast, was a study of the effects of saturation brought about through the juxtaposition of colors, and one of the most important results of his experiments was a contrast-diagram (Figure 14; the plate from the French edition has been reproduced as Figure 15), in which twenty-two colors

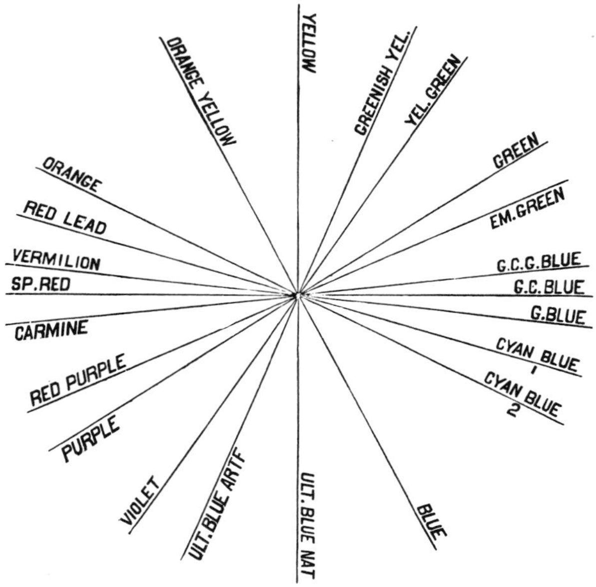

Figure 14. Contrast-Diagram (from Rood, *op. cit.*).

were paired off in exact complementary relationship. This device was to be particularly valuable to the Neo-Impressionists as a convenient means of locating complementaries, especially since the colors were named as painters' pigments, not in physicists' terms. We shall have occasion to refer frequently to this contrast-diagram because Seurat is known to have been interested in it: a copy he made of it was found among his effects after his death (Figure 16).[73]

Rood also conducted experiments on various optical effects of contrast, including the intensification and reduction of the apparent saturation of color by juxtaposing similar and contrasting hues. However, his remarks on this subject, rather than being particularly original in content, merely echo Chevreul's discoveries.

On the subject of gradation, Rood asserted that colors could be made richer and more agreeable in appearance by composing

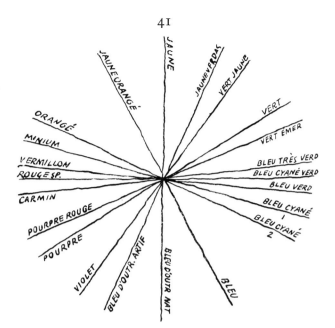

Figure 15. Contrast-Diagram (from Rood, *Théorie scienti-fique des couleurs*).

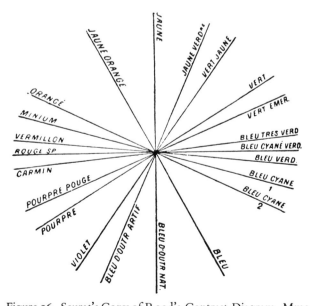

Figure 16. Seurat's Copy of Rood's Contrast-Diagram, Mme. Ginette Signac Collection, Paris.

them not of flat, unmodulated tones, but by putting side by side colors that are close to each other on the chromatic circle — in "small intervals." Ruskin is cited as a major proponent of this method of enriching color, and he is quoted at some length in Rood's book. Also the author mentioned another related phenomenon, under the heading of gradation, which, significantly, contains the seeds of the pointillist technique:

> There is . . . another lower degree of gradation which has a peculiar charm of its own, and is very precious in art and nature. The effect referred to takes place when different colours are placed side by side in lines or dots, and then viewed at such a distance that the blending is more or less accomplished by the eye of the beholder. Under these circumstances the tints mix on the retina, and produce new colours, which are identical with those that are obtained by the method of revolving discs.[74]

In this context, Rood also called attention to the work of the German physicist Heinrich-Wilhelm Dove, who had discovered that "when two masses of light simultaneously act on the eyes, lustre is perceived, provided we are in any way made conscious that there are actually *two* masses of light. . . . According to Dove's theory, we have here the conditions necessary for the production of more or less soft brilliancy."[75] Owing to the importance of this passage for Seurat's art, we shall have occasion to return to it later in this book.

In one of the least scientific portions of his text, Rood tried to discover pleasing combinations of colors by arranging them in pairs and triads. He arrived at a general principle governing such combinations, which may be summarized as follows: hues separated by more than 90 degrees on the color circle will be harmonious. Also, he divided the chromatic circle into a warm and a cool half, advising that, if possible, warm colors should predominate in pictorial compositions.

Rood's concluding chapter deals with the practical application of many of the principles discussed earlier in the book, and he suggests here what the artist's aims in painting should be. Although he believed that color should be subordinate to form, "its impor-

tance still remains very great, and it is trifling to attempt to
adorn with colour that which is really only a light-and-shade
drawing."[76] As to the aim of painting, he observed

> The object of painting is the production, by the use of colour, of more
> or less perfect representations of natural objects. . . . If the work is done
> directly from nature, and is at the same time elaborate, it will consist of
> an attempt to represent, not all the facts presented by the scene, but only
> certain classes of facts, namely, such as are considered by the artist most
> important or most pictorial, or to harmonize best with each other.[77]

In summary, Rood's recommendations for good color in painting
are the following: a well-planned chromatic composition; a firm
foundation in light and shade; the use of gradation; and pure, clear
colors. In the end, however, Rood suggested that the student of
painting should also study the work of good colorists and not
cling too closely to rules[78] — a remarkably liberal point of view
for one trained as a physicist.

### Sutter's "Les Phénomènes de la vision"

For our present purposes, the most important of the six installments of David Sutter's[79] "Les Phénomènes de la vision" are the
last two; the first four are concerned mainly with questions of
"esthetic lines," composition, and the analysis of antique sculpture.
The fifth article deals at length with chiaroscuro and color in terms
that, as we shall point out, are particularly relevant to Seurat's art.
Early in this installment Sutter restated Leonardo's principle of
value contrast, here referred to as "irradiation," which he defined
as follows: "Irradiation is a phenomenon of light which makes
objects stand out one from the other, setting them in sharp
relief."[80] Sutter urged the painter to include such effects in his
pictures: "Observe a white wall standing out against the sky. You
will see a white line lighter than the surface of the wall, and a blue
or gray line darker than the mass of the sky. This line of irradiation
remains unnoticed by the majority of painters, and, nevertheless,
it is of the greatest importance to copy it exactly."[81]

After proposing further aphorisms concerning the handling of light and shadow, Sutter turned to the question of color. In discussing this subject he followed Chevreul's example by identifying the complementary pairs as red-green, orange-blue, and yellow-violet. He also admired Goethe's method of setting up a color diagram which placed these complementary pairs on the points of two superimposed color triangles (Figure 17),[82] which appear to be almost identical to Charles Blanc's diagram (Figure 9, page 31). And, like Blanc and Chevreul, he saw that complementaries could neutralize each other. In summarizing the nature of color, Sutter added little to the theories postulated by Blanc and Chevreul.[83] Thus on this particular level, Sutter's ideas merely reinforce concepts of color developed earlier in the nineteenth century, rather than serving as a major source of new data for Seurat.

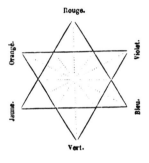

Figure 17. Chromatic Diagram (from David Sutter, *Philosophie des beaux-arts*).

Sutter believed, too, that color had an intrinsic symbolic and emblematic character: "Red, the most powerful of all colors, is the symbol of height, force, and authority; lilac or violet of the solar spectrum, the symbol of coquetry, instability, and weakness. Orange is the image of pride and vanity; blue, that of modesty and candor, etc."[84] The value of this statement and others like it will be pointed out in Chapter 4; as far as this writer can determine, it does not appear to be relevant to Seurat's early work. But Sutter's remarks on color harmony do concern us here. He believed that "the laws of the esthetic harmony of colors are learned as one learns the rules of musical harmony. The knowledge of harmony in music makes one understand immediately the laws of unity and esthetic harmony of colors."[85] These sentiments, it will be noted, are remarkably close to those expressed by Blanc.

The sixth and last installment in Sutter's "Les Phénomènes de la vision" is particularly interesting because it recommends to painters a knowledge of scientific principles. Here the author argued succinctly for the use of law in art: "It is impossible to render exactly the parts of a whole without knowing the laws which govern the whole. In the experimental sciences, one can understand perfectly the parts of a whole without going back to general laws; but, in the arts, since the parts of a whole must be ordered among themselves and with the ensemble, a knowledge of these laws is indispensable."[86] Following this statement, Sutter asserted that there were two types of esthetics: the speculative, dealing with the means of analyzing beauty in nature; and applied esthetics, which provides "the formula of all the rules which constitute grandeur, order, and harmony."[87] It is chiefly this latter aspect that concerned him, both in the articles now under discussion and in his books. In this context, the following aphorisms embody his views on the role of reason and rules in art:

> Instinct is unchanging; reason progresses ceaselessly.
> Reason rests upon positive facts, not on pompous and senseless words.
> True criticism is based upon precise rules.
> Feeling accepts truth without proof; reason gives proof of its judgments.
> In all artistic creation, feeling and reason lend each other mutual support.
> In any science, the role of reason is greater than that of instinct.
> Art is one facet of the laws of order and harmony in nature; through observation, a group of positive ideas, realized in practice, has been drawn from these laws.[88]

Here instinct must bow before law; yet both must be present, even though reason should have the upper hand. Science, in relation to feeling and genius, is important, yet it is limited to a foundational role which can be learned.

Sutter summed up these relationships by stating: "When this science becomes fixed in the mind, the rules become second nature and come forth, like the rules of grammar, without thinking about them."[89] This belief, as we shall see later, was apparently held by Seurat; his friends and associates confirm it in their reports concerning his convictions about the role of science and rules in art.

But in this article perhaps the most concise statement of the value of science is the following:

> Science relieves one of all uncertainties, permits one to move about in complete freedom and in a greatly extended area; therefore, to believe that one necessarily excludes the other is to doubly wrong both art and science. Does science not enable us to give a reason for all things, to know the limits of each genre, the character of each passion, of each situation of the soul, and to express it with the color and degree of power which suits it?[90]

Sutter also believed that there were rules governing the expression of the passions that transcend the tastes of individuals and schools: "Only analysis permits one to establish a necessary rapport between the style and the expression of the passions; it considerably shortens the path of observation and experience and promptly places the artist ... in a situation of incontestable superiority."[91] Because teaching in art schools had degenerated so much in his own time, Sutter felt that it was necessary to resurrect a knowledge of rules and principles, just as the Carracci had done after a century of "decadence."[92] (Seurat must have felt acutely, about 1880, the kind of degeneration in teaching to which Sutter referred. We have noted that he became dissatisfied with the codified methods practiced in Lehmann's *atelier* and turned for inspiration to the principles embodied in the art of the old masters. Indeed, Sutter's articles may have been one of the catalytic agents that discouraged him from returning to the École des Beaux-Arts after his discharge from the army in November, 1880.)

Exactly what appealed to Seurat in this last article of the series is known because he marked with an asterisk the following passages, which will be quoted in their entirety:

There is one thing in common to all kinds of painting, all feelings and styles: the perfect application of the laws of unity, order, and harmony. And as all the arts have the same foundation, the same rules should serve as a basis for all artistic instruction.

It was necessary then to find the clear and precise formula for the harmony of lines, of light and color, and to give the scientific reason for these rules. It was all the more necessary that the artist, dedicated to routine, not attain relative perfection until his hair began to gray and until the best years of his life were spent in endless groping and research.

We stress this essential point: all rules having been derived from the laws of nature themselves, nothing is easier to learn by principles nor more indispensable. In the arts, everything should be willed.[93]

.    .    .    .    .    .    .    .    .    .

With the support of rules, which are simple, as is everything which is true, one proceeds with confidence to analyze the works of all the masters of every school of painting, sculpture, and architecture; one clearly proves that there is no beauty without a logical relation of taste, subjected to the laws of harmony, and that these laws are constant, however lofty the subject may be.[94]

In Sutter's "Les Phénomènes de la vision" we find a strong reaction against imprecise Romantic esthetic theories that relied so heavily on instinct and personal sensibility. As a countermeasure, Sutter turned both to French academic theory (and the artists admired by this view) and to the results derived from the scientific disciplines of physics and optics. In effect, Sutter asked the artist to follow time-tested laws of harmony and order, and yet also advised him to take advantage of the proofs furnished by modern science that confirmed these laws. He thus maintains a position rather close to that of Charles Blanc: both are firmly grounded in French academic theory and both took much from Leonardo's *Trattato della Pittura*; but they both recognized that nineteenth-century science also had much to offer artists of their own time.

It should be noted, too, that Sutter wanted to reduce the expression of the "passions" to irrefutable rules; similar ideas, as we shall see, were later espoused by Seurat and his friend Charles Henry. Though grounded in academic theory, these questions came to be studied increasingly by another scientific discipline, experimental esthetics, that arose about the middle of the nineteenth century, and which we shall consider in Chapter 4.

## STYLISTIC SOURCES
### Delacroix

What did Seurat see in Delacroix's art? To answer this question we may turn to his notes of 1881 on a group of the master's paintings, some of which were then in the hands of Parisian art dealers.[95] In these pictures Seurat discovered a number of principles that were later to become part of the Neo-Impressionists' artistic credo. First, he admired Delacroix's ability to harmonize colors, particularly through contrasting complementary pairs. In the color scheme of *Les Convulsionnaires de Tanger* (Jerome Hill Collection, Minneapolis) Seurat observed: "Grayish-green white material accompanied by an underlinen, streaked with rose, which shows on the arm and at the bottom of the leg (harmony of the red and green street)." Or again, "On another part of the roof hangs a blue drapery, grayed by the distance, harmonizing with the orange-white of the wall." Seurat noted, too, that in some of Delacroix's paintings, complementaries "exalted," or intensified, each other: "One of the fanatics . . . has a red undergarment. This red is exalted by the green edge which borders his gray-white-yellow burnoose." Throughout these pictures — particularly in the shadows — Seurat found vibrancy, freshness, and delicacy of color. For example, about the *Cortège de l'empereur du Maroc*, he wrote: "There is not much heavy brushwork . . . the exceedingly fine tones become even more so through the superimposition [of color] which is quite visible." Furthermore, he praised Delacroix's subtle handling of colored grays, particularly as seen in the distance of this picture.

Because these notes are relatively brief, we must also turn to Paul Signac's *D'Eugène Delacroix au néo-impressionnisme* for additional evidence concerning Delacroix's importance for the Neo-

Impressionist painters. This book, while not by Seurat, is by his closest friend, who shared his interest in Delacroix and whose esthetic had much in common with Seurat's. Writing on the ways in which he paved the way for the art of Seurat and his circle, Signac saw in Delacroix's work the application of the principles of gradation, optical mixture, harmony of color through contrast and analogy, and the use of simultaneous contrast in order to obtain greater hue intensity.

On Delacroix's use of gradation in his repainting of the *Scène du Massacre de Scio* (Louvre, Paris) — presumably under Constable's influence — Signac wrote: "He completely repainted his canvas, working over the color, which he had laid on smoothly until then, with unblended touches of pigment, making it vibrate with the help of transparent glazes. At once he saw the canvas being unified, becoming airy, luminous, and gaining in power and also in truthfulness." [96] Signac added that, during his stay in Morocco, Delacroix had discovered that the "orientals" used the principle of gradation in their decorative arts: "He understood that the elements of which they are composed, intense and almost gaudy by themselves, are reconstituted into extremely delicate hues and are juxtaposed according to the immutable rules which assure their harmony. He ascertained that a colored surface is pleasing and brilliant only to the degree that it is neither smooth nor uniform, and that a color is beautiful only if it vibrates with a flickering lustre which gives it life." [97]

Signac perceived that optical mixture was another essential feature of Delacroix's method, the use of which permitted him to obtain lustrous combinations of colors widely separated from each other on the chromatic circle by hatching, rather than mixing them on the palette:

[Delacroix] creates by the juxtaposition of two colors . . . a third hue resulting from their optical mixture. His rarest colorations are created by this ingenious artifice and not by mixtures on the palette. Does he want to modify a color, calm it down, or reduce it? He does not muddy it by mixing it with an opposite color: he obtains the desired effect by superimposing light hatchings which influence the hue in the requisite direction without altering its purity.[98]

Through this technique — optical mixture — Delacroix was able to obtain "unmuddied grayish tones, whose fineness and lustre no amount of trituration on the palette could produce."[99]

Signac saw in Delacroix's work two kinds of color harmony — harmony by contrast and harmony by analogy — which, he pointed out, could be found in *Femmes d'Alger dans leur appartement* (Louvre, Paris). In this painting he discovered the following examples of harmony by contrast: "The negress' red turban stands out against a curtain of different colored bands, but it encounters only a greenish area of cloth — precisely that which forms the most satisfying accord with the red. The woodwork of the closet alternates between red and green and is another example of binary harmony."[100] The juxtaposition of areas of complementary color, however, had a second purpose; in addition to being harmonious, they could intensify each other. Signac pointed out the dual role played by the complementaries in *Femmes d'Alger dans leur appartement*: "The orange-red jacket of the woman reclining at the left has a blue-green lining. These surfaces of complementary hues excite and harmonize with each other, and this favorable contrast gives to the materials an intense *éclat* and lustre."[101]

On the subject of harmony by analogy, achieved through the "accord" of similar elements, Signac wrote: "One would have to mention, as an application of the accord of similar elements, almost all parts of the picture. They quiver and vibrate, thanks to touches of tone upon tone or of almost identical hues, whose diverse colors, placed flatly at first and to which he returns through that ingenious method of gradation, this subtle master has worked over, dabbed, caressed, and hatched."[102]

The crowning masterpiece of Delacroix's career, in Signac's opinion — which was undoubtedly shared by Seurat — was his decoration of the Chapelle des Saints-Anges at Saint-Sulpice (1856–1861; Figures 18 and 19). Signac's comments on these frescoes will be quoted in their entirety in order to gauge his, and very probably also Seurat's, reaction to them:

> For the decoration of this chapel, he no longer paints with any but the most simple and pure colors; he definitively renounces subordinating his color to chiaroscuro; light is spread everywhere; not a single black hole, not a single dark spot out of harmony with the other parts of the picture, no more opaque shadows, no more flat colors. He composes his colors with all the elements which should heighten and enliven them, unconcerned about imitating appearances or natural coloration. Color for color's sake, with no other pretext! Flesh, décor, accessories — everything is treated in the same way. There is not a single fragment of the painting that does not vibrate, shimmer, or glisten. Each local color is pushed to its maximum intensity, but always in harmony with its neighboring color, influenced by it and influencing it. All fuse with the shadows and lights in a harmonious and colorful whole, perfectly balanced, where nothing clashes."[103]

In this laudatory account, Signac obviously viewed these frescoes with the eyes of a Neo-Impressionist, and thus from a strictly historical point of view misjudged Delacroix's intentions. But what is important to note is that the younger painters saw in the chapel a triumph of vibrant, harmonious color, the handling of which contained many lessons for their own work.

### Impressionism

In his rebellion against the École des Beaux-Arts Seurat turned not only to the art of Delacroix but also to Impressionism. There is, however, considerable confusion about how much influence the Impressionists exerted on Seurat's painting, as well as about the time when this influence was felt. Some of this confusion was brought about by Paul Signac, who implied that Seurat ignored Impressionism before the spring of 1884[104] (that is, when *Une Baignade* was first exhibited), and many subsequent writers have followed Signac's statements on this matter without turning to documentary, critical, and pictorial evidence to the contrary.

Significantly, several contemporary critics who wrote about *Une Baignade* saw its Impressionist qualities immediately. In 1884,

Figure 18. Eugène Delacroix, *La Lutte de Jacob et de l'ange*, Chapelle des Saints-Anges, Saint-Sulpice, Paris. (Photo Bulloz.)

Figure 19. Delacroix, *Héliodore chassé du Temple*, Chapelle des Saints-Anges, Saint-Sulpice, Paris. (Photo Bulloz.)

for example, Claude Roger-Marx referred to it as an "Impressionist painting"[105] and observed that Seurat applied "without awkwardness and even with much accuracy the system of multicolored touches dear to Camille Pissarro."[106] Gustave Kahn realized, too, that *Une Baignade* "marked Seurat's passage into the Impressionist technique."[107] And even an anonymous New York critic observed in 1886 that in this canvas "the uncompromising strength of the impressionistic school is fully revealed."[108]

Furthermore, in the writings of Seurat's friends, certain Impressionist painters — Renoir, Monet, and Pissarro — are mentioned as having influenced him. According to Kahn, "He allied himself with Renoir (the Renoir of the portrait of Mme. Charpentier: comma-like strokes)."[109] In another article the same writer observed: "He had been intensely attracted to Renoir's early technique and also to Pissarro's, two painters, in fact, trying to obtain modeling on their canvases by the interlacing of small colored lines."[110] Again, Kahn cited Seurat's attitude toward the Impressionists: "From earlier Impressionism, he willingly declared that his three most important sources, by example of their work and the direction imposed upon painters close to them, were Degas, Renoir, and Pissarro."[111] And, as we have seen, Seurat stated in a letter to Fénéon that he was struck by the intuition of Monet and Pissarro.[112] Unfortunately, we have little documentary evidence, as we do in the case of Delacroix, informing us of what Seurat saw in the work of the Impressionists at this time. But there is abundant stylistic evidence in the preparatory oil studies for *Une Baignade* to indicate that Seurat drew much from Impressionism. The nature and degree of this influence will be discussed shortly.

## *UNE BAIGNADE*: STYLISTIC AND THEORETICAL SOURCES

We have reviewed the contents of five texts Seurat studied and have considered his interest in the art of Delacroix and the Impressionists; it will now be our task to show how these sources were utilized in his search for "a formula for optical painting," as exemplified pictorially by *Une Baignade*. In the following pages, therefore, a number of different, but interrelated, aspects of the painting and its preparatory studies will be analyzed — aspects that were of special interest to Seurat and his friends: namely, light-shadow relationships, the separation of elements and their optical mixture, gradation, contrast, the system of color harmony, pigments, and procedure and method. In discussing *Une Baignade*, we shall point out specific correspondences between Seurat's style, technique, and theory and the texts he read (including writings of lesser importance by Couture, Corot, and Leonardo), as well as the work of artists he is known to have studied by 1884. We shall have a triple aim in mind: to show that a firm theoretical foundation for *Une Baignade* exists in these texts; to demonstrate the ways in which specific prescriptions in such writings were applied in this canvas; and, where possible, to cite stylistic precedents in the work of other painters.

The subject of *Une Baignade* is a group of young men bathing and lounging on the bank of the Seine at Asnières, an industrial suburb of Paris. Although representing an outdoor scene, the canvas was undoubtedly painted in the studio; but Seurat did execute at the site a series of small preparatory oil studies, which he called "*croquetons*," or "sketchettes." In addition, he studied the position and form of the figures that populate the landscape in a group of conté crayon drawings, which were done from models in the studio. These figure studies, along with the *croquetons*, served as a means of collecting visual data to be incorporated in the final canvas, which was, in the last analysis, a studio painting.[113] (It should be noted that Seurat repainted a few areas of *Une Baignade* in a pointillist technique about 1887.[114]) Because of their obvious dependence on the Impressionist vocabulary, we shall turn first to the oil studies for *Une Baignade*.

*Impressionism and the Oil Studies* (Croquetons) *for* Une
Baignade

Although there is some argument among art historians about
the nature and scope of the Impressionist movement, it is generally
agreed that the mature, or "high," phase of Impressionism existed
during a brief period of time, namely, from the early 1870s to the
early 1880s. Before 1874, the year of the first exhibition of the
Impressionist group, their artistic aims had not been codified, and
in many respects each of the major participating painters was
experimenting in his own individual way. But from 1874 to 1882,
most of the Impressionists were in close touch with each other,
exhibited together, and discussed mutual artistic problems.
Moreover, their styles, techniques, and aims had much in common
during this brief span of years. About 1882, however, this loosely
knit group began to dissolve, and some of the painters — Renoir
and Pissarro, for instance — sought to revise or reform their
styles. Following the example of Venturi[115] and Schapiro,[116] we
shall view Impressionism as that narrowly defined style and
approach practiced by Monet, Renoir, Pissarro, and Sisley, among
others, between about 1874 and 1882, the basic tenets of which
will be outlined in the following paragraphs.[117]

One of the Impressionists' chief aims was to record the appearance of their subject, as conditioned by the light falling on it,
without preconceptions of any kind.[118] They felt that they must
execute their paintings at the site and add nothing more to them in
the studio.[119] Because they were fascinated by effects of natural light
which changed with the weather and the time of day, the Impressionists had to work rapidly; indeed, according to Laforgue's
authoritative report, they sometimes spent as little as fifteen
minutes on a canvas at a given time of day[120] (however, the artist
could continue working on the same painting on subsequent days,
provided that the lighting conditions remained unchanged).[121]
Since the Impressionists believed that nature should be seen chiefly
as patches of colored light, strong local colors in their paintings

were often minimized in an effort to capture the character of the illumination, atmospheric effects, or reflections that modified the appearance of the subject.[122] In seeing nature in terms of color and minimizing chiaroscuro as a major pictorial device, they portrayed shadows as blue or blue-violet and treated sunlight as orange or yellow-orange in hue. The Impressionists' mode of vision implied that line, as the tangible boundary between objects, had to be eliminated, and that the composition of the painting should be determined almost entirely by the actual position of color areas seen in nature; marked alterations in design by arbitrary pictorial means were not permitted.[123]

While the Impressionists eliminated exaggerated contrasts between values as a major formal element, they did rely heavily on hue contrast in two ways: to sharpen the visual distinction between objects and their background by surrounding them with strokes of their complementary color, and (as in Delacroix's paintings) as a means of obtaining greater hue intensity by placing relatively large areas of complementary colors beside each other. Complementaries were used, too, not only to intensify each other mutually but also to cancel each other through optical mixture. Necessary to this kind of mixture and to the recording of diverse elements of color was a small, irregular brushstroke. It appears in Impressionist paintings as comma-shaped, in short dashes, spots, hatching, and in a multitude of other indefinable forms. Common to all these varieties of brushwork, however, was the function of documenting the complex fabric of color that nature presented to the Impressionist's unspoiled eye.

In addition, they frequently (though not always) eliminated earth colors from their palette, concentrating instead on pure pigments approximating the hues of the solar spectrum. These were defined by Signac, who would have known the Impressionists' views on color through personal contact with Guillaumin, as "yellows, oranges, vermilions, lakes, reds, violets, blues, and intense greens, such as Veronese and emerald greens."[124]

To what extent did Seurat adopt an Impressionist approach in

Figure 20. *Étude finale pour "Une Baignade,"* The Art Institute of Chicago, Bequest of Mrs. David Levy.

Figure 21. *Vêtements, étude pour "Une Baignade,"* Tate Gallery, London.

executing the *croquetons* for *Une Baignade*? In the *Baigneur assis* (D.-R. 96), *Chevaux dans le fleuve* (D.-R. 88), and *Étude finale pour "Une Baignade"* (D.-R. 97; Figure 20), he treated many of the forms that receive the direct light of the sun as tinged with orange or yellow-orange; the shadowed side of these forms are tinted with blue or blue-violet. Also, in many of the *croquetons* the brushstrokes are unmistakably inspired by the Impressionists. The water in *Chevaux dans le fleuve* (D.-R. 88), *Vêtements* (D.-R. 89, Figure 21), and *Garçons se baignant* (D.-R. 91), for example, is executed in a series of short, overlapping horizontal strokes, and the riverbank and sky are represented by broadly brushed *balayé* (that is, swept over or crisscrossed) strokes. In most of these panels, however, Seurat did not use the irregular commalike strokes found so frequently in Monet's paintings of the late 1870s; rather, Seurat's more rationally controlled execution has closer affinities to Pissarro's technique of the early eighties, when he relied heavily on the *balayé* stroke, as seen in *Paysannes au repos* (d. 1881; Toledo Museum of Art; Figure 22). Renoir's technique of sweeping the brush over the forms very lightly in a series of short parallel strokes (seen in *Rocky Crags, L'Estaque* [detail]; d. 1882; Museum of Fine Arts, Boston; Figure 23) was also echoed by Seurat in some of his *croquetons*, as in the seated figure in the center of *Étude finale pour "Une Baignade"* (Figure 20).

Seurat, like the Impressionists, frequently used myriad small strokes to record the multitude of hues corresponding to the local colors, the color of the sunlight, and various reflections. This approach is exemplified in his treatment of the river in *Une Baignade*, to mention only one example. We need only turn to Monet's *River Scene, Vétheuil* (d. 1880; Metropolitan Museum of Art, Figure 24) to find a similar technique used in transcribing the multiplicity of elements contributing to the surface of the water. The Impressionists' practice of recording the effects on the grass of the color of the light (orange or yellow-orange) and reflections from the blue sky overhead, as seen in Monet's *Fisherman's Cottage on the Cliffs at Varengeville* (d. 1882; Museum of Fine Arts,

Figure 22. Camille Pissarro, *Paysannes au repos*, Toledo Museum of Art, Gift of
Edward Drummond Libbey, 1935.

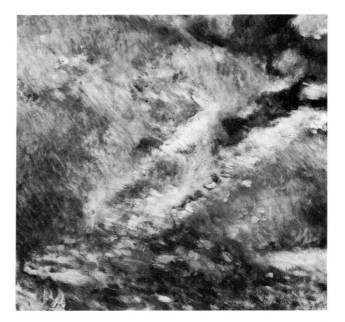

Figure 23. Pierre-Auguste Renoir, *Rocky Crags*, *L'Estaque*
[detail], Museum of Fine Arts, Boston.

Boston), is also echoed by Seurat in some of the *Baignade* oil
studies; an instance of such division of color may be found in the
riverbank of *Chevaux dans le fleuve* (D.-R. 88), where, over
the local color of green, separate strokes of light blue and yellow-
orange are superimposed.

When one views such *croquetons* as *Baigneur assis* (D.-R. 96)
and *Étude finale pour "Une Baignade"* (D.-R. 97; Figure 20) from
a distance of about five feet, one finds that their various colors
tend to lose their individuality as separate hues and undergo partial
optical mixture. In many cases, however, as Webster pointed out
in his study of the technique of Impressionism,[125] the dominant
local colors — blue-green in the water and green on the riverbank — frequently retain their identity and are merely modified
by the hues that are superimposed over them in smaller quantity.

Figure 24. Claude Monet, *River Scene, Vétheuil*, The Metropolitan Museum of Art, New York, Bequest of William Church Osborn, 1951.

The final effect, then, in both of these panels is one of shimmering, vibrating color, which may be found as a common characteristic of most "high" Impressionist paintings.

In summarizing the Impressionists' style and methods, we observed that they relied heavily on hue contrast so as mutually to intensify juxtaposed or neighboring colors (much as Delacroix had done) and to enhance the separation of objects from their background, thereby creating a sense of space surrounding them. An excellent example of the application of the former device may be found in Monet's *Path in the Île St. Martin, Vétheuil* (d. 1880; Metropolitan Museum of Art), where bright spots of red representing flowers are placed against a green background, which is complementary to it; as a result, the green and the red both appear more intense. The latter principle is employed effectively in the *Saint-Lazare Station* (d. 1878; David Rockefeller Collection) by the same artist. Here Monet succeeded in making the building in the upper right-hand quarter of the painting seem to exist in space and at the same time to stand out from its background by applying a broad patch of light yellow-orange in the sky where the bluish-gray outline of the roof meets it; conversely, where the yellow-orange vertical wall at the extreme left of the building meets the sky behind it, a broad stroke of pronounced blue near the line of juncture serves to reinforce the contrast between the two planes.

Seurat applied both of these principles in his *Étude finale pour "Une Baignade"* (Figure 20). Pairs of complementary colors in close proximity that intensify each other mutually are the orange hat of the boy in the water at the far right against the blue water; the light orange of the flesh of the large seated figure in the center of the picture against the blue background; and the muted orange of the clouds of smoke in the center against the blue sky. Also, the tan-orange dog is juxtaposed over the blue shadowed side of the reclining figure at the lower left.

Like Monet, Seurat also followed the principle of juxtaposing complementaries wherever it was necessary to reinforce the separa-

tion between planes or areas. The major contrasts of this type in
*Étude finale pour "Une Baignade"* are as follows: the blue-green
and green foliage at the horizon is surrounded by strokes of pink
and red-orange; similarly, where the yellow-orange planes of the
factories meet the sky, the sky is colored blue. But when the bluish
shadowed sides of these same buildings meet the sky immediately
behind them, it turns to yellow-orange. This same pair of alternating complementary colors may be found in the areas surrounding the central seated figure; where yellow-orange meets the
background, the background is blue; when the blue shadows of
the boy (as in his face) meet the water, they are juxtaposed against
yellow-orange.

There are, of course, significant differences between the style of
Seurat's *croquetons* and that of the Impressionists. For our purposes,
the most pronounced difference is found in his brushwork, which
is usually more mechanical and regular in size and appears more
abstractly detached from the actual contours and textures of the
objects represented. Further obvious discrepancies between
Seurat's and the Impressionists' style may be found in composition
and in the treatment of the human figure, but these matters are
not of particular concern to us here.

Having considered the influence of Impressionism on the
preparatory oil studies, let us now turn to the completed canvas.
In the process of analyzing *Une Baignade*, we shall take up the
problem of identifying Seurat's sources and of determining
the way in which they contributed to the style and technique of
this painting.

## *Light-Shadow Relationships*

Seurat represented the sunlight permeating *Une Baignade* as a
warm, light orange hue, which sometimes becomes pink-orange
or yellow-orange; conversely, most of the shadows take on a blue
or blue-violet cast, the exceptions being the shadowed side of the
trousers of the reclining man in the left foreground and the other

dark brown accents on the riverbank. This mode of treating light and shade is exemplified particularly well in subject matter whose local color is white or nearly white, such as the flesh of the semi-nude figures or the pile of clothing. In this clothing, the area exposed to the direct light of the sun is represented by white pigment tinted slightly with pink-orange; the shadow cast by the hat, which blocks the sun's rays, is distinctly bluish in tone. The same kind of color relationship may be seen in the boy bathing at the far right: here the portion of the figure that receives the full light of the sun is colored with very light pink-orange tones. But the shadowed side of the body and the areas from which direct sunlight has been blocked are bluish in color. Similarly, in the grass under the direct light of the sun, Seurat recorded its action on the local color, green, by introducing strokes of yellow-orange and orange; touches of blue, on the other hand, are applied in the cast shadows (Plate A). Generally, then, Seurat used a light dominated by variations of orange throughout most of *Une Baignade* and frequently introduced the complementary of that light, blue or blue-violet, in the shadows.[126] However, he did not always apply orange in the lighted areas as a separate element; in the flesh of the figures and in the white drapery the color of the sunlight was mixed with the local color on the palette before being applied to the canvas.

The explanation for Seurat's treating light consistently as orange or yellow-orange and shadows as blue or blue-violet (that is, as complementary to the color of the light) can, of course, be found in his allegiance to the Impressionists' approach at this time. We have already noted that he had followed their method of handling light and shadow in some of the *croquetons* for *Une Baignade*, and it is not surprising to find it carried over in the execution of the final canvas.

Interestingly, this same kind of light-shadow relationship was recommended, in different ways, by Chevreul, Blanc, and Rood. Chevreul's remarks on this subject are particularly relevant:

When the sun is on the horizon, and when it strikes opaque bodies with its orange light, the shadows that these bodies project, illuminated by the light which comes from higher parts of the atmosphere, appear blue. This colorisation is not due to the colour of the sky, as many persons believe; for if, instead of the bodies being struck by the orange light of the sun, they were struck by red, yellow, green, or violet light, the shadows would appear green, violet, red, or yellow.[127]

The law of color stated in this excerpt — that the shadows should be complementary in hue to the light — was clearly obeyed by Seurat in painting much of *Une Baignade*.

Chevreul also made additional, more specific recommendations about the importance of indicating the effects of the illuminating light upon objects. Here, significantly, he discussed "modifications produced by two different lights—as, for example, the light of the sun, and diffused daylight — each lighting distinct parts of the same object,"[128] a lighting situation similar to that found in *Une Baignade*. He illustrated these modifications by listing the effects that orange light has on every color of the spectrum, thus providing theoretical justification for, and a useful set of rules to guide, Seurat's handling of orange light in his paintings.[129]

Blanc, as we have seen, was also aware of bluish shadows and recommended that the artist incorporate the effects of colored light in his pictures:

In nature the light comes to us variously colored, according to climate, the medium, the hour of the day. . . . If the light is orange like that of the sun, this same [blue] drapery will seem much bluer in the shade and less so in the light.[130]

It is interesting to note, parenthetically, that Chevreul and Blanc, whose books are dated 1839 and 1867, respectively, had already observed and published their ideas about blue shadows long before the Impressionists "discovered" them around 1870.

Rood, from whom we should expect more about the color of light and shadow, referred to the subject only occasionally. But he was certainly conscious of the phenomenon of warm light and cool shadow in the following statement, which might well apply to *Une Baignade*: "Grass in the sunshine acquires a yellowish-green hue; in the shade its colour is more bluish."[131] Rood was also aware of the dual illumination of objects in nature from the sun and sky, particularly in sunsets:

> There is another mode of mingling coloured light, which is not much used by physicists, though it is of constant occurrence in nature. We refer to the case where two masses of coloured light fall simultaneously on the same object. Sunsets furnish the grandest examples of these effects, the objects in a landscape being at the same time illuminated by the blue sky and the orange or red rays of the sinking sun.[132]

### Separation of the Elements and Optical Mixture

In painting the grass in *Une Baignade*, Seurat separated the orange and yellow-orange strokes, representing sunlight, from the underlying local color. The application of this method, which Fénéon and Signac referred to as the "separation of the elements," can be detected throughout the painting. It is most pronounced, however, in the river, where a multitude of different colors are reflected from the rippling surface of the water. The local color of the water is blue-green, but this, in turn, is influenced by two other hues: the pale yellow-orange of the sunlight, already mentioned, and reflections from the blue sky. While these three colors — blue-green, yellow-orange, and blue — occupy the majority of the water area, additional hues are introduced through the presence of reflections from the factories on the opposite bank, the sailboats, and the rowboat at the far right. A particularly complex set of reflections is projected onto the water from the local color of the rowboat (blue-green), the clothing of the figures (white, blue-violet, tan) and the sail (red, white, blue). As we might expect, these elements are expressed by individual strokes of pigment that do not mix physically with each other on the surface of the canvas (see Plate B).

Far fewer elements contribute to the color of the grass on the riverbank, because it does not encourage reflection of extraneous hues. Here, however, in addition to the modifying factor of the sunlight, another element enters into the picture: strokes of blue or blue-violet — hues that are complementary to the color of the light, and which also represent reflections from the sky into the shadow areas (see Plate A). Furthermore, certain forms that are in close proximity to the grass — such as the back of the young man wearing a straw hat seated at the left, the arm of the man reclining in the foreground, and the hat on the pile of clothing in the center of the picture — show the effects of green and blue-green, colors that are reflected from the grass. The technique of separating colored elements described here imposes two requirements on the artist. First, he must allow each layer of the painting to dry before adding subsequent dosages of pigment, in order to avoid fortuitous mixtures on the canvas that might damage the purity and intensity of the colors; and second, he must rely on full or partial optical mixture as a means of blending the various tones that contribute to the areas in question.

Seurat utilized optical mixture in *Une Baignade* for several different purposes. First, as indicated in the foregoing paragraphs, over a fundamental local color he superimposed dosages corresponding to the hue of the illuminating light. In the grass, for example, orange strokes were applied over a green underbody (Plate A). As one moves away from the painting, these two colors gradually coalesce until they mix optically to form a lively yellow-green tinged with orange. If, however, these same hues are mixed subtractively on the palette, the result will be a dull, desaturated olive-green.

The quality of color vibration experienced in Plate A may also be found in the water (Plate B), where, at a distant view, the small individual strokes recording the various elements of color and light undergo partial optical mixture. It should be pointed out here, however, that Seurat was not attempting to produce radically new colors from these components. Rather, he used optical mixture as a means of varying and modifying an area of one dominant hue — such as the green of the grass or the blue-green of the water — according to the character of the light and reflections that strike it, without soiling the individual colors that enter into its composition. In this way he obtained greater luminosity and intensity than if he had mixed these hues physically; and at the same time he created an illusion of shimmering vibrancy in the canvas.

A similar kind of mixture is found in many of the shadows. In the shadows on the boy at the far right or on the central figure, for example, Seurat simultaneously recorded the local color of the flesh (pink to yellow-orange) and the color of the shadow (blue). Because these two colors were applied in about equal quantity, when viewed at a distance they fuse into a luminous "optical gray" in which the two components appear to "cancel out" each other. In these shadows the orange tends, at times, to be stronger, and at other times, blue triumphs over the orange, producing, respectively, an orange-gray or a gray of bluish cast.

We have already seen that the Impressionists frequently applied a host of diverse colors to their canvases by means of small, separate brushstrokes and allowed these hues to mix fully or partially in the eye of the observer. Clearly inspired by Impressionism is the concept of painting much of *Une Baignade* in small multicolored touches of pigment that record the various aspects of light and hue appropriate to the subject. An excellent example of this treatment may be seen in the rowboat in the distance and the reflections surrounding it, which appear as irregular dashes of paint corresponding to every color ingredient falling upon, or reflected from, the water (Plate B). Indeed, such a detail is remarkably close in handling to Renoir's treatment of a similar subject in the distance of his *Boating Party at Châtou* (d. 1879; National Gallery of Art, Washington; Figure 25).

In certain ways, Delacroix also practiced the "separation of the elements," but his artistic goals were obviously less naturalistic than those of the Impressionists. His reason for "dividing" his colors, we learn from Charles Blanc, was to create tones of un-

UNE BAIGNADE

Figure 25. Pierre-Auguste Renoir, *Boating Party at Châtou*, National Gallery of Art, Washington. Gift of Sam A. Lewisohn.

usual freshness and delicacy through optical mixture, rather than by mixing pigments on the palette. This meant that small touches of a complementary color might be juxtaposed over an area of a given hue in order to reduce its intensity without soiling the pigments in question; or — if the complementaries were about equal in quantity — to create the luminous optical grays that Delacroix called "half-tints." [133]

Seurat could have found numerous instances of this kind of optical mixture in Delacroix's frescoes at Saint-Sulpice. An examination of their shadows and half-lights reveals that Delacroix relied very heavily on this means of neutralizing colors without sacrificing luminosity. In the shadows of these frescoes, particularly, he managed to create a wide range of indescribable colored grays that result from the optical mixture of hues quite distant from each other on the chromatic circle. [134] Such effects in the Senate and in the Chamber of Deputies were described eloquently by Signac:

> One could easily verify that the freshest and most delicate flesh tones are produced by coarse juxtaposed hatchings of green and red and that the luminous *éclat* of the skies is obtained by an analogous process. From a distance, these hatchings disappear, but the color resulting from their optical mixture reveals itself powerfully, whereas a flat hue seen from this distance would fade out or become obliterated. [135]

Blanc and Rood both wrote at some length about optical mixture, but, paradoxically, Chevreul mentioned it only on a few pages of his book. On the subject of weaving with colored threads, he observed several principles of optical mixture which, incidentally, are similar to those followed by Delacroix (and which, indeed, may have influenced him):

> When we mix red and green, orange and blue, yellow and violet, the colours are more or less completely neutralized according as they are more or less perfectly complementary to each other, and as they are mixed in proper proportions. The result is a grey, the tone of which is generally higher than that of the colours mixed, if these latter are of a suitably high tone. [136]

The type of gray obtained by mixing these complementaries in painting would, of course, be called an "optical gray" — to use Signac's term. And it is especially significant that Chevreul here observed a principle later to be reiterated by Rood, and in turn, by the painters themselves: that the optical mixture of complementary colors yields resultant tones that are higher in value than if the components had been mixed physically (subtractively). Also, Chevreul described a method of creating colored grays by diminishing the dosage of either of the two complementary colors. Two examples will suffice here:

> 3 yellow threads with 1 violet give a greyish-yellow.
> 3 violet threads and 1 yellow give a greyish-violet.[137]

Blanc, as we have seen, also discussed this principle as it applied to painting, especially to the work of Delacroix. Common to both Blanc and Chevreul is the notion that the optical mixture of complementaries in different proportions will produce various tones of gray; Blanc, however, saw the distinct *artistic* advantages of this system, which resulted in fresh, transparent, delicate tones — precisely the qualities Seurat perceived in Delacroix, as witnessed by his notes on the work of that painter. As pointed out in our discussion of *Une Baignade*, this method was used particularly for the shadows on the flesh of the figures, where the underlying local color, orange, intermingles with the bluish hue of the shadows. Seen at a distance, the resultant is a delicate optical gray, which inclines either to warm or to cool gray, depending on the proportions of the components.

In a similar vein, Seurat could have read Couture's ideas on reducing mixtures of pigments on the palette to a minimum in his *Méthode et entretiens d'atelier* (Paris, 1868). Here the academic master wrote:

> As much as possible, use your colors pure, without mixing; if it is absolutely necessary to employ several colors to obtain exactly what you need, never go beyond three; if you increase this number, you introduce into your picture a bad element. If you use four, five, six, then your picture has no longer any life, it becomes scrofulous, it vegetates and dies.[138]

This technique, according to Couture, would give *finesse* to the colors and prevent them from changing over a long period of time.[139] He also proposed a system of color separation and mixture that is remarkably close to Seurat's procedures, and to Chevreul's ideas as well: "Mix your three colors as you would twist three differently colored threads, so that they could be distinguished."[140]

Veronese, too, was praised by Couture for the *finesse* of his color, which was applied in separate touches: "He seldom mixes his colors; in the skin which requires many, he gives samples, as it were, he places grey greenish tones by the side of red tones; but so manages as to give an extreme fineness to his color."[141] This excerpt immediately calls to mind the treatment of the central figure of *Une Baignade*. Here, Seurat succeeded in modeling the face through the use of alternating warm and cool tones, and at the same time kept his colors pure and clean: a gray-green, as mentioned by Couture, is superimposed over the red-orange in many parts of the flesh. The former hue not only assists in the modeling, but at a distance tends, in places, to mix optically with the red-orange, forming a fresh, optical gray.

Blanc, Chevreul, and Couture discussed methods of creating from two juxtaposed complementary colors neutralized resultant tones that were fresh and delicate, but these were very much reduced in intensity. Rood, however, explained how colors located *anywhere* on the chromatic circle, as well as complementaries, could be mixed optically. By following the methods he proposed, the artist could obtain greater luminosity and, at the same time, could duplicate nature's mode of operation. As we pointed out earlier, Rood conducted experiments in which he demonstrated the laws governing the mixture of colored light, on the basis of which he formulated charts in which the optical mixture of different colored lights on surfaces could be predicted.[142] His pronouncements, of course, are relevant to the handling of the grass plot in *Une Baignade*, where Seurat first established the local color of the grass as green, and then super-imposed over it uniform, individual strokes of orange and yellow-orange. The resultant optical mixture, as we have shown, is a luminous yellow-green tinged with orange. It is very likely that Seurat knew Rood's tables governing these phenomena, since the results obtained in *Une Baignade* are just as the scientist predicted them.

Seurat's application of the technique of optical mixture in painting the water also reflects a knowledge of Rood's ideas on the subject of color mixture:

> The result of this imperfect blending of colours . . . by the eye is to com-municate to the surface an appearance of clearness, and to remove any idea of hardness or chalkiness. . . . As an example in nature, we have the somewhat distant sea under a bright-blue sky: the waves will be mainly green, the spaces between them blue; these colours then blend into a sparkling greenish-blue, which cannot be imitated with a simple mixed pigment.[143]

In painting *Une Baignade*, Seurat imitated this effect by the means suggested by Rood; indeed, the sparkling quality of the river is made even more pronounced because small strokes corresponding to the orange of the sunlight have been added to the blue and blue-green of the water.

Rood also explained that the optical mixture of a number of different colors in any given area actually occurred *in nature*. Seurat's handling of the colors on the riverbank of *Une Baignade* almost certainly reveals his acquaintance with the following passage:

> In grasses viewed at some distance, the yellowish-green, bluish-green, reddish, purplish, and brown tints, and the glancing lights, blend more or less together, and produce an effect which cannot be reproduced by a single sweep of the brush.[144]

And Rood recommended that in his pictures the painter follow this method of mixing colors — optical mixture — which actually takes place in his experience of the subject:

This same method of mixing colours on the retina of the observer is also used more or less in oil painting with excellent effect; it lends to them a magical charm, the tints seeming purer and more varying; the very fact that the appearance of the painting changes somewhat according as the observer advances or retires from it being an advantage, communicating to it, as we might say, a certain kind of life.[145]

## Gradation

The technique of gradation — the juxtaposition of hues or values close to each other on the chromatic circle or value scale — was used throughout most of *Une Baignade* (the exceptions are the seminude torsos of the bathers and the jacket of the figure stretched out on the riverbank). By eliminating almost all flat, unmodulated tones through the process of gradation, Seurat gave the colors of the picture a rich, vibrant — almost "fluttering" — quality. Probably the best example of these effects may be found in the execution of the grass, which is comprised of numerous strokes of bluish green, green, and yellow-green that intermingle ; in addition, small quantities of white were mixed with some of these components, so that gradation of value as well as of hue would be brought into play (Plate A).

Delacroix, as we observed, frequently enriched his colors through gradation, and at Saint-Sulpice (to select a prime example) this technique served to create a remarkable sense of scintillation and vibration in the colors of the frescoes, particularly in the grass (Plate C). Here the tones are not of one single hue, but are composed of neighboring colors gradated through the range of blue-green, green, and yellow-green. Also, some of these colors were gradated in value by the addition of white. Seurat's *Une Baignade* shares much of the over-all effect of color vibration found in the frescoes at Saint-Sulpice; but more specifically, it is possible to find areas in both paintings that are extremely close in their use of gradation, such as the grass plots already mentioned (cf. Plates A and C).

Earlier, the Impressionists were equally fond of gradation as a means of recreating pictorially the effects of vibrating color and light they perceived in nature. Seurat showed that he was well acquainted with this technique in his Impressionist-inspired *croquetons* for *Une Baignade*, and many of the same characteristics of hue gradation were carried over in his execution of the final canvas.

The elements of color and value gradation in *Une Baignade* also have a firm basis in some of the theoretical texts Seurat read. Gradation, as we have indicated, may be understood in two senses: either as a technique of enlivening and enriching colors, or as a means of creating harmony through the use of analogous hues (a discussion of the latter aspect will be postponed for the moment). The former mode of handling color was recommended strongly both by Rood and Blanc. The latter praised the methods practiced by the "orientals," and on this subject quoted the following passage from the writings of Adalbert de Beaumont: "The more intense the color, whether red, lapis-lazuli, or turquoise, the more the Orientals make it *miroiter* [shimmer], shade it upon itself, to render it more intense and lessen its dryness and monotony, to produce, in a word, that vibration without which a color is as insupportable to our eyes as under the same conditions a sound would be to our ears."[146] Blanc cited Delacroix, too, as a master of gradation. Not only did he make the surfaces of his pictures seem to vibrate by placing tone over tone, but he also enhanced this quality through his method of applying the paint: "Instead of applying his color horizontally, he dabbed it with the brush over a preparation of the same, but stronger, hue which was to show through a bit here and there, yet enough to produce an impression of unity from a distance, while giving a singular depth to the tone thus modeled upon itself, thus *vibrant*, that is quite the right word."[147]

Rood, however, was more explicit about gradation in a passage that undoubtedly interested Seurat:

One of the most important characteristics of colour in nature is the endless, almost infinite gradations which always accompany it. It is impossible to escape from the delicate changes which the colour of all natural objects undergoes, owing to the way the light strikes them, without taking all the precautions necessary for an experiment in a physical laboratory. Even if the surface employed be white and flat, still some portions of it are sure to be more highly illuminated than others, and hence to appear a little more yellowish or less greyish; and, besides this source of change, it is receiving coloured light from all coloured objects near it, and reflecting it variously from its different portions. If a painter represents a sheet of paper in a picture by a uniform white or grey patch, it will seem quite wrong, and can not be made to look right till it is covered by delicate gradations of light and shade and colour.[148]

## Contrast

Seurat relied heavily on the principle of value contrast, which he used in *Une Baignade* to create an illusion of pictorial depth and to throw figures and objects into relief. The application of this principle is well illustrated in his treatment of the figure at the far right. The mass of the body, taken independently of its background, is illuminated on the top and right-hand side and is shadowed on the left-hand side and lower portions. The tone of the background adjacent to the figure (that is, the water) is, in turn, adjusted arbitrarily so as to contrast with whichever value is juxtaposed to it. For example, the boy's back, neck, and hat are in shadow; thus the area of water that meets these parts of the figure becomes noticeably lighter toward the line of demarcation between them. On the other hand, the front of the body, which is fully illuminated, has as its background a considerably darker value. These tonal adjustments are unusually effective in creating the illusion of space surrounding the figure, which, when seen in isolation, is actually modeled very slightly. The application of the principles of value contrast that we have described here may be seen in operation throughout the painting, following the rule that, when placed beside each other, the difference between two tones is always strengthened. Too, the value contrasts in *Une*

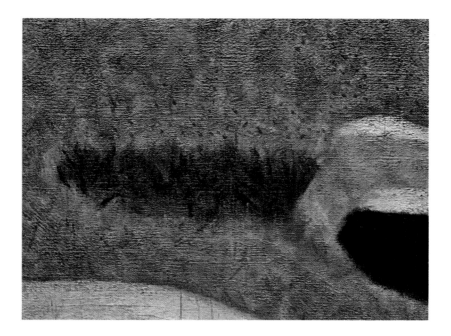

Plate A.  *Une Baignade, Asnières* [detail, center].

Plate B.  *Une Baignade, Asnières* [detail, right].

*Baignade* are strongest at the line of juncture between any given pair of tones and diminish as one moves away from this line.

A second type of contrast is that which exists between hues, and it is governed by laws similar to those for value contrast. However, Seurat took advantage only sporadically of hue contrast in *Une Baignade*. A major instance of its use may be found in the three seminude figures whose flesh is painted a very light yellow-orange. In each case this color is surrounded by a background that is forced toward the complementary of this color — blue — as the line of demarcation is approached, thus making the figures appear separate and distinct from their background. But Seurat failed to be consistent: when the bluish shadows of these same figures meet their background (the river), little effort is made to introduce the complementary hue there.

Seurat employed hue contrast in several other parts of the canvas where he wished to reinforce value contrast as a means of throwing a figure into relief. Behind the seated young man wearing a straw hat, for example, an extra dose of yellow-orange in the grass serves as complementary to the blue of the vest juxtaposed to it. Similarly, when the light yellow-orange of his straw hat meets the trees behind it, an additional dosage of blue is introduced there in order to strengthen the contrast, and hence the apparent difference, between the two areas. Following the same principle, the hue of the grass near the shadowed side of the arm of the reclining man in the foreground is adjusted so that it will be complementary to it, thus making the arm seem to stand out distinctly from the grass plot.

Another variant of hue contrast was used in establishing the relationship between the lighted portions of the grass and the shadows (Plate A). Here Seurat exaggerated the difference between the two areas by adding an extra dosage of white to the region immediately surrounding the blue-green shadow in order to strengthen the contrast between values; further, he added yellow there to accentuate the chromatic difference between the bluish tone of the shadow and the illuminated green area of the grass. In addition, he followed the principle that every color projects its complementary onto its neighbor: in this same shadow, strokes of purple and violet are found which are complementary to green and yellow-green, the local colors of the grass in the light (see Plate A). Also, the orange strokes corresponding to the sunlight striking the riverbank invoke their complementary, blue, several flecks of which appear in the shadow. Of course, Seurat was here following a principle already discussed: that the hue of the shadow should always be complementary to the color of the light. (It should be noted that the hues of the complementary pairs mentioned here are based on Rood's contrast-diagram (Figures 14 and 15, pages 40 and 41, respectively), not on Chevreul's or Blanc's color systems.) Hue contrast, however, was not employed consistently in *Une Baignade*. Frequently plane meets plane without this convention being brought into play.

There are many possible sources for Seurat's use of arbitrarily forced light-dark contrasts along the edges of the forms in *Une Baignade*. The laws and principles governing such contrasts were enunciated, as we shall see, in the writings of Leonardo da Vinci, who also frequently practiced this method of separating figure and ground in his drawings and paintings. But it is Paolo Veronese who stands out as a more influential source, both because one of Seurat's friends testified to his interest in the Venetian painter's work,[149] and because of the similarities between their techniques of applying the principles of value contrast: the type of carefully contrived contrasts along the edges of the forms in a painting such as Veronese's *Il Calvario* (Louvre, Paris; Figure 26), to select a typical example, very probably served as a model for Seurat's solution to the same problem in *Une Baignade*. Interestingly, Seurat could have found a similar method of forcing the contrasts between dark and light in Delacroix's frescoes at Saint-Sulpice, which we know he studied. And Delacroix, in turn, based much of his decorative style on Veronese; as he said: "All that I know I have gotten from Paolo Veronese."[150]

Figure 26. Paolo Veronese, *Il Calvario*, Louvre, Paris. (Photo Archives Photographiques, Paris.)

As we have seen, Seurat occasionally reinforced value contrasts through the application of hue contrast at the line of juncture between planes and masses — though this technique was not used consistently in *Une Baignade*. It is the work of the Impressionists, who were the first to apply hue contrast as an integral part of their style, that must have turned his attention to this pictorial device. And among the Impressionists, Seurat probably learned valuable lessons from Renoir, whose work he knew and who, according to Signac, almost always observed the laws of contrast.[151]

Simultaneous contrast of color and value was discussed at length by Chevreul, Blanc, and Rood. It is Chevreul, however, who rightly receives credit for being the first to formulate a specific law governing the principles of contrast and for proposing ways in which this law might be applied in painting and decoration. Two varieties of the phenomenon of contrast cited by Chevreul are relevant to Seurat's treatment of *Une Baignade*. The first type occurs when noncomplementary colors are juxtaposed; the second, when complementaries are juxtaposed. In the first case, Chevreul found that the difference between the two hues was mutually intensified:[152] for example, when green and blue are placed side by side, the green inclines toward yellow and the blue toward indigo.[153] Similarly, when two different tones of gray are juxtaposed, the darker one seems darker and the lighter one becomes lighter in appearance. (The illustration Chevreul used to demonstrate value contrast has been reproduced as Figure 27.) In both hue and value, Chevreul found that the effects of contrast diminished as one's eye moved away from the line of demarcation between the two areas. Also it is important to realize that, as a rule, simultaneous contrast of both color and

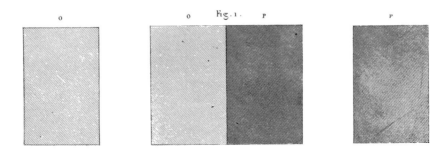

Figure 27. Plate Illustrating Value Contrast (from Chevreul, *op. cit.*).

value occurs at the same time when two different tones are placed next to each other. The law governing these phenomena was formulated by Chevreul as follows: "In the case where the eye sees at the same time two contiguous colours, they will appear as dissimilar as possible, both in their optical composition and in the height of their tone."[154]

As to the second type of contrast (previously mentioned), Chevreul found that when complementaries were juxtaposed there occurred "a simple augmentation of their intensity."[155] Concerning the contrast phenomena seen when blue and orange are juxtaposed, he wrote:

> When we put a blue stripe beside an orange stripe, whether we admit that the first appears to the eye to receive some blue from the proximity of the second, as this latter appears to acquire orange through the vicinity of the blue stripe — or, which is the same thing, whether we admit that the blue stripe appears to destroy the effect of the blue rays of the second stripe, as this latter appears to destroy the effect of the orange rays of the blue stripe — it is evident that the colours of the two objects in contact will purify each other, and become more vivid.[156]

Chevreul observed, too, that when a disc colored with any given hue is placed on a white background, an aureole (or halo) corresponding to its complementary, which gradually diminishes in intensity, will be seen surrounding the disc[157] (one of Chevreul's plates illustrating this phenomenon has been reproduced as Figure 28).

After having observed these laws, we should expect Chevreul to give precise instructions about the ways in which they could be applied in painting, but as we pointed out in our résumé of his book, only general suggestions, such as the following, were proposed:

> Now what do we learn by the law of *simultaneous contrast of colours*? It is, that when we regard attentively two coloured objects at the same time, neither of them appears of its peculiar colour, that is to say, such as it would appear if viewed separately, but of a tint resulting from its peculiar colour and the complementary of the colour of the other object. On the

other hand, if the colours of the objects are not of the same tone, the lightest tone will be *lowered*, and the darkest tone will be *heightened*; in fact, by juxtaposition they will appear different from what they really are.[158]

Seurat's execution of certain portions of *Une Baignade* indicates that he was well aware of Chevreul's laws of contrast. His application of these laws in the treatment of the light-shadow relationship in the grass plot has already been pointed out. And, as we have noted, he took advantage of hue contrast whenever he wished to create a marked sense of separation between an object and its background. In this painting, too, the effects of contrast are reduced as the distance from the line of juncture between forms is increased, following Chevreul's advice.

Blanc reiterated Chevreul's principles of contrast without adding any new theoretical material. But he did point out the

Figure 28. Plate Illustrating Simultaneous Contrast of
Color (from Chevreul, *op. cit.*).

distinct artistic advantages that could be derived from following these principles and cited Delacroix as one who had a profound understanding of the role of contrast in painting.[159]

Leonardo da Vinci's precepts on this subject are also relevant here. He wrote more extensively on the elements of chiaroscuro than did any of the nineteenth-century authors Seurat is known to have studied. In his *Trattato della Pittura*, a book that Seurat probably read in a French translation,[160] Leonardo enunciated the principle of value contrast, which Seurat used frequently in his work of 1882–1884. The function of contrast, as Leonardo conceived of it, was to throw objects into relief and to make them appear as though separated from their background. Such effects are referred to repeatedly in different ways in the sections of the *Trattato* dealing with chiaroscuro. Indeed, the aim of the painter, according to Leonardo, should be to handle his whole picture according to this principle:

> The great design of a painter, is so to manage a plane surface, as that on it may appear a body raised and standing out from the said plane. . . . It follows that a painter, in being sparing of his shadows, where they are necessary, does an injury to himself. . . . In painting, 'tis much more difficult, and requires a great deal more thought and reflection, to give the shadows to a figure, than to design its contours.[161]

Leonardo described as follows the means by which these effects of relief could be achieved:

> Two colours, one whereof serves for a ground to the other, whether they be illumined, or supposed in a shadow, will appear free and loose from each other in proportion as they are found in different degrees; that is, one obscure colour must never serve as a ground for another; but for that use you must choose some very different colour, as white, or some other colour bordering in the same degree upon white, as the other appears bordering upon black.[162]

Unfortunately, we cannot be absolutely certain that Seurat read Leonardo's *Trattato della Pittura*. However, Leonardo's ideas about value contrast were echoed in Sutter's "Les Phénomènes de la vision" and in Blanc's *Grammaire des arts du dessin*, two texts we know the artist studied. In the latter we find Leonardo's principle of contrast summarized: "Leonardo da Vinci says we should place a light background in contrast to a shadow and a dark background to a mass of light, and it is a general principle, a precept not to be attacked." [163]

Returning to nineteenth-century writers who investigated the problem of contrast, we will recall that Rood reviewed Chevreul's discoveries and derived additional general rules from the French scientist's basic premise, which he paraphrased as follows: "When two coloured surfaces are placed in contiguity, each is changed as though it had been mixed to some extent with the complementary colour of the other." [164] Rood then applied Chevreul's principles to his own improved color circle (which we shall discuss shortly), devising the following law:

> When any two colours of the chromatic circle are brought into competition or contrasted, the effect produced is apparently to move them farther apart. In the case, for example, of orange and yellow, the orange is moved toward the red, and assumes the appearance of reddish-orange; the yellow moves toward the green, and appears for the time to be greenish-yellow. [165]

Like Chevreul, Rood realized that complementaries, unlike noncomplementary colors, could not follow this principle: "Colors which are complementary are already as far apart in the chromatic circle as possible; hence they are not changed in hue, but merely appear more brilliant and saturated." [166]

Rood stated that if the painter wished to take advantage of the effects of contrast, the color circle would have to be arranged carefully: "If the angular positions of the colours are laid down falsely, the results, in the matter of increase or diminution of brilliancy or saturation, will also be false." [167] He presented the results of his experiments on color saturation in a contrast diagram (Figures 14 and 15, pages 40 and 41, respectively) in which the distances between the radii corresponding to the different hues were measured with great care. We know that Seurat was familiar with this diagram because a copy he made of it (Figure 16, page 41) was found in his studio. Furthermore, upon close examination, the hues of the "induced" complementaries in *Une Baignade* will be found to be based on this diagram.

*Brushstroke*

Seurat used three different types of brushstroke in *Une Baignade*, each of which is confined to a specific area, or areas, of the painting. The first and simplest of these is found in the flesh and clothing of the figures: here broad, wide strokes were employed. In the fully lighted areas, the paint was applied heavily and opaquely, and the resulting surface often assumes a hard, rather waxy appearance. But in the half-lights and shadows the pigment was frequently dragged across the rough surface of the canvas so that the uppermost portions, but not the interstices, were covered. As a result, this technique engenders some optical mixture, since the hues that remain undisturbed in the hollows of the canvas may mix optically with the superimposed color. In the hat on the pile of clothing in the center of the picture, for example, Seurat lightly scumbled blue and blue-green tones over the underlying yellow-orange; because these covering hues were picked up only by the projecting threads of the canvas, some of the yellow-orange of the hat remains visible in tiny patches and thus mixes optically with the blue and blue-green, forming a luminous optical gray. Interestingly, this variety of brushwork closely approximates Seurat's later "pointillism," inasmuch as dragging and scumbling broad strokes over the rough canvas of *Une Baignade* frequently produce small spots and points of color that are unusually conducive to optical mixture.

A second type of brushwork, made up of *balayé* strokes, is found in the grass of the riverbank and, in modified form, in the trees. These strokes tend to be short and of uniform length, and are applied in every possible direction. Such a technique permits disparate elements of color to be applied to the same area and enables them to mix optically with little difficulty, since a generous dosage of these opaque, multidirectional strokes may serve as a uniform web or mesh to conceal part of the underlying hue while simultaneously adding a new component (see Plate A). These brushstrokes usually appear as extremely regular cross-hatchings, which are applied without regard for the inherent texture or contours of the subject matter.

A third variety of brushwork, composed of long, thin, parallel strokes, is found mainly in the water. These, like the *balayé* strokes, are used as a means of adding numerous elements of color to the canvas without relying on the physical (subtractive) mixture of pigments. But the parallel strokes are not quite so conducive to total optical fusion as are the two types already mentioned. Yet because they are thin, a variety of hues may be compressed into a small area of the canvas which, when viewed at a distance, gives an impression of vibrating, shimmering color. Such an effect is particularly noticeable in the area of water surrounding the rowboat in the distance (Plate B).

Thus, Seurat used three distinctly different types of brushstroke in *Une Baignade*, and each was confined to a particular area or to a specified task. As a rule, fully illuminated, opaque areas, such as the figures and drapery, are represented by broad, heavily loaded brushstrokes that are often dragged across the surface of the canvas. The local color of the grass, trees, and some articles of clothing are depicted by the *balayé* stroke which also records the distinct action of the sunlight on these areas. Finally, parallel horizontal strokes are reserved for the river. The end result is that the surface of the painting is composed not only of three distinctly different visual textures but also presents three different degrees of optical mixture of color.

We may observe at the outset that the *balayé* and short horizontal strokes merely represent a disciplined formalization of the brushwork frequently used by the Impressionists. The *balayé* stroke, as we saw earlier, was favored by Camille Pissarro (among others) about 1880, and knowing that Seurat admired his work, it is not surprising to find this technique utilized in the *Baignade croquetons* and then in the completed canvas. His use of multi-colored horizontal strokes in the river cannot be traced to the influence of a single painter; it was a technique shared by most of the Impressionists, particularly Monet and Renoir (as seen in Figures 24 and 25, pages 63 and 71, respectively).

In those portions of *Une Baignade* where small brushstrokes were not used, similarities in surface treatment to parts of Delacroix's frescoes at Saint-Sulpice may be found. As we have seen, Seurat sometimes applied his pigments in broad, flat strokes that adhered to the uppermost surfaces of the canvas but allowed some of the underlying coat of paint to show through, as in the illuminated parts of the flesh in strong light or in the white articles of clothing on the riverbank. Certain portions of Delacroix's frescoes are treated in this manner, especially in the lighter tones, where hatching was not as necessary as it was in the half-tones and shadows. An excellent example of this technique may be found in the handling of the white drapery lying on the ground at the lower right in *La Lutte de Jacob et de l'ange* (Figure 18, page 52). In Delacroix's painting, as in Seurat's, such roughly dragged strokes are extremely conducive to the optical mixture of different, superimposed layers of pigment.

While both paintings have in common a technique that usually relies on the application of innumerable small strokes of pigment throughout the canvas, Seurat's brushstrokes in *Une Baignade* are more mechanical and uniform than Delacroix's at Saint-Sulpice. In the latter's case, this type of execution occurred, as Signac suggested, as a by-product of the artist's use of gradation, which made the entire surface seem to vibrate. Thus we find that Delacroix tended to treat the surface of the painting in a rather abstract way, without being overly concerned with the material texture of the objects represented. As Signac said: "Flesh, décor, accessories — everything is treated in the same way. There is not a single fragment of the painting that does not vibrate, shimmer, or glisten." [168] A similar abstractness of surface was achieved through the use of relatively uniform brushstrokes in *Une Baignade*, and indeed in many parts of the painting this quality is even more pronounced than at Saint-Sulpice.

Curiously enough, the few specific instructions about the technique applying color proposed by Blanc and Rood were not explicitly followed by Seurat in painting *Une Baignade*. As we saw in our summary of their books, both recognized the advantages of a "pointillist" method of execution as a means of inducing optical mixture, but in 1883–1884 Seurat was not quite ready to follow their advice. Indirectly, of course, Chevreul, Blanc, and Rood may have been responsible for the methodical, unspontaneous manner in which the artist applied paint to the canvas, since, in a variety of ways, these three writers all championed the idea of rigorously controlling the division of color and its optical mixture.

*Pigmentary Materials and Mixtures*

Signac pointed out that Seurat used both prismatic and earth colors in *Une Baignade*: "This picture was painted with large flat strokes, swept over each other and issuing from a palette comprised, like Delacroix's, of pure and earth colors." [169] While many of the middle values of the painting were executed with the pure colors of the solar spectrum, Seurat employed earth colors and black in many of the dark areas and in some of the lights. [170]

But the function of earth colors is limited here, first, to creating large accents corresponding to the local colors of objects which, like the trousers, shoes, and earth, would in reality have been composed of nonspectral colors. And, second, the earths mixed with hues of higher value are intended to reduce the over-all intensity of the color effect of the painting — as Signac said: "Because of these ochres and earth colors, the painting was dulled and seemed less brilliant than those which the Impressionists painted with their palette reduced to the colors of the prism." [171] After examining *Une Baignade* carefully, the writer concluded that very few mixtures of pigments other than neighboring ones on the color circle took place in the painting. That is to say, it appears that Seurat almost entirely avoided reducing the intensity of his colors by mixing complementaries with them on the palette (the exceptions are the dark areas of clothing, already mentioned). Furthermore, he avoided accidental mixtures of pigments on the surface of the canvas, presumably by waiting for each layer to dry completely before adding subsequent layers of paint.

In using earth colors and black, Seurat revealed his allegiance to the pre-Impressionist tradition of nineteenth-century painting. Specifically, there are obvious analogies between his palette of 1883–1884 and Delacroix's, as Signac pointed out. Yet the *croquetons* for *Une Baignade* testify that Seurat was well acquainted with the intense spectral colors of the Impressionist palette, even though at times he did introduce earth colors here and there. However, in the final painting, which was destined for the Salon, he toned down the intensity of color found in some of the small oil studies and added generous accents of black, tan, and dark brown.

## System of Color Harmony

Seurat used several different, but interrelated, methods of harmonizing the colors in *Une Baignade*: a "triad" of colors; pairs of complementary colors; and colors close to each other (analogous colors) on the chromatic circle. The first type is seen in the relationship of the hues comprising the major areas of the painting, which are drawn from three regions of the chromatic circle separated from each other by about 120 degrees. The dominant colors in the water and sky fall between ultramarine-blue and blue; those of the riverbank fall between yellow-green and green; and various color accents on the riverbank and in the water range from purple to yellow-orange (these relationships have been diagrammed in Figure 29). If the center of each of these groups is located on the chromatic circle, a "triad" of colors will be seen as the unifying framework of the picture. At the same time, harmony through contrast was achieved through the juxta-position of complementary hues, such as the red-orange and blue-green pair found in the river, the yellow-orange hat against the blue water, and the contrast of the pinkish-purple of some of the clothing of the seated figures with the green grass.

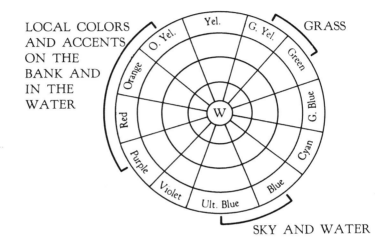

Figure 29. Diagram of Color Relationships in *Une Baignade*.

Seurat also obtained color harmony by relying on a number of hues close to each other on the chromatic circle. Such "analogous" colors in the red-orange to yellow-orange range may be found distributed as accents across the surface of the canvas, beginning with the red-orange hat and trunks of the bather at the far right, moving to the yellow-orange head of the boy in the water to the left, to the straw-yellow hat in the center of the picture, and finally to the tan-orange dog at the lower left. Similarly, closely related hues in the red-purple range have been spotted along the riverbank in the trunks of the central bather, in the bands of the hat behind him, in the sash of the seated figure in the middle distance at the left, and in the shirt of the reclining man on the bank in the far distance.

Intimately associated with such analogous color relationships is Seurat's use of hues separated by small intervals in the over-all composition of almost every major area in the picture, and which was referred to earlier as the technique of gradation. This method, then, has a dual function: to make areas of color seem richer and more vibrant, and to harmonize by "analogy" the individual, but closely related, hues that enter into their composition.

In the matter of color harmony, Seurat undoubtedly learned many practical lessons from Delacroix, particularly from his frescoes at Saint-Sulpice. As we observed earlier, Seurat and Signac discovered that Delacroix had achieved harmony of color by using complementary or near-complementary pairs of hues. In *Héliodore chassé du Temple* (Figure 19, page 53) at Saint-Sulpice, for example, the artist relied on the following color pairs, which are either juxtaposed or placed close to each other in the painting: moving from right to left, the soldier carrying the metal vessel on his shoulder, red-green; the figure in the right foreground, blue-orange; the inside of the helmet of Heliodorus and the neighboring drapery, orange-blue; and the two pieces of drapery in front of him, yellow-green *versus* red-violet. The flying figure above Heliodorus is clothed in a violet garment and is placed against a yellowish-tan background; and the flying figure approaching from the left wears a green garment adorned with a pink scarf.[172] In addition to relying on these complementary pairs, Delacroix utilized the relationship between analogous colors to achieve harmony. For example, the figure riding the horse at the left is clothed in orange, yellow-orange, and yellow, which are, of course, neighboring colors on the chromatic circle; similar hues echoing these are placed as accents on the steps at the right. (The principle of using such closely related hues was referred to as "harmony by analogy" by Chevreul, Blanc, and, later, by Signac.)

There is also a firm foundation in the theoretical texts Seurat read for the system of color harmony in *Une Baignade*. His juxtaposition of the complementary pairs enumerated in our analysis of the painting followed one of Chevreul's most important principles of harmony: "The harmony of contrast of colours, produced by the simultaneous view of colours belonging to scales very far asunder, assorted according to the law of contrast." [173] Harmonies of analogous colors, as found in *Une Baignade*, were also recommended by Chevreul. These are: "The harmony of hues, produced by the simultaneous view of tones of the same height, or nearly so, belonging to scales more or less approximating." [174]

While Chevreul was interested primarily in establishing rules for the harmony of pairs of colors, Rood attacked the problem of arranging colors in "triads." The American scientist noted that, in general, colors rather far apart on the chromatic circle produce good combinations. With the aid of his contrast-diagram (Figures 14 and 15, pages 40 and 41, respectively), he reduced this observation to a rule: "Colours less than 80° or 90° apart suffer from harmful contrast, while those more distant help each other." [175] After recommending triads of color as harmonious combinations, Rood explained how they could be selected:

> The studies that we have made with the contrast-diagram render it easy for us to select a series of triads that are free from the defect of hurtful contrast; for this will be the case with all colours that are equally distant from each other in the diagram, or are separated by an angle of 120°; and, when we examine the triads that have been most employed by artists and decorators, we find that this principle has actually been more or less closely observed.[176]

In arranging the major colors of *Une Baignade* as a triad (see Figure 29, page 92) it is almost certain that Seurat was following Rood's recommendations on the subject of color harmony. The scientist also suggested that the colors constituting the triad could be varied within the "small interval" much in the way Seurat did in his painting.[177]

Referring specifically to the problem in landscape painting that Seurat faced in *Une Baignade*, Rood recognized the difficulty of harmonizing large areas of green and blue, which he felt were intrinsically unharmonious colors:

> It by no means follows that the introduction of large masses of positive green into paintings is always to be avoided; it is not advisable, unless it can be accomplished *successfully*, and without injury to the work as a chromatic composition. The ability to solve this problem in a brilliant manner is one of the signs which indicate an accomplished colourist; and, when the green is combined with blue, the task becomes still more difficult and success more praiseworthy.[178]

Having stated the problem, he proposed several solutions to it, including the idea of introducing "a third colour situated at a considerable distance in the chromatic circle."[179] Seurat, as we have seen, did just this by adding accents from the orange-red-purple range of the chromatic circle, opposing the two other legs of the triad, blue and green (see Figure 29, page 92).

It is worth noting that Rood and Blanc believed that artists should enhance their color schemes by the use of white and black. The latter, who devoted a section of his chapter on color to this question, felt that white and black, when applied properly, could contribute to harmony in paintings; "acting as non-colors [they] will serve to rest the eye, to refresh it, by moderating the dazzling brilliancy of the whole representation."[180] But Blanc warned that white and black must be applied sparingly and "should be divided and repeated upon narrow spaces as a sordine to the color in a lugubrious picture."[181] White, alone, has a definite value in harmonizing as well as intensifying colors: "Applied against a particular color, the white heightens, the black lowers it."[182] Although this principle had been stated earlier by Chevreul, Blanc pointed out the way in which Delacroix had applied it: "At other times this powerful colorist [Delacroix] uses white to correct the contiguity of two colors like red and blue. In one of the pendentives that so magnificently decorate the Library of the Corps Legislatif, the executioner who has cut off the head of John the Baptist is dressed in red and blue, two colors whose juxtaposition is softened by a little white which unites them without sacrificing the energy suitable to the figure of an executioner." [183]

Seurat's use of white and black in *Une Baignade* clearly echoes Blanc's prescriptions on the subject: white is distributed in small doses throughout the painting and, as Blanc suggested, serves as a harmonious link between different areas of color. White areas appear between the reddish trunks of the central bather and the grass, and between the second and fourth figures in depth at the left; black and blackish accents are also found in the foreground of the picture. Rood, too, admitted the artistic value of white and near-black. After his discussion of harmonious triads in painting — such as those used in *Une Baignade* — he wrote: "White or gray can be introduced, and is often used with a happy effect, particularly, in the triads." [184]

A few words should be added here apropos of Corot's remarks on pictorial harmony. He believed that paintings should be unified by the presence of a single luminous area, which may be placed anywhere the artist chooses. As he said: "There is always in a picture a luminous spot of which there must be only one." [185] Seurat clearly followed Corot's advice in *Une Baignade* by emphasizing one — but only one — luminous spot: this is found in the area of white cloth in the center of the picture. While some tones come close to it, this single area is in fact the highest value and is equaled by no others in the painting.

## Procedure and Method

Seurat gathered material for *Une Baignade* in two ways: he drew from models posed in the studio so as to understand the anatomy and posture of the individual figure units. And he went out to the banks of the Seine where he painted a number of small quasi-Impressionist panels in which he recorded the main masses of color in his subject. But it is obvious that the art of the Impressionists could not furnish him with much assistance in composition, since they rejected the concept of rigorously planned designs.

Thus, for a compositional matrix, he turned for inspiration to the art of Pierre Puvis de Chavannes,[186] a radical within the academic tradition and well-known creator of monumental mural decorations. In painting *Une Baignade*, Seurat seems to have wanted to combine Puvis' sense of decorative design with a modern divisionist approach and contemporary subject matter — all of which was governed by a controlled value scheme. These elements were brought together in a studio painting that he thought would be suitable for the official Salon, but which was rejected by the jury.

Seurat's decision to send *Une Baignade* to the Salon and his training at the École des Beaux-Arts provide important clues to the sources of his method of painting. A glance at the nature of the French academic tradition will indicate that he was conforming to a procedure in painting that had been followed for well over two centuries, particularly by the more classical wing of this tradition. David, Ingres, and Puvis de Chavannes (to mention only three artists) had frequently used a highly rationalized system of studying individual figure units and groups through drawings and oil sketches, and had continually revised and perfected their designs through prolonged study. Indeed, in some of his paintings Delacroix, too, had subscribed to this kind of methodical procedure and had warned artists of the dangers of improvisation.

In spite of the similarities, one major difference between these painters' and Seurat's approach should be pointed out. He added one further step to the documentation of his subject: oil sketches made directly from nature. In so doing, he revealed his allegiance to a viewpoint held by artists of the Barbizon School, many of whom accumulated data from nature by making oil sketches out-of-doors but usually finished their paintings in the studio. Interestingly, the revolutionary idea of painting *en plein air* consecrated by the Barbizon School and the Impressionists was accepted even at the École des Beaux-Arts in Seurat's day, for we have accounts of the students' custom of painting from nature in the outskirts of Paris[187] — a practice followed by Seurat in executing *croquetons* at Asnières and in other nearby suburbs. Yet, he did not accept the Impressionists' idea of considering a painting done exclusively at the site as the final and complete work of art; for Seurat, working out-of-doors in an Impressionist manner was only a means of collecting data to be modified and perfected by further work in the studio.

Of particular note is the high degree of correspondence between Seurat's method of painting *Une Baignade*, as well as *La Grande Jatte*, and the advice given by Rood in the last chapter of his book. The scientist felt that two things were required of the artist in painting, the first of which was a good "chromatic composition," the plan of which "should be most carefully considered and worked out beforehand, even with reference to minor details; the colours should be selected and arranged so that they all help each other either by sympathy or by contrast." [188] Second, he insisted that good color depends on a well-composed scheme of light and shade: "Powerful drawing adds enormously to the value of the tints in a coloured work when they are at all delicate, or when the combination contains doubtful or poor colour-contrasts, which in point of fact is a case common enough in nature." [189] Rood then provided instructions for the artist about how to study light-and-shade and color, recommending that he master chiaroscuro before moving on to painting:

> The advance from drawing to painting should be gradual, and no serious attempts in colour should be made till the student has attained undoubted proficiency in outline and in light and shade. Amateurs almost universally abandon black and white for colour at a very early stage, and this circumstance alone precludes all chance of progress. . . . If it is impossible for him to draw the objects in full light and shade in a rather masterly way, then there is no use in attempting colour. [190]

These statements are relevant to Seurat's career in three ways. First, the artist planned the "chromatic composition" of the picture very carefully and, unlike the Impressionists, left almost nothing to chance. Second, we have seen that he relied heavily on value drawings in studying the figures and accessories of *Une Baignade*, and that these drawings were quite complete as statements of the value scheme of the individual units that appeared in the finished painting. Third, and equally important, the advice given in the preceding excerpt may have been followed explicitly by Seurat in devoting the majority of his time during the early 1880's to drawing, rather than to painting. Indeed, his first major canvas — *Une Baignade* — was not begun until 1883, even though he had been working independently since his return from the army in November, 1880.

Let us turn momentarily from Rood's remarks to some of Corot's observations on the importance of value relationships as the foundation for color, which Seurat knew. Among Corot's utterances, which Seurat copied from notes taken by Mme. Aviat, the following statements occur: "What there is to be seen in painting, or rather what I look for, is the form, the ensemble, the value of the tones: color for me comes after." [191] Putting the same idea in another way, Corot said: "Color comes after, because I like, above all, the ensemble, the harmony in the tones; while the color sometimes gives you a violent contrast which I don't like." [192] These excerpts also contain the following affirmation of the importance of light and shade: "We do not attach enough importance to chiaroscuro in our canvases: enthusiastic as we are for color, we forget the tone. Without that science of black and white, without that composition of chiaroscuro, the picture seems incomplete." [193] These remarks constitute one more piece of evidence Seurat gathered concerning the importance of a firm value structure to which color could be added.

Returning to our account of Rood's influence on Seurat's methods, we find that the scientist suggested that the artist first work out the color scheme of his pictures in the studio on the basis of notes taken from nature. Then, and only then, should the artist go out of doors to make color sketches directly from his subject. In effect, he suggests the procedure that Seurat followed in his *croquetons*:

After some progress has been made, the colour-sketches that are attempted directly from nature should be simple and executed with reference to *colour*, the element of form being kept quite subordinate. The very natural desire to make something that will afterward look like a picture is to be suppressed, and the work performed rather with an eye to the remote future. Beginners always neglect the large relations of light and shade and colour, dwelling on those that are small; whereas the aim of the true artist is the production of a broad general effect by the use of a few masses of colour, properly interchanged and contrasted, variety being gained not so much by the introduction of new colours as by the repetition of the main chords.[194]

An approach such as that described in this passage was used by Seurat, as we have seen, in the small oil studies for *Une Baignade*. In these, color alone is his main concern; form and correct drawing are almost entirely ignored. And significantly, the *croquetons* are kept small in size, following the advice of Rood, who suggested "making the colour-sketches so small that there is hardly room for anything but the main masses of colour, the use of small brushes meanwhile being avoided." [195]

A final warning, however, was issued by the scientist: he suggested that, instead of trying to imitate nature's complexity through sheer observation, chromatic effects, particularly those of contrast, be worked out conceptually in the studio:

The hues of all objects are also greatly affected by their surroundings, . . . and this is another source of perplexity and confusion to the beginner, who is constantly led astray by appearances due to this cause. The extent of the difficulty can be appreciated when we remember that contrast affects not only the intensity of the colour, but its position in the chromatic circle, and also its apparent luminosity, and is particularly lively in the case of the pale colours of nature. It is as well to meet this difficulty fairly face to face, and, instead of spending all the disposable time in endeavoring to solve the riddles of contrast presented by nature, to reverse the process, and occasionally to construct in the studio simple chromatic composition founded on the known laws of contrast, and thus study its effects by experiment as well as by observation.[196]

In this excerpt we have in concise form a justification for Seurat's abandoning an Impressionist-inspired approach (where a premium was placed on pure sensation) to studio painting that, though based on specific experiences in nature, is determined by the laws governing visual phenomena.

## THE ROLE OF THE PREPARATORY DRAWINGS FOR *UNE BAIGNADE*

Seurat's main concern in his preparatory drawings for *Une Baignade* was to study the position, lighting, and mass of five of the human figures and the pile of clothing on the riverbank.[197] When the drawings are compared to their respective motifs in the final painting, very few differences will be found. In addition to defining the posture of the figures, these preparatory studies incorporate a carefully planned system of value contrasts — a feature of paramount importance in *Une Baignade* and in the forthcoming Neo-Impressionist style. In our initial discussion of this picture, we pointed out that Seurat used value contrasts as a means of throwing a figure into relief and separating it from its background. In the preparatory drawings, these contrasts were worked out according to the following principle: if the area of the object in proximity to the background is light, then the ground will be darkened; if the edge of the object is dark, the adjoining background will be lightened. Through the use of this pictorial device, Seurat obtained a convincing sense of separation between the figures and the background and created an effect of space surrounding them.

In these preparatory drawings, Seurat also utilized the principle of optical mixture, which is invoked almost automatically by the use of rough Ingres paper as the material on which his conté crayon was applied. In such drawings as *Écho* (D.-R. 97a; Figure 30), *Garçon assis* (D.-R. 97b), and *Chapeau, souliers, linge* (D.-R. 97e), the crayon could not penetrate the deepest hollows of the surface of the paper (except in the darkest blacks), thus creating an almost uniform grid in which white spots of different sizes are interspersed among the covering blacks and grays. Accordingly,

Figure 30. *Écho, étude pour "Une Baignade"* (conté crayon drawing), Edith Wetmore
Collection, New York.

tones applied by the crayon and the underlying specks of white paper mix optically when the sheet is seen at a distance, and an effect of atmospheric transparency and luminosity is the result.

Interestingly, the kind of optical mixture found in these drawings of 1883–1884 has something in common with Seurat's pointillist technique, which was not fully developed in his paintings until 1886. Seen abstractly, the drawings are composed of a series of juxtaposed points of dark and light, many of which, when scrutinized closely, are often found to be quite different from each other in value. Only at a distance, through optical mixture, will a more-or-less uniform resultant tone be perceived. In his preliminary oil studies for *Une Baignade*, curiously enough, Seurat seems not to have grasped the possibilities of the "pointillist" execution implicit in these drawings.

To what extent was the conception of optical mixture in the drawings applied in painting *Une Baignade*? A major point of similarity may be found in those areas of the picture where Seurat achieved a kind of "proto-pointillist" effect by dragging his paint across the rough surface of the canvas. The result, as we mentioned earlier, is that optical mixture of the color of the underlying and superimposed layers takes place. When, however, the method of mixing the elements of color in *Une Baignade* is compared to that used in the preparatory drawings, it appears far less controlled.

Thus far we have considered only the broad brushstroke that dragged the pigment across the canvas, creating effects that are analogous to the "pointillism" of the drawings. But a further similarity should be mentioned here: the use of a *balayé* stroke in some of the drawings, which is echoed in the technique used in painting the riverbank of *Une Baignade*. In *Homme étendu* (D.-R. 97h; Figure 31), for example, long interwoven cross-hatchings, which are conducive to the optical mixture of values, appear in the area above the reclining figure. Their function in the drawing is almost the same as it is in the painting: to apply additional

Figure 31. *Homme étendu, étude pour "Une Baignade"* (conté crayon drawing), Ernst Beyeler Collection, Basle.

elements, either of color or value, while retaining the distinct identity of the stroke itself.

In the drawings for *Une Baignade*, the strokes of the crayon rarely follow the contour or imitate the texture of the objects they depict. Seurat's chief methods of applying the crayon were either to scrub it across the paper, leaving no visible strokes, or else to use cross-hatchings, which are multidirectional and independent of the form of the subject portrayed. In such drawings as *Écho* (D.-R. 97a; Figure 30), he permitted the figure to emerge from an abstract and undifferentiated mass of luminous tone, accented here and there by heavier dark lines that pull the image into focus. His attitude of detachment toward the tangible identity of the subject in the drawings has interesting parallels in the color technique used in *La Grande Jatte*, where a similar abstractness of surface prevails. This is a question, however, that remains to be taken up in the next chapter.

In the final synthesis of pictorial elements in *Une Baignade*, what role did the drawings play? It was here that Seurat worked out in advance the chiaroscuro not only of the figure units themselves, but also of their relationship to the background. By doing so he provided a systematic value structure to which the desired hues could be added. In both value and hue, as we pointed out in our analysis of the painting, Seurat followed the principle of simultaneous contrast, and in the preliminary drawings these basic contrasts were worked out exhaustively. And the drawings enabled Seurat to experiment within a narrow range of means on an effect that was to be of paramount importance in Neo-Impressionism: luminosity through optical mixture.

Before proceeding to an analysis of his next major painting, *Un Dimanche à la Grande Jatte*, it would be well to summarize Seurat's artistic position as of 1883–1884. In so doing, we hope to indicate how much he owed to various aspects of past art and theory, and to determine just how close he came to evolving the major tenets of Neo-Impressionism at this time. We attempted to show in the foregoing discussion of *Une Baignade* that Seurat developed the painting from a solid foundation in traditional styles and drew a large part of its color scheme from the art of Delacroix and the Impressionists. At the same time, there is much in this canvas that cannot be explained without reference to the scientific and theoretical texts that he is known to have read. What is the relationship between these sources, as applied in *Une Baignade*?

First, a few words should be said about the sources themselves. It should be noted that the problems that interested the painters to whom Seurat was attracted were frequently similar to those taken up by the theoretical texts he read. These problems may be divided into three general classes: how to obtain luminosity, *éclat*, vibration, and intensity of color; how to create a sense of relief and/or space surrounding pictorial forms; and how to establish color harmony. All five of the major texts studied by Seurat — by Chevreul, Blanc, Rood, and Sutter — discussed these questions and in some instances overlapped in taking information from one another. Furthermore, a connection can sometimes be found between such theoretical sources and the painters in whom Seurat was interested. For example, Sutter and Blanc, who drew much from Leonardo's ideas, suggested that effects of relief could be obtained by exaggerating value contrasts at the line separating an object from its background. Chevreul, too, was interested in the problem of contrast, devised laws by which color and value could be intensified and/or harmonized, and proposed the concept of the optical mixture of complementaries. Similarly, Blanc recognized the importance of contrast and added further suggestions about how to obtain delicacy and vibration of color, both through optical mixture and gradation. We shall recall that he had based his remarks about color largely on Chevreul and illustrated many of his ideas by referring to Delacroix, who also knew Chevreul's theories. Seurat, in turn, studied both Chevreul's book and Delacroix's paintings. Rood, who seems not to have known

Sutter's or Blanc's writings, summarized some of Chevreul's discoveries, which he used as a point of departure for his own more developed theories of contrast. Interestingly, the American scientist's taste in art ran to Turner, whose work he praised in his *Text-Book of Color* and who exerted a strong influence on the Impressionists. Although Rood did not discover Impressionist painting until after his book was published,[198] it is significant that he should see in Turner many "proto-Impressionist" qualities. And without consciously intending to do so, he also provided scientifically valid solutions to many of the problems explored by Delacroix and the Impressionists.

A similar interaction of interest occurred among the painters whose work Seurat studied. We know, for example, that Delacroix was very much absorbed by Constable's division of color and use of gradation. And among the Impressionists, Monet and Pissarro discovered in Turner's and Constable's paintings techniques of breaking up color and of achieving luminous, transparent atmospheric effects. In addition, one of Delacroix's major sources was the work of Veronese, in whom Renoir was particularly interested. Seurat, in turn, studied not only the paintings of Delacroix and Renoir but those of Veronese as well. Finally, many of the Impressionists drew inspiration from Delacroix. It is significant, then, that both the painters and writers who interested Seurat dealt with almost identical problems, the solutions to which he had discovered partially at the time that he executed *Une Baignade*.

In discussing Seurat's early style, we witnessed the dual influence of Delacroix and Impressionism on *Une Baignade*; but he clearly derived different things from this pair of sources, even though there is considerable overlapping between them. Both, for example, took advantage of hue contrast in order to increase the intensity of neighboring color areas; and they used this method to create the illusion of an object's separation from its background. Each used small brushstrokes as a means of recording separately the numerous colored elements appropriate to their subjects. And these elements, in turn, were frequently combined, either fully or partially, through the process of optical mixture. Moreover, both Delacroix and the Impressionists enriched the surfaces of their paintings through gradation of color.

But from this point on, the differences become more pronounced than the similarities. In Delacroix's work Seurat found a system of color harmony based on the planned contrast between, or similarity of, color areas — the Impressionists, of course, denied any such arbitrary arrangements, believing that only colors perceived in nature should be recorded in their paintings. Their irregular, rapid brushwork, too, was determined by the need to transcribe their sensations during a very brief period of time; Delacroix's strokes, with which Seurat's have many affinities, were applied slowly and methodically and are much more regular in size and shape. Furthermore, the colors recorded by these individual strokes, in each case, are quite different: the Impressionists depicted elements derived solely from their visual transaction with nature — local colors, orange sunlight, blue shadows, and diverse reflections. These hues were often used at full intensity and earth colors were rarely present. Delacroix, on the other hand, also noted a multiplicity of elements in his frescoes at Saint-Sulpice, but the local colors, first of all, were arbitrarily chosen. The hues of the light and shadow, while often in a complementary relationship to each other, were not based on his unprejudiced optical sensations but, rather, were freely adjusted to suit his personal expressive ends. And these frescoes, like most of his other paintings, depend heavily on the use of earth colors. Seurat eschewed much of the conceptual nature of Delacroix's light and avoided murky shadows in *Une Baignade* but, at the same time, failed to eliminate earth colors entirely.

The tonality of *Une Baignade* is thus lighter than Delacroix's decorations at Saint-Sulpice, and the colors are purer and more intense, following Impressionist practice. Nevertheless, Seurat's canvas still lacks the *éclat* and high value range of most Impressionist paintings; he continued to rely on earth colors to reduce the intensity of some of the hues and insisted on incorporating many accents from the lower end of the tonal scale. He also carefully planned the value structure of the painting in advance, a procedure that is non-Impressionist in character.

Thus we may regard the relationship between the artistic and theoretical sources which Seurat studied at this time as being a mutually complementary one. As we have seen, the visual-pictorial framework of *Une Baignade* was based on the work of several earlier artists, but the guiding rules and principles by which he perfected their achievement were drawn from the theoretical texts discussed above. This perfecting, to repeat, was carried out on three levels: that of achieving increased richness, *éclat*, and vibrancy of color; effects of relief through value and hue contrast; and color harmony.

In 1883–1884, the more practical side of Seurat's early "science" was still imperfect and in some ways capricious and arbitrary. While he relied heavily on the colors of the solar spectrum in *Une Baignade*, earth colors and hues possibly soiled by mixture with their complementaries were also introduced; thus he contradicted the view that all of nature's hues are the result only of various combinations of the colors of the solar spectrum. Furthermore, while he applied colors separately and used optical mixture in large areas of the painting, in many parts, such as the reclining figure in the left foreground, he did not employ this principle at all, but instead relied on flat, opaque strokes. And while the principle of value contrast was observed consistently at the edges of the figures, it was reinforced only occasionally by hue contrast, thus doing violence to the concept of the physical world operating according to unified principles that govern the behavior of color and value.

Also, the light in the painting, while convincing in places, is handled in an arbitrary manner: the sky and water are rather uniform in tone, as if seen on an overcast day; yet the shadows are dark, implying much stronger sunlight than is actually evident in the picture. And the light-shadow relationships in the figures are curiously unbalanced: while parts of the flesh are bathed in a warm light and have convincing bluish shadows, contiguous areas that should obey the same laws, such as the hair of the central figure or the hat of the boy at the far right, are painted in flat tones of a single, almost unmodified color that denies the presence of sunlight. A variant of this type of inconsistency may be seen in the broadly painted dark trousers of the two figures at the left; they seem to be placed there as formal accents, and participate neither in the lighting scheme nor in the over-all chromatic composition of the picture.

Many of the reasons for these irregularities may be found in Seurat's ambivalent artistic position in 1883–1884. When he began painting *Une Baignade*, he had already looked carefully at the art of the Impressionists, but instead of allowing the perceptual qualities implicit in their work to dominate the painting, he perfected and "improved" this style by relying heavily on the conceptual pictorial vocabulary of Delacroix and Puvis de Chavannes (among others), both of whom were little concerned with recording their exact sensations of color and light in nature. In a sense, he might be regarded as moving backward stylistically in relying on a traditional pictorial framework that negated many of the perceptual elements that can be found in his small oil studies for the painting. Although Seurat's later structuring of Impressionism in color technique and composition may, about 1886, be interpreted as manifestation of an advanced Post-Impressionist spirit, this was apparently not the dominant attitude underlying *Une Baignade*. On the contrary, at this stage he merely seems to have wanted to "modernize" a conservative pictorial idiom by relying on the language of Impressionism as a means of gathering color data and infusing the final canvas with a sense of outdoor light. But in the last analysis, *Une Baignade* denies many of the discoveries about the appearance of the physical world made by the Impressionists.

Another reason why *Une Baignade* reflects only partially the theories of physics and optics current in Seurat's day may be found in the artist's dependence on the less reliable texts among the books he consulted. While the most up-to-date and scientific of these — Rood's *Text-Book of Color* — corrected many of the mistakes inherent in Chevreul's and Blanc's writings, Seurat followed Rood's concepts only sporadically, preferring to draw many of his ideas from the less advanced "science" of the former pair of authors.

Between 1884 and 1886 many of the traditional, unscientific elements in Seurat's art were sloughed off in favor of a new approach that was guided more rigorously by the precepts of modern physics and which in some ways depended more completely on the premises of Impressionism. Still, as we shall see, Seurat retained in his next major painting, *Un Dimanche à la Grande Jatte*, many of the elements of color harmony and compositional structure apparent in *Une Baignade*, while attempting to make his canvas operate according to the scientific laws that govern the appearance of color and light in nature. It is his progress toward this end that will be considered in the following chapter.

# 3

# The Theory, Technique, and Methods of Chromo-luminarism (1884—1887)

THE MONTHS THAT ELAPSED between the first public appearance of *Une Baignade* in 1884 and the spring of 1886 witnessed the creation of the style that Félix Fénéon christened in the latter year as "Neo-Impressionism."[1] During this period Seurat undertook a second major canvas, *Un Dimanche à la Grande Jatte* (Figure 32), in which he reformed the artistic language of *Une Baignade* in several ways. First, he eliminated earth colors and black as contributing elements to pigmentary mixtures and as components in large color areas. Second, he corrected some of the methodological irregularities inherent in Impressionism by making his brushstrokes more uniform in size and shape, and by controlling his colors according to the principles of

Figure 32. *Un Dimanche à la Grande Jatte*, The Art Institute of Chicago, Helen Birch Bartlett Memorial Collection.

light and color he had found operating in nature, rather than purely by sensation. And third, he attempted to treat the entire canvas according to a consistent set of laws of optics and physics proposed by such scientists as Rood, Maxwell, Helmholtz, and Dove.

After almost two years of labor on *La Grande Jatte*, Seurat exhibited the painting at the eighth and last Impressionist exhibition, which opened on May 15, 1886. In order to make more explicit their unified aims as "scientific" Impressionists — to use Pissarro's term [2] — Seurat and his friends (Signac, Camille and Lucien Pissarro, and Dubois-Pillet) had their work hung together. This is not the place to review the critical storm that broke upon them, but suffice it to say that by the end of the exhibition it was clear to the more perceptive observers that a new artistic language had been created. True, it had much in common with Impressionism, but the fundamental premises held in 1886 by Seurat and his circle were different enough from those of the established Impressionists to identify them as an independent group. Referring to this exhibition, Signac enumerated the underlying principles of the new style: "It is there for the first time that works appeared which were painted solely with pure, separate hues in equilibrium, mixing optically according to a rational method: the basic principles of Neo-Impressionism." [3] In addition, most of the critics saw *La Grande Jatte* as the first definitive formulation of the style that shortly came to be known as Neo-Impressionism — Signac, in fact, called the painting the "*tableau-manifeste*" of the movement. [4]

In executing *La Grande Jatte*, Seurat followed a procedure similar to that used in *Une Baignade*: he recorded the requisite color data at the site in small oil sketches, and the figure units were studied in conté crayon drawings. But to these preliminary studies, a third type was introduced — oil sketches for the final composition executed in the studio. [5] Fortunately, we have several dated accounts from Seurat's own hand concerning his progress in working on this painting. In one of these (a letter to Fénéon, of June 20, 1890) he wrote:

1884, Grande Jatte study [*étude*], exhibition of the Indépendants
1884–1885, Grande Jatte composition
1885, studies [*études*] at la Grande Jatte and at Grandcamp
Resumption of La Grande Jatte composition, 1886 [*sic*, read 1885], October.[6]

In another version of this letter, Seurat provided additional information about the stages of his work on *La Grande Jatte*:

1884, *Ascension Day*, Grande Jatte, the studies [*études*] and the *painting* [*tableau*]
This canvas was ready to be exhibited in March, 1885, at the Indépendants (canceled)
Taken up again and completed after a trip to Grandcamp (1885) and exhibited on May 15, 1886.[7]

It is clear from these accounts that Seurat made the first *croquetons* at the island of la Grande Jatte during the spring and summer of 1884 and had completed the painting during the winter of 1884–1885 so that it could be shown at the Indépendants, which was to open in March, 1885, but instead was canceled. From the artist's statement "1885, studies at la Grande Jatte," we learn that more studies were made in that year, but it is not clear whether he meant the spring or fall of 1885. We know, however, that Seurat spent the summer of 1885 painting at the Channel town of Grandcamp, and that in October, after this excursion, he reworked *La Grande Jatte*, completing it in time to be shown at the eighth Impressionist exhibition, which opened on May 15, 1886.

## THE PREPARATORY STUDIES FOR *LA GRANDE JATTE*

### Oil Sketches (Croquetons)

Many of Seurat's oil sketches, or *croquetons*, for *La Grande Jatte* were painted at the site, and it is likely that most of these date from the spring and summer of 1884, though some of them, following the artist's own account, must have been executed at the island in 1885. Yet a number of these oil sketches give evidence of having been executed in the studio, and thus were undoubtedly done in 1885 as a means of working out more developed schemes of color, which Seurat incorporated in the final large canvas. If we cannot provide exact dates for these *croquetons*, it will at least be possible to place most of them in one of two general classes: "early" exploratory panels done from nature, in which the spontaneous technique and loose compositional organization characteristic of the Impressionist style are still evident;[8] and "later" oil studies in which Seurat structured his design in a manner approximating the final picture and used a more mechanical, regular execution.[9]

In brushstroke and color relationships the "early" *croquetons* for *La Grande Jatte* display several marked changes over the most advanced oil studies for *Une Baignade*. We may compare, for example, the *Étude finale pour "Une Baignade"* (D.-R. 97; Figure 20, page 58) with *Vue du fond avec quelques personnages* (D.-R. 114; Figure 33), one of Seurat's freer transcriptions of the riverbank of the island of la Grande Jatte. In the later panel the most noticeable change is in the increased presence of light and atmosphere. Seurat lightly flecked the grass, trees, and water with strokes of orange and yellow-orange, which make the picture appear to be inundated by a unifying warm light; in the *Baignade* study, however, the action of the sunlight is confined to a few areas, such as the figure and parts of the water. Seurat also achieved a more pronounced atmospheric quality in the *Grande Jatte* panel by softening the brushstrokes and reducing the intensity of color in the far distance — devices that were not used in the earlier *croqueton*. And just as the lighted areas in the *Grande Jatte* panel have been flecked consistently with orange, so the shadows have received a dosage of blue, particularly on the underside of the trees and in the foreground shadow.

Another important difference between the two studies may be found in the impressionistic softening of contours in the *Grande Jatte croqueton*; this is in contrast to the *Baignade* panel, where Seurat insisted on delineating the planes sharply, thus creating a

Figure 33. *Vue du fond avec quelques personnages, étude pour "La Grande Jatte,"* Mr. and Mrs. Robert Lehman Collection, New York.

marked and rather artificial separation between the riverbank, water, sky, and trees in the background. In the *Grande Jatte* panel, on the other hand, sunlight, atmosphere, and local colors were fused in a quasi-Impressionist mode; none of the forms are particularly distinct, and all are bathed uniformly and consistently in a golden light.

The pictorial qualities apparent in this study for *La Grande Jatte* may be found, with minor variations, in several other *croquetons* that belong to the same "early" group, namely, *Moyenne distance, gauche, avec homme debout* (D.-R. 108); *Moyenne distance, gauche* (D.-R. 110); *Vue générale, avec groupement de personnages* (D.-R. 119); *Centre, moyenne distance, "femme à la jupe rose"* (D.-R. 127); *Section de gauche, groupement de personnages* (D.-R. 128).[10] All of these share the Impressionist-inspired quality of shimmering, vibrating color — a characteristic enhanced by the use of small touches of pigment over the entire surface of these panels. In this group of oil studies the paint was applied either in very loose *balayé* strokes, short horizontal strokes, or else in spots of near-oval or circular form, once more echoing the techniques favored by the Impressionists.

Seurat employed the principles of contrast and gradation freely in these "early" *croquetons* for *La Grande Jatte*, in accord with Impressionist procedures outlined in the previous chapter. Gradation of color, particularly, is found throughout the panels: as a rule, the fundamental hue of each area will be varied within the "small interval" (to use Rood's terms) — a practice that gives the color a vibrant, pulsating quality similar to that experienced in nature under intense summer light. The laws of contrast, however, were followed somewhat less rigorously. At this time, Seurat seems to have been interested in transcribing the main colors of his subject as they appeared in bright sunlight, without systematically recording the effects of hue and value contrast.

More consistent in this group of studies was the artist's application of separate strokes of orange to record the distinct action of the sunlight on the local colors. This procedure is particularly evident in the treatment of the figures seated near the riverbank in *Vue générale avec groupement de personnages* (D.-R. 119) and in the woman at the far left of *Section de gauche, groupement de personnages* (D.-R. 128). Similarly, Seurat usually added strokes of blue to the shadowed side of fully illuminated figures or objects in the landscape. In applying orange or yellow-orange pigments consistently in the light areas and blue in the shadow, using strokes distinct from those representing the local colors, he engaged in the practice that was to be referred to in Neo-Impressionist parlance as "the methodical separation of the elements" or, simply, "divisionism."

Although some optical mixture takes place in these informal sketches, it has not yet become a major component in his color technique. At this point, Seurat was interested chiefly in recording the hues of the subject and allowed the tones he put down to mix optically at random. Apparently it was his aim in this group of studies to transcribe accurately the colors he perceived in nature, not to create finished images that worked in accordance with scientific laws.

In these "early" *croquetons* for *La Grande Jatte*, Seurat comes as close as he ever will to recording his sensations of the natural world without the intercession of preconceived theories. That his art could be firmly grounded in an optical awareness of his subject was attested by Paul Signac, who provided the following description of the artist at work before the motif:

> In front of his subject, Georges Seurat, before placing a touch of paint on his little panel, looks, compares, and squints to see the play of light and shadow, perceives contrasts, distinguishes reflections, plays for a long time with the box-lid which serves as his palette, struggling with matter as he struggles with nature; then, he picks from the little piles of prismatically arranged pigments the diverse colored elements which constitute the hue destined best to express the mystery which he has discovered. From observation to execution, from stroke to stroke, the panel is covered.[11]

Further evidence concerning Seurat's optical sensibilities at this time may be found in some remarks by his friend Charles

Angrand: "On the Boulevard Courbevoie, recently built along the river, they had just planted some trees. Seurat was delighted to point out to me that their green mass against the sky was haloed with pink." [12] Here, of course, Seurat was probably following, consciously or unconsciously, Chevreul's suggestion that, once aware of the law of simultaneous contrast, the artist could perceive its effects in nature more readily.

Quite different in conception from the "early" group of *croquetons*, which had been based on the close observation of nature, is a second, "later" group of panels that were undoubtedly painted in the studio as a means of working out the color composition of the picture away from the motif. In these, the relationship of the figures to their landscape setting was studied and the effects of light and shadow explored more carefully than in the panels executed at the site. While many irregularities may be found in the "early" group of *croquetons*, most of the later ones were guided by a set of uniform principles, which, as we shall see, are very close to those followed in the final painting. It is here, then, that Seurat made the transition from an art of sensation guided, in part, by an Impressionist point of view to one in which nature's colors could be recreated in the studio according to fixed laws.

Typical of the later group of *croquetons* for *La Grande Jatte* is *Vue du fond avec quelques personnages* (D.-R. 122; Figure 34). There are several important differences between this and the earlier studies for the painting, the most noticeable of which is Seurat's use of a more mechanical, regular brushstroke. And while he continued to use the technique of gradation and treated light as orange and added blue to the shadows, he now carefully observed and recorded the complementary hues, or "reactions," invoked by the juxtaposition of the illuminated area of the grass and the shadow in the foreground. (Such effects, it will be recalled, were incorporated in the painting of the grass plot of *Une Baignade*, undoubtedly as a result of following Rood's and Chevreul's advice.) Close to the line of demarcation, the patch of grass in the light inclines toward orange, while near this line the blue-green

Figure 34. *Vue du fond avec quelques personnages, étude pour "La Grande Jatte,"* Wertheim Collection, Fogg Museum of Art, Harvard University, Cambridge, Mass.

plot in shadow reveals the addition of purple and violet strokes. Seurat thus followed the principle that, when two colors are juxtaposed, each tints the other with its complementary. (These same induced complementaries were recorded in the shadow areas farther back on the riverbank.)

In this panel, and in those painted about the same time, Seurat finally achieved his goal of "the purity of the spectral elements": earth colors have been eliminated, and hues far from each other on the chromatic circle, such as the purple projected on the blue-green grass, are applied in separate strokes. And there is no evidence of mixture on the palette of any colors but neighboring ones. Furthermore, he carefully avoided fortuitous subtractive mixtures of pigments on the surface of the picture, presumably by allowing it to dry completely before adding alien color elements to it. In order to maintain the unadulterated purity of brushstroke, Seurat had to rely on optical mixture of the component colors, just as he did in parts of *Une Baignade*. But in *Vue du fond avec quelques personnages*, this technique was utilized everywhere in the picture, not just in selected areas.

One of the most difficult problems for Seurat to solve, following his insistence on the purity of color, was that of painting shadows. While shadows traditionally had been reduced in value by the addition of black, some dark earth color, or by the use of complementaries mixed together on the palette, Seurat applied a generous dosage of blue in the shadows in *Vue du fond avec quelques personnages*, following the principle that they should be tinted with the complementary of the color of the light. When seen at a distance, the intense greens and blue-greens constituting the local color of the grass in the shadow are "achromatized" (that is, reduced in intensity) and made cooler in tone by optical mixture with the superimposed strokes of blue pigment.

Seurat relied on *balayé*, or criss-cross, brushwork throughout much of this panel as a means of effecting the optical mixture of colors. As in the grass plot of *Une Baignade*, strokes of almost uniform size are applied in every possible direction, and as a result the contour and texture of the materials portrayed are almost completely disregarded. In the water, however, the strokes are short horizontal ones, rather than of the *balayé* type, and are thus reminiscent of those used in the river in *Une Baignade*.

The method and technique Seurat applied in *Vue du fond avec quelques personnages*, which is representative of many of the later *croquetons* for *La Grande Jatte*, were also followed in a larger canvas that served as a final oil study for the entire painting: the *Étude finale pour la composition de "La Grande Jatte"* (D.-R. 138; Figure 35). This picture, undoubtedly executed in the studio, is important because it embodies the advances that Seurat had made just prior to undertaking the final canvas. In addition, it gives us some idea of what *La Grande Jatte* must have looked like before it was re-worked during the autumn of 1885. (There is some repainting in this final study, as Dorra [13] has pointed out; however, it is confined to the border and a light sprinkling of orange dots adjoining it.) In this study Seurat equaled, or even surpassed, the degree of luminosity found in many of the *croquetons* discussed earlier, and handled the whole painting consistently according to a set of scientific principles, the nature of which will be discussed shortly. And it embodies many of the tenets of Seurat's *"peinture optique"* developed during the previous eight years.

In the *Étude finale pour la composition de "La Grande Jatte,"* he preserved "the purity of the spectral elements" by applying individual strokes over each other whenever mixture or modification of color was necessary; no mixtures on the palette, except of neighboring hues, appear to have taken place here. Many of the colors, of course, have been mixed with white, but this in no way detracts from their purity: it is merely a means of raising them in value. To use Seurat's own terminology, the painting is "divided [*divisée*] in purity of hue"; [14] by "divided" he evidently meant that any given area must be broken down into its component elements, which are then applied in touches of pure color that will mix optically at a distance in order to produce the desired resultant tone.

Figure 31. *Homme étendu, étude pour "Une Baignade"* (conté crayon drawing), Ernst Beyeler Collection, Basle.

The painting is remarkably effective in conveying a sense of pulsating sunlight and luminous shadow. Perhaps the most appropriate way to describe the picture is to say that it abstracts the essence of our experience of color and light in nature and recasts it on the canvas. True, much of the visual data of the seen world has been omitted, but in so doing, Seurat strengthened the intense sensation of light as the dominant element in the painting. Also, it corresponds in another way to our experience of nature: the effects of simultaneous contrast that scientists had pointed out, and which may be confirmed by observation, have been incorporated in the picture.

Before turning to the final, large version of *La Grande Jatte*, the role of value drawings as preparatory studies will be considered here, both in relation to the painting and to the drawings Seurat executed one or two years earlier for *Une Baignade*.

### *Preparatory Drawings for* La Grande Jatte

Just as he did for *Une Baignade*, Seurat studied the figures that were to appear in *La Grande Jatte* through the medium of conté crayon drawings. While only individual figures were drawn for the earlier painting, he represented larger groups in his preparatory drawings for *La Grande Jatte*. Their function was twofold: to establish the form and position of the models, without including the background,[15] and to study the figures in relation to their environment in a general tonal scheme that is close in appearance to the final painting.[16] The latter category, rather than the former, will concern us at present, since it is from these drawings that we can gain a clear idea of Seurat's method of planning the value relationships for *La Grande Jatte*.

Two of the most developed drawings of this type are *Vieille femme et nourrice* (D.-R. 138c; Figure 36) and *Trois femmes* (D.-R. 138d; Figure 37). In both Seurat moved away from the deep, rich blacks and harsh highlights that characterized the *Baignade* drawings, concentrating instead on subtle gradations of tone in the

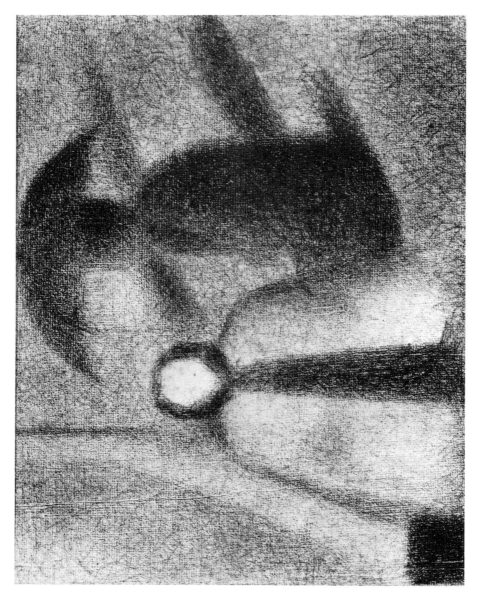

Figure 36. *Vieille femme et nourrice, étude pour "La Grande Jatte"* (conté crayon drawing), General A. Conger Goodyear Collection, Old Westbury, Long Island, New York.

Figure 37. *Trois femmes, étude pour "La Grande Jatte"* (conté crayon drawing), Smith College Museum of Art, Northampton, Mass.

middle range of the value scale and indulging only rarely in the use of heavy blacks and intense white accents. As a result, these two drawings display a luminous, atmospheric quality greatly surpassing that of the *Baignade* studies.

While Seurat utilized the rough surface of the paper in the drawings for *Une Baignade* in order to gain luminosity through the optical mixture of tones, he went much further in these two studies for *La Grande Jatte* in allowing the surface of the sheet to sparkle as a result of the multitude of small white spots showing through the covering crayon strokes. It is apparent that Seurat here considered the paper as a screen of uniform texture from which forms defined only as unclear masses of shadow emerge; accordingly, firm contours have almost disappeared. Rather than treating his subject as something that can be touched and understood in a three-dimensional sense — a point of view implicit in most of the *Baignade* drawings — Seurat represented the forms in *Vieille femme et nourrice* and *Trois femmes* as slightly modeled silhouettes that are brought into existence by being hewn out of an unarticulated mass of gray shadow. One feels that the human figures almost swim in a sea of luminous shadow and that light, rather than being thought of as external illumination, actually emanates from the paper. In this sense, the drawings are quite close in general effect to the final painting, for in both the surface is treated as an abstract grid or mesh in which appropriate modulations of luminous color or tone serve to define the subject matter. As we shall see in *La Grande Jatte*, unlike *Une Baignade*, Seurat employed optical mixture uniformly throughout the canvas — a technique that was fully explored in this pair of preparatory drawings.

In both of these sheets Seurat utilized value contrast to throw forms into relief and to place them convincingly in space. (Leonardo da Vinci, we recall, advocated the use of this principle, and it was placed on a scientific basis by Chevreul.) In *Vieille femme et nourrice*, for example, the background is lightened slightly as it approaches the silhouette of the human form and umbrella at the right, following Chevreul's law of contrast, which states that when two areas are juxtaposed, the difference between their values should be intensified; or, to put it another way, any given tone will be surrounded by its complementary. Conversely, when a light tone is placed against a darker background, the background becomes appreciably darker near the line of juncture, as seen in the tree at the left of this drawing.

By studying the effects of contrast in black and white before executing *La Grande Jatte*, Seurat was observing a principle that Fénéon later put into words: "this contrast [of value] is the regulator of the contrast of hues."[17] We have seen that several of the writers Seurat studied had affirmed the importance of a solid value foundation as the basis for color, and have already observed that he followed their advice in *Une Baignade*. The drawings for *La Grande Jatte* likewise serve to establish a set of value relationships ranging from almost black to white, which the painting follows explicitly, at least in the areas for which drawings have been found. The difference between the drawings and final painting, of course, is that color is added in the latter; but significantly the framework of values established in the drawings is always respected in the completed canvas.

Having considered the role of the preliminary studies for *La Grande Jatte*, we may now turn to the final painting. First, we shall enumerate those scientific and theoretical sources that Seurat is known to have studied before 1886 and then examine the ways in which he utilized them in the execution of this canvas.

## Scientific and Theoretical Sources

In 1886, Seurat began to receive considerable attention from critics associated with *avant-garde* magazines and newspapers, and most of them attempted to indicate which scientific sources had inspired the young artist. The most important of these critics, Félix Fénéon,[18] made a conscious effort to document the evolution of Neo-Impressionism and was careful to mention relevant sources and dates whenever possible. In his first major article to discuss Seurat's *La Grande Jatte*, "Les Impressionnistes," he cited the following book as one of the artist's sources: "*Théorie scientifique des couleurs et ses applications à l'art et à l'industrie*, 1881, par M. N. O. Rood, de New York."[19] He also mentioned the importance for Seurat of demonstrations conducted with "Maxwell's discs."[20] (It is very likely that Seurat studied Rood's account of James Clerk Maxwell's experiments, rather than consulting any of the English physicist's writings at firsthand.) Another writer close to Seurat, Emile Hennequin, also confirmed his use of Rood's book as a source when painting *La Grande Jatte* and, in addition, mentioned Seurat's interest in John Ruskin's ideas on color, as explained by Rood.[21] We have already seen that the latter had admired Ruskin's *Elements of Drawing* and quoted long excerpts from it in his *Théorie scientifique des couleurs*.

Oddly enough, Fénéon did not mention Chevreul's name in his article "Les Impressionnistes." But it appears, among other places, in an important letter by Camille Pissarro to Durand-Ruel in which he enumerated Seurat's sources as "the theory of colors discovered by Chevreul, the experiments of Maxwell, and the measurements of O. N. Rood."[22]

Also, in 1884, after their meeting at the Indépendants, Signac, probably accompanied by Seurat, paid a visit to Chevreul[23] at Les Gobelins. According to one account, Signac and his friends had an argument about the division of light and decided to call upon the scientist to clarify the matter.[24] Although Signac referred to the meeting with Chevreul as "our initiation to the science of color,"[25] it is difficult to assess the actual value of this personal contact, since Chevreul was then ninety-eight years old and apparently was losing his faculties.[26] But the fact that the artists consulted him suggests that their discussions had reached a rather advanced scientific level.

Another of the artist's sources at this time was a text that Gustave Kahn called "*le papier de Gauguin*," said to have been written by the Persian poet Vehbi Mohamed Zunbul-Zadé

(d. 1809), a copy of which Seurat probably obtained from Gauguin.[27] It contained numerous precepts on color and instructions
about drawing the human figure. Seurat, according to Kahn, was
very much taken by this text, but felt, at the same time, that it did
not embrace all questions of technique.[28] Unlike the writings
enumerated thus far, we have no certain indication of when
Seurat gained knowledge of Zunbul-Zadé's text, but it was
probably between 1884 and 1886; after June, 1886, Seurat was on
poor terms with Gauguin, and it is unlikely that they would have
known each other before the spring of 1884.

Thus, with Seurat's recognition in 1886 by a substantial number
of art critics, many of whom became his personal friends, the
theoretical and stylistic sources upon which he relied may be
identified with some degree of certainty. Through their writings
and from statements by artists participating in the Neo-
Impressionist movement, we know that the writers on color
theory who contributed particularly to the evolution of *La
Grande Jatte* are Chevreul, Zunbul-Zadé, and Rood; and through
Rood's book Seurat became acquainted with the theories of
Maxwell, Ruskin, and Helmholtz.[29]

It is worth noting that Charles Blanc's name appears in-
frequently in writings that discuss the sources of Seurat's art and
theory between 1884 and 1886. It is likely that the painter saw the
serious limitations of the color theories set forth in the *Grammaire
des arts du dessin* when judged by the discoveries of such modern
physicists as Rood, Helmholtz, and Maxwell.[30] Blanc's writings,
however, were to have renewed interest for Seurat in the last few
years of his life.

## UN DIMANCHE À LA GRANDE JATTE (1884–1886)

### Theory, Color Technique, and Method

Completed after almost two years of work, Seurat's *Un
Dimanche à la Grande Jatte* (Figure 32, page 113) stands a definitive
formulation of the technique, method, and theory of Neo-

Impressionism in its first, or "chromo-luminarist," phase. As the "*tableau-manifeste*" of the Neo-Impressionist movement, it embodied Seurat's latest discoveries in the realm of scientifically controlled light and color. Close analysis of the painting, with the aid of pertinent writings by artists and critics, will enable us to reconstruct Seurat's procedures, while at the same time tracing the sources of his newly developed theories and color technique. We tried to show in the previous chapter that in 1883–1884 Seurat had formulated many of the tenets of the artistic language that was to be termed "Neo-Impressionism" in 1886. In the following discussion of *La Grande Jatte*, therefore, we shall point out similarities in conception to *Une Baignade* whenever possible.

Fortunately, Seurat's friend Félix Fénéon wrote three definitive articles on the Neo-Impressionists' procedures, two of which Seurat considered excellent expressions of his ideas on painting;[31] these will serve as a guide to our analysis of *La Grande Jatte*. In one of the articles Fénéon explained and enumerated, in sequence, the elements that entered into the chromatic composition of Seurat's pictures:

> The innovation of Seurat, already implicitly contained in certain works by Camille Pissarro, is based on the scientific division of tone. Here it is: instead of triturating on the palette the pigments whose resultant mixture will approximate the hue of the surface to be represented, the painter will place on the canvas touches representing the local color, that is, the color that the aforesaid surface would have in white light (appreciably, the color of the object seen from up close). This color, which he has not achromatized on the palette, he will indirectly achromatize on the canvas, according to the laws of simultaneous contrast, through the intervention of other series of touches, corresponding:
>
> 1. To the portion of colored light that is reflected unaltered from its surface (this will usually be solar orange);
> 2. To the feeble portion of colored light which penetrates below the surface and which is reflected after modification by partial absorption;
> 3. To reflections projected by neighboring objects;
> 4. To ambient complementary colors.[32]

The initial application of paint, according to Fénéon, would correspond to the local colors, which in *La Grande Jatte* are mainly green for the grass, blue for the water and sky, and red-orange and blue-violet for the clothing of the figures that populate the landscape. However, Fénéon did not mention one all-important element in the application of the local colors: the use of gradation. In *Une Baignade*, we saw that gradation was used as a fundamental means of making the tones vibrate and appear richer in color, echoing the technique used by Delacroix and the Impressionists, as well as the advice of Blanc and Rood. Close examination reveals that Seurat employed just such gradated local colors in *La Grande Jatte* within the following hue ranges: for the illuminated area of the grass, yellow-green to green; for the shadowed grass in the foreground, green to blue-green; and for the water, blue to ultramarine blue. In addition, he introduced gradations of value by mixing white with some of the hues just enumerated, thereby raising them somewhat in tone.

While Fénéon failed to mention gradation, its importance in Seurat's technique was pointed out in an article by Émile Hennequin, who also suggested that Ruskin's ideas on this subject were transmitted to the artist through Rood's *Théorie scientifique des couleurs*;[33] Ruskin, as we have noted, argued for the value of gradation in his *Elements of Drawing*, excerpts from which were quoted in Rood's book. Seurat undoubtedly meditated on a passage such as the following:

> Ruskin, speaking of gradation of colour, says: "You will find in practice that brilliancy of hue and vigor of light, and even the aspect of transparency in shade, are essentially dependent on this character alone; hardness, coldness, and opacity resulting far more from *equality* of colour than from nature of colour." In another place the same author, in giving advice to a beginner, says: "And it does not matter how small the touch of colour may be, though not larger than the smallest pin's head, if one part of it is not darker than the rest, it is a bad touch; for it is not merely because the natural fact is so that your colour should be gradated; the preciousness and pleasantness of colour depends more on this than on any

other of its qualities, for gradation is to colours just what curvature is to lines. . . ."[34]

The next element added to the local color, according to Fénéon, was the "colored light" — usually a solar orange — "that is reflected unaltered from its surface." We have already seen that Seurat recorded just such a "solar orange" as a distinct element in the grass and water of *Une Baignade*, but did not apply this color consistently in the shadows of that painting. However, strokes of "solar orange" permeate every corner of *La Grande Jatte*, thus creating a sense of all-pervading sunlight that is distributed according to the laws of nature, rather than at the caprice of the artist. Fénéon pointed out, too, that this "solar orange" was not only a major element of color in the lighted area of the grass but that small quantities also appeared in the shadows in order to express "the barely perceptible action of the sun" (see Plate D).[35]

Just as Seurat recorded the effects of orange light on the illuminated side of objects, he also applied blue to their shadowed side in *La Grande Jatte*; in addition, blue was added generously to the cast shadow on the grass and to the figures that are placed within this area. Again, we observed in the last chapter that Seurat used blue and blue-violet in most of the shadows of *Une Baignade*. The main difference in the treatment of shadow between that painting and *La Grande Jatte* is that the blue was added in small spots in the latter picture and in broad strokes in the former; and in *La Grande Jatte* every shadowed area was influenced consistently by blue, while Seurat occasionally omitted this color in the shadows of *Une Baignade*.

In one of his later explanations of the method and technique of Neo-Impressionism, Fénéon accounted for the presence of blue in the shadows of such paintings as *La Grande Jatte*: it belongs there as a "reaction" of the orange light; that is to say, it is complementary to orange and is invoked according to the law of simultaneous contrast.[36] This law, the reader will recall, had been articulated by Chevreul, Blanc, and Rood and was applied

Plate C.  Eugène Delacroix, *La Lutte de Jacob et de l'ange,*
Chapelle des Saints-Anges, Saint-Sulpice, Paris [detail].

Plate D.  *Un Dimanche à la Grande Jatte* [detail].

by Delacroix and the Impressionists. Seurat, too, mentioned the role of complementary "reactions" in his letter to Maurice Beaubourg of August 28, 1890, where he wrote that his technique was based upon the optical mixture of values and hues "of the local color and the color of the illuminating light: sun, oil lamp, gas, etc., that is to say, of the lights and their reactions (shadows) in accordance with the laws of *contrast*, gradation, and irradiation."[37] In this statement we have further evidence of Seurat's belief that "reactions," or induced shadow color, should be guided by the laws of contrast. In other words, he felt that the hue of the shadows should be represented as being complementary to that of the illuminating light. Significantly, in painting *La Grande Jatte*, Seurat carefully derived the exact complementary of the color of this light from Rood's contrast-diagram. (Through direct study of the painting the present writer found that Rood's sets of complementaries — rather than those of Blanc, Chevreul, or Sutter — were used; furthermore, in their writings on Seurat's technique, Fénéon and Signac almost always refer to Rood's color system.)

On the subject of reflections, which also enter into the chromatic composition of *La Grande Jatte*, Fénéon observed that "a shiny surface sometimes reflects its own color upon a surface placed at an angle — and it may happen that these reflections, almost always negligible, will take precedence over the manifestation of complementaries; but the latter is absolutely general, the former fortuitous."[38] Because the figures in *La Grande Jatte* are rather isolated from each other physically, reflections from one to another rarely occur. Green reflections from the grass, however, were recorded in some of the figures, such as the canoeist, the dog at the right, and the skirt of the woman with the monkey. And in the water, as in *Une Baignade*, the local color was modified considerably by reflections from the sky, the trees, and boats.

Very noticeable in *La Grande Jatte* are those modifications of color brought about through Seurat's observation of the laws of simultaneous contrast. Fénéon explained the operation of these laws, as applied to hue and value, as follows:

> Two adjacent colors mutually influence each other, each imposing upon the other its own complementary: green a purple, red a blue-green, yellow an ultramarine, violet a greenish yellow, orange a cyan blue: contrast of hues.
>
> The lightest becomes lighter; the darkest, darker: contrast of values.
>
> This contrast is the regulator of the contrast of hues: the influence, by way of complementaries, of the lightest region upon the darkest grows with the separation of values, whereas the opposite action is diminished and, for a powerful contrast of values, such as that of dark to light, is almost abolished.[39]

The basis of this conception of color behavior may be found in Chevreul's *De la loi du contraste simultané des couleurs*. The French scientist, we recall, wrote:

> Now what do we learn by the law of *simultaneous contrast of colours*? It is, that when we regard attentively two coloured objects at the same time, neither of them appears of its peculiar colour, that is to say, such as it would appear if viewed separately, but of a tint resulting from its peculiar colour and the complementary of the colour of the other object. . . .[40]
>
> It is easy to prove that the modification is not equally intense over the whole extent of the surfaces . . . but that it becomes gradually weaker from the line of contact.[41]

Although Chevreul proposed the idea that, when juxtaposed, each color projects its complementary onto its neighbor, the pairs of colors listed by Fénéon in the foregoing excerpt are based on Rood's color system, not Chevreul's. Rood, of course, accepted the latter's ideas about simultaneous contrast, but was more careful about determining the exact hue of the complementaries.

Fénéon also described the operation of contrast between the lighted and shadowed area of the grass in *La Grande Jatte* (see Plate D):

> The lawn in the shade: touches for the most part give the local color of the grass; others, of orange, are sparsely scattered, expressing the barely perceptible action of the sun; others, of purple, cause the complementary

of green to intervene; touches of cyan blue, induced by the proximity of a plot of grass in the sun, are accumulated toward the line of demarcation and progressively diminish away from this line. Only two elements combine in the formation of the plot itself: green and solar orange, all other reactions being destroyed under so furious an assault of light.[42]

The complementary colors mentioned here are again based on Rood's contrast-diagram (Figures 14 and 15, pages 40 and 41, respectively). These pairs, interestingly, are the same as those used by Seurat in *Une Baignade*, in which he also must have used Rood's color circle; they are: green and purple, cyan-blue and orange. In short, each of the two component colors of the lighted area of the grass, green and orange, projects its complementary onto the neighboring blue-green area of grass in shadow.

Similar effects in the treatment of the monkey and dog in the foreground of the picture were also noted by Fénéon: "Black being non-light, the black dog will be colored by the reactions from the grass, its predominant tone consequently being deep purple; but it will also be attacked by a dark blue, induced by the neighboring luminous regions. The monkey on a leash will be spotted with yellow, its intrinsic quality, and speckled with purple and ultramarine."[43] Here the "reactions" projected by one hue, the green of the grass, have strongly influenced the color of the two animals that are placed on its surface. What little color there is in the dog, as Fénéon observed, occurs as the induced complementary of the grass, that is, purple.

Also, aureoles, or ambient complementary haloes, are placed consistently around figures to separate them from their background. The torso of the man nearest to the picture plane in the left foreground, for example, wears a red-orange shirt which is haloed with strokes of light cyan-blue which make him appear distinctly separated from the two figures directly behind him. Or, where the blue-violet skirt of the standing woman in the foreground at the right meets the shadowed grass area, it is surrounded near the line of demarcation by an extra dosage of greenish-yellow strokes, which are complementary to it. Similar effects of contrast may be noted in the seven figures located in the foreground shadow whose silhouettes overlap the lighted area of the grass; as the boundaries of the figures are approached, the background becomes appreciably lighter and warmer in tone, as a result of being juxtaposed to the cool blue and blue-violet color of these figures.

Seurat also used the principles of hue and value contrast to separate neighboring planes, such as the skirts of the two seated girls at the edge of the shadow near the center of the painting: here the bluish skirt of the girl at the left is haloed with light orange where it meets the skirt of the girl next to her. Seurat obtained the same kind of separation by scattering an extra dose of yellow-orange dots in the area along the coat of the tall man standing at the right where it meets the bluish dress of the woman beside him. Where necessary, these color relations are reversed; for example, when the dark blue bodice of the woman meets the coat of the man beside her, a yellow-orange aureole is present; but when the face, which is light orange, overlaps this same coat, a bluish halo appears. Similar examples of Seurat's use of ambient complementary colors placed according to the laws of simultaneous contrast may be found throughout the painting.

The principles underlying such color relationships were summarized by Fénéon in the following "synopsis":

| A | B |
|---|---|
| in light: | in shade: |
| 1. Local color. | 1. Local color. |
| | 1a. Reaction of local color of A, that is, its complementary. |
| 2. Solar orange. | 2. Solar orange, rarefied. |
| | 2a. Reaction of the solar orange, that is, its complementary, blue.[44] |

In this synopsis we find repeated many of the propositions concerning color relationships already referred to in our discussion of *La Grande Jatte*: that two major elements — the local color and solar orange — contribute to the lighted areas; that the complementary "reaction" of the solar orange, blue, is projected onto the local color in the shadows; that small quantities of this same orange appear also in the shadows; and that the local color projects its complementary "reactions" into the shadow.

How are these diverse elements to be mixed? Fénéon provided the following answer:

> The mixture of the local color of an object with the diverse colored lights which flow upon it (sunlight, the normal irradiations of complementaries, and accidental reflections), a mixture which constitutes the hue which we perceive in this object, is an *optical mixture*.
>
> The painter enters:
>
> If the painter juxtaposes on his support (canvas, leather, wood, academy board, metal, ivory, etc.) tiny eye-like spots of color, the succession of which corresponds either to local color, or to sunlight, or to reflections, these multicolored spots will not be perceived individually: from a distance, the rays of light which emanate from it will recombine on the retina in an *optical mixture*. The painter's artifice will have rigorously restored the process of reality.[45]

And referring specifically to the phenomenon of optical mixture in *La Grande Jatte*, Fénéon wrote:

> These colors, isolated on the canvas, recombine on the retina. One has, therefore, not a mixture of colored pigments but a mixture of colored light. Need one be reminded that, for the same colors, the mixture of pigments and the mixture of light do not necessarily furnish the same results? It is also known that the luminosity of optical mixture is always much greater than that of pigmentary mixture, as the numerous equations for luminosity established by Rood show.[46]

Rood had demonstrated the advantages of mixing colored light by rotating discs (Maxwell's discs), as opposed to mixing the same colors on the palette, in a series of equations which were published in his *Text-Book of Color*,[47] and one of these equations was actually quoted by Fénéon immediately following the excerpt just cited:

For carmine violet and Prussian blue, which produce a gray-blue:

$$\underbrace{50\ C + 50\ B}_{\substack{\text{mixture of}\\\text{pigments}}} = \underbrace{47\ C + 49\ B + 4\ \text{Black}}_{\substack{\text{mixture of}\\\text{light}}};$$

for carmine and green:

$$50\ C + 50\ G = 50\ C + 24\ G + 26\ \text{Black.}[48]$$

These cryptic formulae may be explained by reference to one of Rood's experiments, in which Seurat and his friends found scientific justification for the superiority of optical mixture of color over subtractive mixture of pigments.[49] In this experiment, Rood first painted a cardboard circle with a pigmentary mixture of fifty parts of carmine-violet and fifty parts of blue paint. Then he tried to match this result by painting each half of a circle with the same colors (carmine-violet and blue) and rotating it at high speed. When the pigmentary mixture was compared to additive mixture of these colors obtained by rotation, the former was found to be grayer, darker, and less saturated. Rood had to add a sector of black to the discs painted carmine-violet and blue in order to make the color obtained by rotation match that derived from the mixture of pigments on the palette; hence we have the equation quoted by Fénéon: "47 C[armine-violet] + 49 B[lue] + 4 Black" for the mixture of colored light. Rood concluded his experiment with the following statement: "The large amount of black which it was necessary to add strikingly illustrates the general proposition that every mixture of pigments on the painter's palette is a stride toward blackness."[50] Here, then, in concise form was convincing scientific proof of the superiority of optical mixture as a means of achieving greater luminosity in painting.

The fundamental importance of optical mixture in Seurat's technique was also revealed in his letter to Maurice Beaubourg, where he wrote: "Granting the phenomena of the duration of the light-impression on the retina, synthesis necessarily follows as a resultant. The means of expression is the optical mixture of values, of hues. . . ."[51] In these remarks Seurat clearly echoes Rood's discussion of the phenomenon of the duration of the light impression on the retina. The scientist has devoted a chapter of his *Text-Book of Color* to this subject where he stated that

> If the light [either white or colored light] be allowed to act for a short time on the eye, when it vanishes . . . the sensation remains for a fraction of a second, this after-sensation being in all respects identical with the original sensation, except that it gradually becomes weaker and weaker; thus, if the original sensation is red, the after-sensation will entirely correspond to this colour. This after-image . . . is called the *positive* image.[52]

A knowledge of this phenomenon, according to Rood, would enable one to mix colored light "in the eye." As he said: "The positive after-images are useful in furnishing us, in the case of revolving disks, with a mode of mixing together masses of coloured light in definite proportions."[53]

It is very likely that Seurat's reading of Rood's account of color mixture through rotating discs — which is, in fact, dependent on the phenomenon of the duration of the light impression on the retina — led him to believe that the same principle was involved in the optical mixture, or "synthesis," of colored lights reflected from myriad small points of pigment used in the pointillist technique. However, the present writer has found no evidence in the writings of Seurat's period or in modern scientific texts asserting that the duration of the light impression is involved in such optical mixtures. Thus Seurat, in his desire to establish a firm scientific basis for his art, appears to have overextended himself by including among the prerequisites for optical mixture in painting a condition necessary only for the mixture of light by Maxwell's rotating discs.

According to Fénéon, one of the chief advantages of using optical mixture was that it enabled the artist to obtain resultant hues that were more *luminous* than those produced by the mixture of colors on the palette. But he did not state that optical mixture invariably yielded resultant hues that were more *intense* than the pure colors in the tubes of paint available to artists. Actually, one of the main reasons why the Neo-Impressionists relied on optical mixture, as many contemporary painters and critics pointed out, was to represent effectively all of the possible varieties of color and light in nature, including the subtle qualities of tone in half-lights and shadows. Seurat's major achievement in *La Grande Jatte* was not, as many have assumed, in making all of the colors appear as intense as possible, but in creating a sense of luminosity in the canvas by the optical, rather than the physical (subtractive), mixture of color, thus duplicating what he believed to be nature's mode of operation.

Seurat's use of optical mixture in *La Grande Jatte* was, in many respects, foreshadowed in *Une Baignade*. In the latter picture we found that he often applied separate strokes corresponding to the local color, the color of the illuminating light and its corresponding bluish shadow, reflections, and ambient complementary "reactions." These, in turn, were to blend by optical mixture, either fully or partially, depending on the distance from which *Une Baignade* was viewed. But, as we pointed out in the last chapter, these elements were recorded only sporadically in that painting, and, in addition, Seurat used several different varieties of brushwork, each of which induced a different degree of optical mixture. In *La Grande Jatte*, however, he discovered the value of treating the entire surface of the picture uniformly and abstractly, and applied the pigment in much more regular brushstrokes.

Intimately related to optical mixture is the phenomenon of "lustre," which is partly responsible for the vibrant, scintillating quality of the color in *La Grande Jatte*. Fénéon was very much aware of these properties when he wrote the following about the painting: "The atmosphere is transparent and singularly vibrant; the surface seems to vacillate. Perhaps this sensation . . . may be explained by Dove's theory: the retina, anticipating distinct rays of light to act upon it, perceives in very rapid alternation both the separate elements of color and their resultant mixture."[54] In reading this, one may be tempted to assume that Seurat turned directly to the writings of the German physicist Heinrich-Wilhelm Dove. However, the present writer has found no evidence to indicate that Seurat knew Dove's writings on color at firsthand;[55] a more logical source would have been Rood's book, which summarized Dove's theory of lustre. Indeed, the terminology and content of the excerpt just quoted suggest that Fénéon knew some of Rood's remarks about Dove, which follow:

> If the coloured lines or dots are quite distant from the eye, the mixture is of course perfect, and presents nothing remarkable in its appearance; but before this distance is reached there is a stage in which the colours are blended, though somewhat imperfectly, so that the surface seems to flicker or glimmer — an effect that no doubt arises from a faint perception from time to time of its constituents. This communicates a soft and peculiar brilliancy to the surface, and gives it a certain appearance of transparency; we seem to see into it and below it. Dove's theory of lustre has perhaps some bearing on this well-known phenomenon. According to Dove, when two masses of light simultaneously act on the eyes, lustre is perceived, provided we are in any way made conscious that there are actually *two* masses of light.[56]

The effects of lustre described by Rood are immediately evident in *La Grande Jatte*, where the degree of optical mixture of the various colored elements depends on the viewer's distance from the canvas. If one stands one foot from the painting, for example, one can see all of the individual constituent colors in any given small area; but upon moving back gradually, these hues begin to fuse and coalesce until one reaches a point about twenty feet from the canvas, where fusion is complete and the individual colored strokes are no longer discernible. But before this point is reached, as Dove pointed out, effects of partial fusion or "lustre" become evident, and it is just this quality that Fénéon observed. (This subject will be taken up in greater detail in our discussion of *Les Poseuses*.)

In *La Grande Jatte*, Seurat finally developed an effective technique that engendered the optical mixture of color — "*peinture au point*," as Fénéon called it.[57] The use of small dots of almost uniform size can be seen nearly everywhere in the painting, but it should be noted that they do not serve as the fundamental underlying brushstrokes for any area; rather, they appear to have been added quite late in the evolution of the painting. To discover what the initial paint layer of *La Grande Jatte* looked like, one must eliminate the dots mentally; underneath one will find a surface made up of *balayé* and long, thin, parallel strokes. The dots that appear in this painting must be interpreted as part of the reworking of the picture after Seurat's return from Grandcamp in the fall of 1885, since they do not appear as part of the original composition of the small version or, with one exception,[58] in the *croquetons*. They fulfill two major functions in the final picture: they distribute a haze of orange and blue tones representing, respectively, sunlight and shadow (or reflections from the blue sky), and they serve as a means of adding ambient complementary colors.

What were the sources of the "*petit point*" employed by Seurat? We have already found that Charles Blanc recommended the application of small spots or stars of pigment to effect optical mixture (see Figure 11, page 33).[59] But surely of greater consequence for the artist were Rood's citations of the work of Dr. Jean Mile and John Ruskin, both of whom suggested the use of a stippled technique in painting. Concerning Mile's method of mixing colors, Rood wrote:

> Another method of mixing coloured light seems to have been first definitely contrived by Mile in 1839, though it had been in practical use by artists a long time previously. We refer to the custom of placing a quantity of small dots of two colours very near each other, and allowing them to be blended by the eye placed at the proper distance. Mile traced fine lines of colour parallel to each other, the tints being alternated. The results obtained in this way are true mixtures of coloured light. . . . This method is almost the only practical one at the disposal of the artist whereby he can actually mix, not pigments, but masses of coloured light.[60]

In this statement we find positive justification for Seurat's use of pointillism as a technique that will enable colors to mix optically. Moreover, the foregoing excerpt is of the utmost importance because Rood states that pigments can be made to behave according to the laws governing the mixture of light.

Seurat could have found in Ruskin, too, arguments in favor of pointillist execution. As we have seen, the critic Émile Hennequin recognized Ruskin's value for Seurat in 1886 and suggested that the English critic's ideas came to the artist *via* Rood.[61] Ruskin's *Elements of Drawing* was of special interest to Rood, who quoted the following lines, which Seurat undoubtedly knew, advocating painting with small points of color: "Breaking one colour in small points through or over another is the most important of all processes in good modern oil and water-colour painting.... In distant effects of a rich subject, wood or rippled water or broken clouds, much may be done by touches or crumbling dashes of rather dry colour, with other colours afterward put cunningly into the interstices."[62]

Interestingly, Seurat also discovered a pointillist technique in Murillo's paintings in the Louvre.[63] In a canvas such as *La Naissance de la Vierge* (Figure 38) (which was on display in the Louvre during the 1870s and 1880s) he could have found very small dots of color distributed on the upper part of St. Anne's garment and along her left arm. When the painting is viewed at a distance, these spots of brown pigment serve to modify the tone of the underlying color. Although Signac failed to mention the fact in his writings, Delacroix, too, used a pointillist execution in applying tiny spots of color to the back and legs of the nude child in the lower right corner of his *Scène du massacre de Scio* (Louvre, Paris; Figure 39), and there can be little doubt that Seurat knew this painting well. Indeed, he could have found in certain Impressionist canvases a similar technique of applying small dots of pigment, among other varieties of brushwork. Monet's *La Chasse* (d. 1876; Louvre, Paris; Figure 40), to select a single example,

Figure 38. Bartolomé Esteban Murillo, *La Naissance de la Vierge* [detail], Louvre, Paris. (Photo Giraudon.)

illustrates how far one Impressionist painter could carry the possibilities of the pointillist brushstroke. There exist, of course, many other instances in Western art where isolated small spots of pigment were used in painting, but only Murillo, Delacroix, and Monet have been cited here as possible sources for Seurat's technique because we have reliable evidence that he studied their work.[64]

## Seurat's Palette

Fortunately, Seurat's palette, from which black and earth colors were eliminated, has survived.[65] He laid out eleven colors in a

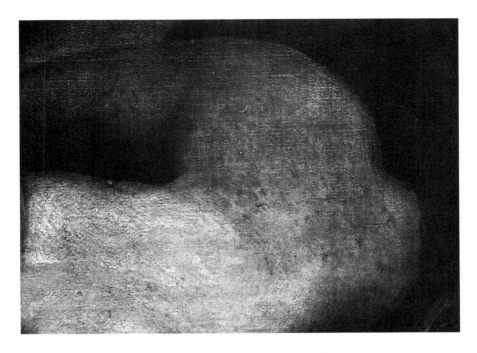

Figure 39. Eugène Delacroix, *Scène du massacre de Scio* [detail], Louvre, Paris.

straight line on the long side of a conventional wooden palette (Figure 41), and parallel to them was placed a second row of colors composed of a mixture of white with each of the pigments of the first row. A third row, parallel to the other two, is comprised of small mounds of white paint. The pigments of the first row correspond closely to the gradual steps around the chromatic circle in a relationship that was described by Fénéon:

> Only prismatic colors play a role in the make-up of the paintings of Signac and Seurat. That is to say, given that the colors from the tube are spread out on the palette in the order of the prism, one would never combine any other than consecutive colors; and the spectral band, thus restorable without any break in continuity, will be, along all its length, capable of being enlarged by the intervention of white, so as to constitute a chromatic rectangle, which would be to the color wheel what a planisphere is to a map of the world. [For an illustration of a "prismatic spectrum" published by Rood, see Figure 42.][66]

Figure 40. Claude Monet, *La Chasse*, Louvre, Paris. (Photo Bulloz.)

*Row 1*: Hues of the
Prismatic Spectrum
(at full intensity) ————→

*Row 2*: Mixture of Hues
in Row 1 with white ————→

*Row 3*: White ————————→

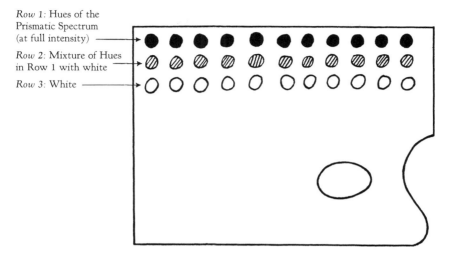

Figure 41. Diagram of Seurat's Palette, Mme. Ginette Signac Collection, Paris.

If, as Fénéon suggests, we arrange Seurat's colors in circular form, the result will be a chromatic circle almost identical to Rood's, in which each of the hues on the periphery is modified by the addition of white until the center, represented by pure white, is reached (Figure 43). We might ask why Seurat used eleven colors, rather than six or seven, which had sufficed for some of the Impressionist painters. The answer is to be found in the fact (pointed out by Rood and Chevreul) [67] that, if separated by too

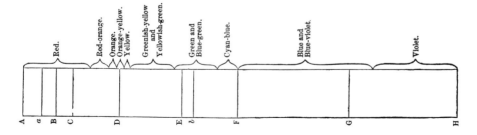

Figure 42. Prismatic Spectrum (from Rood, *Text-Book*).

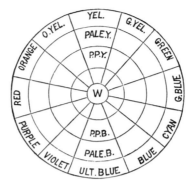

Figure 43. Chromatic Circle
(from Rood, *Text-Book*).

great an interval, neighboring colors, when mixed, lose some of their intensity; for example, red and yellow mixed on the palette will produce orange, but it will not be as pure or intense as orange pigment obtained directly from the tube.

It should be noted that earth colors and black were eliminated from Seurat's palette in favor of hues derived only from the solar spectrum. In taking this step he followed the dicta of modern physics concerning the composition of light. Rood, as well as Chevreul and Blanc, had summarized Newton's experiments showing that white light, when passed through a prism, was sub-divided into all of the colors of the visible spectrum, which, of course, did not include earth colors or black. Considering the Neo-Impressionists' aim of recreating nature's brightness through the optical mixture of hues, it is logical to expect them to eliminate any elements that might interfere with the purity and intensity of their colors.

Another reason why Seurat eliminated black between 1884 and 1886 may be found in his study, presumably at this time, of the treatise of Zunbul-Zadé referred to earlier, which included the following precept: "Discard black and that mixture of white and black they call gray. Nothing is white and nothing is gray.

What seems gray is a composite of pale tints which an experienced eye perceives."[68]

But it is actually Signac who must receive credit for introducing Seurat to the spectrum palette, which had been used by the Impressionists. Although Seurat claimed that he abandoned earth colors between 1882 and 1884,[69] he still relied on them in *Une Baignade*; but after his meeting with Signac in the spring of 1884 they disappear from his paintings. Recalling this encounter, Signac wrote: "Enlightened by their mutual research, Seurat soon adopted the simplified palette of the Impressionists. . . ."[70] We are fortunate in having a description from Signac's hand of the palette to which he must have introduced his friend in 1884 (see Figure 44): "My palette has always been (since 1883) composed of these colors: cadmiums [yellow], vermilion, madder lakes, cobalt violet, ultramarine blue, cobalt blue, cerulean blue, emerald green, composed green no. 1, composed green no. 2, cadmium [yellow] light. I start then in the order or gradation of the prism, from yellow to yellow — complete cycle."[71]

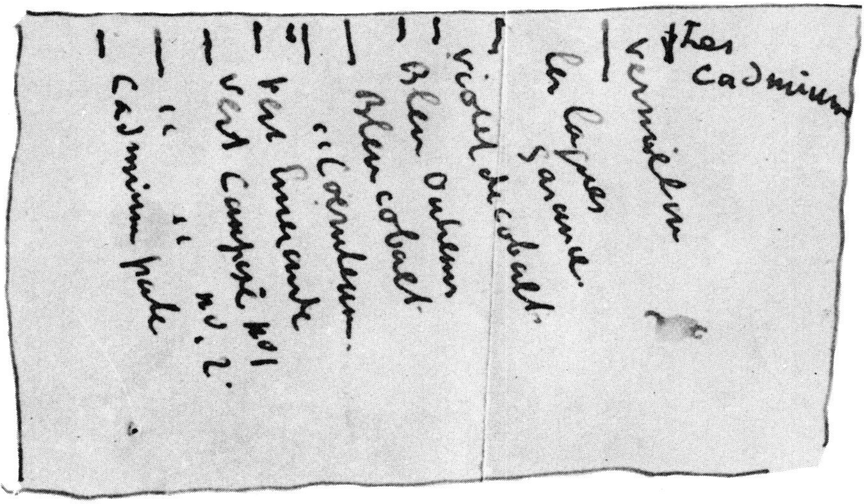

Figure 44. Signac's Palette, drawn by the artist (from a letter in the Amédée Ozenfant Collection, Cannes).

As we have observed, Seurat was willing to mix the spectral colors on his palette with white because their purity would not be compromised thereby. But, Signac pointed out, these mixtures, along with those of adjacent colors on the chromatic circle, were the only kind allowed according to Neo-Impressionist theory:

> They [the Neo-Impressionists] absolutely repudiate all mixtures on the palette except, of course, the mixtures of contiguous colors on the chromatic circle. The latter, gradated amongst themselves and lightened with white, will tend to reconstitute the variety of hues of the solar spectrum and all their tones. An orange mixed with a yellow and a red, a violet gradated toward red and blue, a green passing from blue to yellow, are, with white, the only elements which they have at their disposal.[72]

From one of Signac's letters, we have an even more specific description, accompanied by a diagram drawn by the artist, of this technique of mixing colors without destroying their purity. Referring to a pair of neighboring hues on the palette, emerald green and cerulean blue, he explained the method by which they could be combined with white or mixed with each other (the following remarks accompany the drawing in ink and colored pencil reproduced as Figure 45):

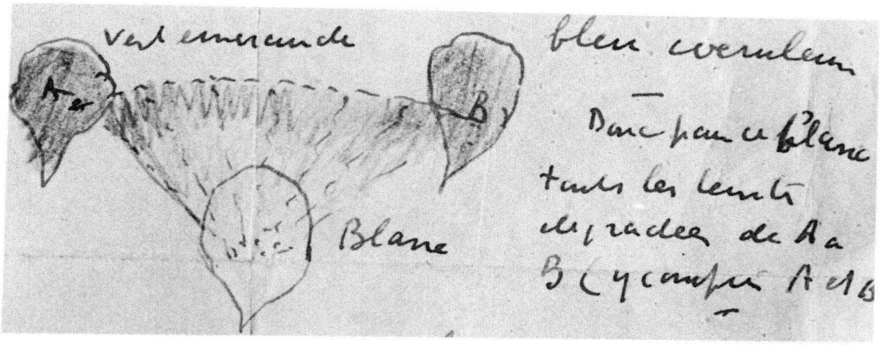

Figure 45. Diagram of Color Mixture drawn by Signac (from a letter in the Amédée Ozenfant Collection, Cannes).

Each pile of white is used to dilute, [not?] a color, but the gradations of hues from one color to another. Consequently, by means of this white all the hues gradated from A to B (including A and B). One brush for each white, and its gradations, so that the purity is respected. . . .[73]

Thus, although they adopted the spectral palette, the Neo-Impressionists consciously avoided the accidental, random elements in the Impressionists' mode of mixing hues, preferring a more methodical, scientifically determined technique that effectively preserved a maximum of intensity, purity, and luminosity of color.

In the foregoing remarks we have been concerned with Seurat's technique and method of representing color and light, his theories, and the origins of these theories. Another important aspect of this painting remains to be discussed: the system of color harmony and the sources upon which it is based.

### System of Harmony

The system of harmonizing colors that Seurat used in *La Grande Jatte* is similar in many ways to that employed in *Une Baignade*. In the earlier painting, we recall, Seurat relied on harmony by contrast and analogy, undoubtedly under the influence of Chevreul and Delacroix; in addition, he harmonized the three main color areas by arranging them as a "triad," as Rood had advised. Seurat's problem in *La Grande Jatte* was to relate not three major hues, as in *Une Baignade*, but four. While the latter picture was based on an outdoor setting that is almost identical in general color scheme to *La Grande Jatte*, a major difference may be detected in the representation of the grass. In *Une Baignade*, the resultant tone of the grass when viewed at a distance is yellowish green, while the deep blue-green shadows occupy a very small portion of the picture and cannot be counted as a major color area. In *La Grande Jatte*, on the other hand, Seurat intensified the yellow-orange illumination of the grass so that it reads as a light yellow-green verging on orange; also, the blue-green shadow in the foreground is sufficiently large to act as a significant element in the color scheme. Thus there are, in effect, four major color components in *La Grande Jatte*: the yellow-green of the lighted surface of the grass, blue-green in the shadow; and in the figures there are two dominant colors: red-orange and blue-violet. The water, too, ranges between blue and blue-violet in color, as did the river in *Une Baignade*.

If Rood's contrast diagram is consulted — we have already shown that it was used for *La Grande Jatte* — these four colors will be found to be separated from each other by angles of 90 degrees. This relationship was recommended by Rood in his chapter "On the Combination of Colours in Pairs and Triads," where he wrote that "colours less than 80° or 90° apart suffer from harmful contrast, while those more distant help each other."[74] The color scheme of the painting is thus based on two pairs of harmonizing complementaries: yellow-green and blue-violet, red-orange and blue-green. Any one of these colors will harmonize with any other because they will be separated either by 90 degrees or 180 degrees on the color circle (for a diagram of these relationships, see Figure 46).

Seurat also used these same four hues to guarantee the harmony of several figure clusters. For example, the two girls seated on the edge of the shadowed area of the grass are dressed in red-orange and blue-violet garments, which, in turn, harmonize with the areas of blue-green and yellow-green they overlap, since all of these colors are either complementary or are separated by 90 degrees on the chromatic circle. The same color relationships may be found, with slight variations, in the group of three girls sitting in front of the waffle stove at the far right, or in the three seated figures in the left foreground.

Similarly, contrasts of widely separated values within the same hue range — Chevreul's "harmony of contrast of scale" — were also incorporated in *La Grande Jatte*. This type of contrast may be seen at once in the woman with the umbrella in the center of the picture: her jacket is red-orange, and her skirt is tinted with this same color raised to a much higher value by the addition of white. Thus, while the basic hue remains the same, the values are widely separated, and harmony by contrast is the result. The same device is echoed in the woman with the umbrella in the far distance at the right and in the nurse seated beside the tree at the left.

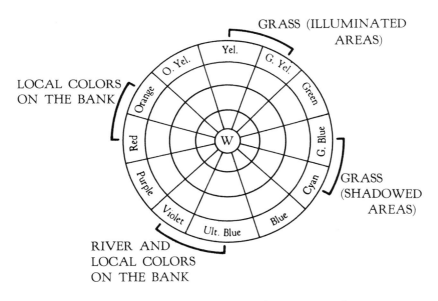

Figure 46. Diagram of Color Relationships in *La Grande Jatte*.

Harmony was also achieved here simply by contrasting complementary hues with each other, as, for example, in the many patches of blue-violet clothing that are superimposed on the yellow-green grass plot. Similarly, one large area of red-orange — the canoeist's vest — overlaps the blue-green shadow of the foreground, which is, of course, complementary to it.

In addition, Seurat took full advantage of harmony through the combination of analogous hues. According to Chevreul, there were two main types of harmony by analogy: hues close to each other on the chromatic circle; and slight variations in the lightness or darkness of the same hue. The first type of color relationship may be found in the many orange and red-orange areas scattered throughout the canvas. These, however, are rarely of an identical hue, but shift from an intense red-orange in the jacket of the woman with the umbrella standing in the center of the picture to almost yellow-orange in the little girl running in the middle distance. The same principle of slight hue variation also holds for the blue-violet areas of the painting.

The second type of harmony of analogous colors — involving the same hue placed at slightly different value levels — may be seen in the woman fishing at the left, where her skirt is a slightly lighter orange than her jacket; in the man playing a hunting horn near the riverbank, where this same relationship exists between his coat and trousers; and in the pair of figures standing in the right foreground, where the dark blue-violet of the woman's jacket is juxtaposed to her slightly lighter skirt as well as to the neighboring coat of her male partner.

Although it was written about four years after he completed *La Grande Jatte*, several passages from Seurat's letter to Maurice Beaubourg are valuable in helping us to understand his conception of pictorial harmony in this painting. He defined harmony as "the analogy of opposites, the analogy of similar elements of *value*, *hue*, and *line*. . . ." The "opposites" [*contraires*] of hue and value he explained as follows:

The opposites are:

For value, a more $\left\{\begin{array}{l}\text{luminous}\\\text{light}\end{array}\right\}$ for a darker one.

For hue, the complementaries, i.e., a certain red opposed to its complementary, etc.

$\left\{\begin{array}{l}\text{red-green}\\\text{orange-blue}\\\text{yellow-violet}\end{array}\right.$[75]

Unfortunately, he did not give exact illustrations of "similar elements" [*semblables*], but these may easily be established by implication: for value the "similars" would be tones close to each other on the tonal scale, and for hue, neighboring colors on the chromatic circle, such as red and orange.

In this statement from his "esthetic" Seurat suggests that harmony of color and value may be established in two ways: through the relationship of opposites, or through the association of similar elements. As we have tried to show, he used just such a system of creating harmony in *La Grande Jatte*; the source of this system is not difficult to find: once more we may turn to Chevreul's *De la loi du contraste simultané des couleurs*.[76]

Finally, it should be noted that at the center of *La Grande Jatte*, as in *Une Baignade*, there is a white area brighter than any other in the picture: the dress of the little girl beside the woman with the umbrella. In isolating this light spot, Seurat again appears to have been following Corot's advice: "There is always in a picture a luminous spot, of which there must be only one."[77] And in placing the point of greatest light in the center of the picture Seurat also followed Couture's precept: "The dominant light bright and central."[78]

### The Artistic Advantages of Seurat's Chromo-luminarist Technique and Method

We have seen that between the spring of 1884 and May 1886 Seurat extended and modified the pictorial language of *Une Baignade* in an increasingly scientific way: the result was his Neo-Impressionist "manifesto," *Un Dimanche à la Grande Jatte*, in which he finally perfected a "formula for optical painting" — to use his own words — that he had sought since 1876. In order to gain a more complete understanding of this first, or chromoluminarist, phase of Neo-Impressionism, we should also consider briefly the distinctive artistic goals toward which Seurat and his friends directed their efforts about 1886. Because he wrote so little about his own aims in painting, it will be necessary to turn to accounts furnished by such critics as Félix Fénéon and George

Moore, who knew Seurat and the Neo-Impressionists well and obtained valuable information directly from the artists.

Like the Impressionists, Seurat was deeply involved with the problem of recording as accurately and convincingly as possible the intense, scintillating quality of sunlight, but he was simultaneously interested in making his paintings operate according to the laws governing the behavior of color and light in nature. As Fénéon put it, his aim was to "synthesize the landscape in a definitive aspect which perpetuates the sensation of it."[79] The importance of sensation was again mentioned in Fénéon's defense of optical mixture: "Such a process will permit the painter to objectify his sensations in their complexity, to translate his fundamental originality with permissible assertiveness."[80] According to Fénéon, the artist's sensations of nature, which were so important to the Impressionists, are still considered as part of the Neo-Impressionists' program; however, they are to be controlled and disciplined "in a precise and conscious manner."[81] In the critic's words: "Among the swarm of mechanical copyists of externalities, these four or five artists [Seurat, Signac, Camille and Lucien Pissarro, and Dubois-Pillet] impose the sensation of life itself, for objective reality is simply a theme for the creation of a superior and purified reality where their personalities are transfused."[82]

Through scientific division of color and optical mixture Seurat was able to materialize the sensation of luminous color he received from nature. As Fénéon observed:

A pigmentary hue is weak and drab compared to a hue born of optical mixture; the latter, mysteriously vivified by a perpetual process of recombination, shimmers, elastic, opulent, and lustrous. . . . Consequently, one might speculate on the prerogatives of optical mixture. All the constituent colored elements will combine without muddying. Their polychrome mass of small dots is ordered according to the play of light and dark: justifying the perspective, making the air quiver over the scenes. The relief is continuously formed: the antagonistic energies of hues are calmed from the lines of collision and beyond, and better than in good *surimonos*, the shading of skies, of beaches, and of seas rivals the delightful gradation of a rose petal. The flight of each color is free and the interdependence of each is strict: the painting is unified under their surge.[83]

As we pointed out in discussing the sources of Seurat's theories, as applied in *La Grande Jatte*, optical mixture was found to yield greater luminosity than the mixture of pigments on the palette. However, as one moves away from such Neo-Impressionist pictures as *La Grande Jatte*, one reaches a point where both the individual colored elements and their optical mixture may be experienced in rapid alternation, according to Dove's theory of lustre.

Fénéon also suggested indirectly the distance from which the spectator should view the canvas in order to see it as the painters intended it to be seen. In response to critics who condemned Neo-Impressionist paintings because they looked like tapestries or mosaics, he wrote: "Take a few steps back and all the multi-colored specks melt into undulant, luminous masses. The technique, one might say, vanishes; the eye is no longer attracted by anything but that which is essentially painting."[84] In using optical mixture, then, Seurat not only gave greater luminosity to color but actually followed the principles of the behavior of color and light in nature — as Fénéon said: "The painter's artifice will have rigorously restored the process of reality."[85] On this subject, the Irish novelist and critic George Moore reported some of his conversations with the Neo-Impressionists concerning the advantages of their technique and method. Of particular interest is the following account from his *Modern Painting*, in which their works are defended because they duplicate nature's mode of operation:

A tone is a combination of colours. In Nature colours are separate; they act and react one on the other, and so create in the eye the illusion of a mixture of various colours — in other words, of a tone. But if the human eye can perform this prodigy when looking on colour as evolved through the spectacle of the world, why should not the eye be able to perform the same prodigy when looking on colour as displayed over the surface of the canvas? Nature does not mix her colours to produce a tone; and the reason of the marked discrepancy existing between Nature and the Louvre is owing to the fact that painters have hitherto deemed it a necessity to prepare a tone on the palette before placing it on the canvas; whereas it is quite clear that the only logical and reasonable method is to first complete the analysis of the tone, and then to place the colours which compose the tone in dots over the canvas.... If this be done truly — that is to say, if the first analysis of the tones be a correct analysis — and if the spectator places himself at the right distance from the picture, there will happen in his eyes exactly the same blending of colour as happens in them when they are looking upon Nature.[86]

By applying pigments in very small strokes, as part of their technique of divided color, the Neo-Impressionists were able to exercise a high degree of control over the various hues contributing to any given area. As Fénéon said: "The tones are decomposed into their constituent elements: they are presented in a mixture where their respective proportions are, one may say, variable from millimeter to millimeter; thus pacific gradations of hues, supple modeling, and the most delicate colorations are obtained."[87] When *La Grande Jatte* was exhibited in 1886, Seurat's technique of applying pigment in small dots, later labeled "pointillism," came under attack by hostile art critics, so his friends felt a special need to defend the artistic advantages of this method. Fénéon correctly saw the "*petit point*" as a means of slowly and carefully changing the tonality of the surface of the canvas according to the representational effect desired by the artist. And, equally important, the pointillist execution also engendered the uniform optical mixture of tones — a fundamental aspect of Seurat's method.

### Impressionism, Chromo-luminarism, and Science: Summary

Thus far we have devoted considerable attention to an analysis of Seurat's technique, methods, and theories, and have attempted to trace their sources in the works of art and writings he studied. The following question must now be posed: what is the relationship between the Neo-Impressionist esthetic, as of 1886-1887, to the Impressionist achievement and to nineteenth-century scientific thought?

Writing in 1886, Fénéon isolated the failings of the Impressionists and in two major articles [88] pitted the Neo-Impressionists against them. He began, however, by pointing out some of the Impressionists' virtues: they had successfully captured the effects of sunlight *en plein air,* had eliminated "tenebrous sauces," and applied separate touches of pigment that mixed optically. But their analysis of color, according to Fénéon, was effected in an arbitrary way, while Seurat and his friends "divide tones consciously and scientifically." [89] On at least four different occasions Fénéon referred to the changes instituted by Seurat and his friends as a "reform," implying that the Impressionists had failed to carry their discoveries far enough. [90] Pissarro's new style, of course, was triumphantly hailed both by Fénéon and Signac as exemplifying the true direction the Impressionists should have taken. The former wrote: "As for the new recruits to Impressionism, it is toward the analyst Camille Pissarro, and not toward Claude Monet, that they orient themselves." [91] Expressing similar sentiments, Signac referred to the Impressionists as "those marvelous precursors who suddenly, except for Camille Pissarro, refused to go any farther and to admit the progressive element and the solution to the problem for which they were searching for such a long time, and which was provided by a new generation of artists." [92] Their opinion of Impressionism was shared, if not inspired, by Seurat, whose attitude was related in a letter Pissarro wrote to his son Lucien (May 15, 1887): "Seurat, who is colder, more logical and more moderate, does not hesitate for a moment to declare that we have the right position, and that the Impressionists are even more retarded than before." [93]

It should be pointed out, too, that the terms "*néo-impressionniste*" and "*néo-impressionnisme*" came into use somewhat casually. Rather than being devised consciously as names for a totally new movement, they occur initially as a means of distinguishing between the older generation of Impressionists — Monet, Renoir,

Sisley, and their circle — and the "new" Impressionists. The term "*néo-impressionniste*" was used for the first time, as far as this writer can determine, in Fénéon's review of the second Exposition de la Société des Artistes Indépendants, published on September 19, 1886. Here, however, the word occurs only once, and it is used in adjectival form: "*la méthode néo-impressionniste.*"[94] The term "*néo-impressionnisme*" was popularized by Fénéon's brochure *Les Impressionnistes en 1886*, which appeared in December, 1886. From this time on, the name was used almost universally by critics and historians to refer to the art of Seurat and his circle.

It is apparent from the writings of Fénéon, who recorded most of the changes in the painters' aims and theories, that in 1886 Seurat and his friends did not envision themselves as creators of a radically new style, but rather as reformers of a random, unscientific type of Impressionism — a style which they considered themselves to be extending and correcting with the aid of modern science. What was the nature of this science and how was it used in the reform of Impressionism? We have seen that Chevreul and Rood are the names mentioned most often as the sources for Seurat's advances in 1884–1886 in transforming the artistic language of Impressionism, which he had adopted briefly as a means of studying nature in preparation for *Une Baignade* and *La Grande Jatte*. Realizing the limitations of the Impressionists' approach, he gradually evolved a more rigorously controlled method and technique by applying laws proposed by scientists who had made exacting studies of physical and optical phenomena and had furnished convincing demonstrations of their conclusions. Chevreul and Rood, for example, not only pointed out general principles of color as discovered in the laboratory but also made numerous observations on the operation of these principles in nature. Interestingly, the Impressionists, too, had observed many of the phenomena investigated by this pair of scientists, but approached their subject matter strictly from the standpoint of sensation, thus eschewing preordained theories in favor of sheer observation.

Seurat, as we have seen, studied the artistic language formulated by the Impressionists *and* scientific treatises that confirmed many of their discoveries. But the writers of these texts went one step beyond the point reached by the Impressionists: Rood and Chevreul, particularly, arrived at general optical and physical principles governing nature's phenomena and provided specific instructions for the painters about how to embody them in their pictures. The Neo-Impressionists' reliance on optical mixture and the separation of elements was, as suggested earlier, a by-product of their belief, inspired by Rood, that much of nature's luminosity was due to the additive mixture of colored light. Thus they felt that the additive method should be used in painting to approximate the scintillating, vibratory quality of light as perceived by the eye.

Chevreul's arguments for painting into one's pictures the effects of simultaneous contrast were based equally on nature's behavior. He had presented proofs, and reduced them to laws, of the fact that an object of a certain color will project its complementary upon its neighboring area or its background. And, as we have seen, Seurat and his friends believed that this principle of simultaneous contrast should be followed uniformly throughout their paintings.

Rood, as reinforced by Ruskin, recommended that the artist use gradation in painting, not only because it would help areas of color harmonize better with each other, but, again, because it was a principle to be found universally in nature. Hence gradation, too, was given status as a law to which painters should consistently adhere.

In summary, Seurat's major achievements in *La Grande Jatte*, as far as this study is concerned, were as follows. First, he discovered and applied physical laws governing the behavior of light and color in nature, rather than merely relying on his sensations; by doing so, he was literally able to make his pictures duplicate nature's mode of operation, thus obtaining a degree of luminosity far greater than that achieved by the Impressionists. Second,

Seurat successfully integrated a carefully thought-out, wide-range value scheme with a color system that could accurately represent nature's hues and values. In other words, he united the traditional elements of chiaroscuro, both in modeling and pictorial planning, with colors that, like those of the Impressionists, were extremely accurate in representing the actual hues present in the subject — local colors, the tone of the illuminating light, and diverse reflections. Third, he harmonized the colors of *La Grande Jatte* according to principles of contrast and analogy drawn largely from the writings of Chevreul and Rood, rather than relying on instinct or rule of thumb.

We have been concerned in the present chapter with Seurat's Neo-Impressionist (or chromo-luminarist) style and theories as manifested in *La Grande Jatte*. Between 1886 and 1888, he extended and refined the artistic language of this painting in two other major canvases: *Les Poseuses* (1886–1888) and *La Parade* (1887–1888). While we do not intend to discuss these pictures in great detail, several aspects of their color technique and mode of operation are of particular interest to us, inasmuch as here Seurat brought to a logical conclusion many of the innovations that appeared for the first time in *La Grande Jatte*.

## ASPECTS OF SEURAT'S CHROMO-LUMINARIST TECHNIQUE AND METHOD: *LES POSEUSES* AND *LA PARADE*

Although Seurat's friends and critics observed that *La Grande Jatte* embodied the main tenets of Neo-Impressionism, it was in many respects an experimental painting in which new discoveries were incorporated only gradually between 1884 and 1886. Henry van de Velde was aware of this when he wrote that the canvas was "incomplete and inevitably suffering from the haste of arriving first and from the poorly estimated intake of breath for the first bugle 'call to arms' of the new formulae."[95] A careful examination of the picture will reveal several vestiges of the earlier stages of Seurat's artistic evolution. The most noticeable of these elements are the *balayé* and short horizontal brushstrokes that serve as an underbody for the multitude of small dots that were added relatively late in the development of the painting. But in the canvases executed shortly after the completion of *La Grande Jatte* — a series of landscapes and seascapes of Honfleur — it is evident that the experimental phase had passed and that Seurat had finally consolidated the discoveries made in *La Grande Jatte* into a consistent artistic credo. As Fénéon wrote in his second definitive article on the Neo-Impressionists, published in September, 1886: "The first efforts in this direction date from less than two years ago: the period of hesitation is over; from picture to picture these painters have consolidated their style, increased their observations, and clarified their science." [96] In such paintings as *Honfleur, un soir, embouchure de la Seine* (D.-R. 171; Figure 47), executed during the summer of 1886, the small dot appears for the first time as a dominant structural element rather than as an afterthought. As a result of the growing uniformity of Seurat's pointillist technique, optical mixture could take place much more easily, and thus his paintings tended increasingly to operate as luminous screens that emit colored light.

The first major picture to embody Seurat's fully developed, perfected Neo-Impressionist technique was *Les Poseuses* (D.-R. 178; Barnes Foundation, Merion, Pa.), the third of his seven large paintings. He started work on it in the fall of 1886, and it was completed in time to be shown at the fourth exhibition of the Indépendants, which opened on March 22, 1888. A second, smaller version of this painting was executed in 1888 as a "*petite réplique*," [97] and although similar in treatment to the earlier version, the brushstrokes were made proportionally larger in relation to the dimensions of the canvas. Because it incorporates some improvements over the painting in the Barnes Foundation and is far easier to study, we shall discuss the second version rather than the earlier canvas.

Figure 47. *Honfleur, un soir, embouchure de la Seine*, Collection, The Museum of Modern Art, New York, Gift of Mrs. David Levy.

### Les Poseuses: *System of Modeling*

Unlike *La Grande Jatte*, *Les Poseuses* (D.-R. 179; Figure 48) was executed almost entirely in small dots, which give the picture a uniform, tapestrylike surface. This technique enabled Seurat to record with unusual subtlety the variations of color in his subject. The merits of this method were, as we might expect, observed by Fénéon, who wrote: "On a very small area, the numerical proportions of colored specks, being capable of infinite variety, the most delicate transitions of relief, the most subtle gradations of hue can be exactly translated."[98] In order to illustrate the appropriateness of Fénéon's remarks, let us consider Seurat's method of executing *Les Poseuses* — a method that serves not only as a means of making delicate adjustments of color but also of recording the chromatic changes in the modeling of three-dimensional forms. In the torso and arms of the central model, for example, we find that the local color in the shadow is pink; as we turn from the shadow toward the fully illuminated areas of flesh, this tone becomes increasingly lighter, through the addition of white, until the highlights are reached. Thus Seurat first modeled the figure monochromatically merely by taking the basic local color and adding white to it in order to obtain the necessary effect of three-dimensionality through variations of light and shade. But following the theory and methods developed in *La Grande Jatte*, the artist believed that the local color should be modified by the color of the illuminating light (in this case, yellow-orange) and that the complementary of this light, blue, should influence the hue of the shadows. Like the local color of the flesh, these modifying hues — yellow-orange and blue — also participate in the general modeling of the figure by being used at almost full intensity in the shadow and gradually moving up the value scale to white as the form turns from the shadow into the light. The yellow-orange, of course, dominates the lights, and blue is restricted chiefly to the shadows. But as the body is modeled from light into shadow, dosages of these two complementary

Figure 48. *Les Poseuses* (small version), Henry P. McIlhenny Collection, Philadelphia. (Photo Giraudon.)

colors intermingle, creating in the half-lights a luminous optical gray. If the observer looks either toward the lights or the shadows, this neutral gray will become tinged slightly with orange or with blue, depending on the direction in which his eye moves around the form. Color and chiaroscuro were thus inseparably welded together by a method that respected the color data supplied by nature — as did the Impressionists — but also retained the solidity of mass characteristic of the Renaissance tradition in Western painting.

In employing such devices, Seurat was gradually abandoning the kind of "divisionism" used in *La Grande Jatte*, where the local color and the illuminating light were kept distinct and separate, and where optical mixture was used chiefly as a means of adding various extraneous elements to large areas of local color. In that painting, the underlying hues were rarely modified so much that they lost their identity, except in infrequent cases where neutrals were produced intentionally through the optical mixture of complementaries. In *Les Poseuses*, however, the local color in many areas is all but lost and is replaced by synthetic resultant tones created by the optical mixture of a multitude of specks of different hues. In certain parts of the painting Seurat seems to have predicted in advance the desired resultant color and then simply juxtaposed the necessary components in small dots to produce this hue. In the rear wall, for instance, he applied almost equal dosages of purple and green, which are complementary to each other and hence mix optically to produce a cool, luminous neutral tone; then throughout this area were scattered spots of blue and yellow-orange, which express the action of light and shadow, respectively, and serve to neutralize further the underlying color. When viewed at a distance, the wall appears as a flickering light neutral tone, swinging sometimes to coolness and at other times toward warmth of color. What is most remarkable about this effect is that when the individual dots are scrutinized closely they are found to be quite intense in color and relatively low on the value scale; but when seen at a distance they lose their identity through optical mixture and blend into a resultant tone that is considerably lighter in value than any of its components.

It should be observed here that Seurat's reason for using optical mixture in *Les Poseuses* was not to create resultant colors that were necessarily more *intense* than their individual components but rather to duplicate the qualities of transparency and luminosity in half-tones and shadows experienced so frequently in nature. Were nature composed entirely of intense, pure colors, then Seurat probably would have found a way to match them; but only a small proportion of the hues we perceive are found at full saturation. More often the artist is confronted with the problem of representing the perplexingly difficult warm and cool neutrals that occur especially in shadows.

In order to succeed at the task he set for himself in painting *Les Poseuses*, Seurat was forced to make certain adjustments in the representation of the visual data presented to his eye. It is obvious, of course, that human flesh is not spotted with myriad colored dots — covered with "colored fleas," as one critic put it.[99] The dots have very little to do with the surface texture of the objects represented, but instead are components of an impartial screen of colored pigments which, through different combinations, represents the seen image. In *Les Poseuses* it is as if we have been presented with the colors of the subject before they were completely synthesized. That is to say, when the painting is seen close up, the architecture of the intended color experience is all too evident. Only when we move back will it begin to resemble the subject matter as we are accustomed to seeing it. At a distance, the roughly dotted surface disappears; as Fénéon observed: "Take a few steps back and all the multicolored specks melt into undulant, luminous masses. The technique, one may say, vanishes: the eye is no longer attracted by anything but that which is essentially painting."[100]

Why, then, did Seurat insist on breaking up the colors into their components and allow them to synthesize in the eye of the observer? The following answer must be proposed: in no other way could the inherent luminosity of his subject be duplicated with artists' pigments. We should remember that the intensity of light is far greater than that of the pigments at the painter's disposal; Seurat thus had to resort to every device known to the science of his day in order to equal nature's brightness. For this reason, he insisted on using pigments at full intensity or else mixed only with white. By juxtaposing them as uniformly sized small dots — a technique that is most conducive to optical mixture — he was almost able to compose, as it were, with colored light, following Rood's advice that paint handled in this way could be made to obey rules governing the mixture of light, not pigments.

In *Les Poseuses*, then, we find Seurat beginning to create luminous images in a much more abstract way than he had in *La Grande Jatte*. The principle of optical mixture had been employed in the latter picture in an effort to record the extraneous hues that influenced the local colors, and in that canvas Seurat pursued an essentially analytical approach to nature. In *Les Poseuses*, on the other hand, he discovered synthetic methods by which he could predict whatever effects of color he desired, largely through obeying Rood's suggestion that, with the appropriate theory and technique, artists could make pigments behave like colored light.

## Les Poseuses: *Viewing Distance and Fusion*

Many arguments between writers on Neo-Impressionism have occurred because some of them — Fénéon and Signac, for instance — saw Seurat's paintings as being much more luminous than those of the Impressionists, while others found them dull and gray. Two examples of the latter opinion should suffice here. The critic Émile Hennequin wrote: "One could hardly imagine anything dustier or more dull than his *La Grande Jatte*, which represents promenaders placed in the half-shadow cast by a full sun." [101] George Moore, too, shared Hennequin's reaction: "They [the Neo-Impressionists' pictures] fail most conspicuously at the very point where it was their mission to succeed. Instead of excelling in brilliancy of colour the pictures painted in the ordinary way, they present the most complete spectacle of discoloration possible to imagine." [102] There is a reasonable explanation for this curious disagreement: the characteristic luminosity of Seurat's paintings may be experienced only by standing at the proper distance from them. If one moves too close or too far away, the desired effect is lost. Unfortunately, Seurat, as far as we know, wrote nothing about the appropriate distance from which his canvases should be viewed; but he undoubtedly gave Fénéon instructions about where to stand, because in the critic's estimates of his friend's pictures he consistently praised their luminosity. A significant hint about Seurat's intentions was supplied by Fénéon in his article "Les Impressionnistes," quoted earlier, where he mentioned the importance for the artist of Dove's theory, which stated that when one perceives the separate colored elements and their resultant optical mixture in rapid succession, effects of "lustre" are produced. In the light of Fénéon's observations, let us examine the various color effects brought about by viewing *Les Poseuses* at different distances.

At a distance of fifteen feet, certain parts of the painting (the flesh, the rear wall, and the floor) do in fact appear desaturated and neutral in tone. But areas such as the red-orange, blue, and green articles of clothing do not become grayish, owing to the intrinsic intensity of their hues. It is, then, only in the portions of the painting where less intense colors have been used that grayness becomes a problem. To find out when these areas become more colorful and luminous, the observer must move closer to the canvas. Upon arriving at a distance of nine feet from it, the individual colored elements become more discernible, and the areas that originally appeared flat and dull now reveal some of their component hues. Although individual colors cannot yet be named, one can detect an alternation between warm and cool tones that was not evident at the fifteen-foot distance.

Moving to a distance of six feet from the painting, the effects of lustre described by Fénéon become pronounced. At this point the whole surface vibrates with color, and a lustrous atmospheric veil seems to hover over the picture. Yet considerable fusion is still found: if, for example, one attempts to separate the individual spots of yellow-orange, representing sunlight, from the local color (green) of the grass in *La Grande Jatte* (seen in the background of *Les Poseuses*), one will find that it cannot be done. As hard as one tries, at a distance of six feet most of the colors can neither be made to fuse completely nor can they be seen individually. One's eye is simply caught between the horns of a visual dilemma.

Moving to a position three feet from the painting, the point of greatest lustre has been passed. With a few exceptions, the hues of the individual dots are now discernible, but they do not blend into a uniform value as they did at the distant view. Instead, there are abrupt transitions in many places, particularly in the flesh of the models. Also, because the different hues of the dots can be detected, the effect is rather spotty, whereas three feet farther back partial fusion would have occurred. One now sees separately the components that comprise the final resultant tones, and because they are disparate colors in many cases, they tend to struggle against each other. This is particularly noticeable when complementaries (such as yellow-orange and blue) appear in a given area, where, instead of neutralizing each other (as they would at a distant viewpoint), they tend mutually to intensify one another.

It is the critical change of viewing distance from six to three feet, then, that destroys the beneficial effects of optical fusion and reveals instead the component colors of the painting. Yet it would be incorrect to say that at three feet all of the colors can be seen individually. There is still some fusion at this distance, particularly in those portions of the painting where Seurat used extremely small dots (as, for example, in the face of the central figure). Our conclusion, at this juncture, must be that effects of fusion work by degrees, moving from grayness to lustre, and then to the point where separate elements can be discerned, still without being able to rule out fusion entirely. The final step is to close in on the canvas until no evidence of fusion can be detected, that is, until the individual colored elements reveal themselves with perfect clarity.

Thus if one stands too far away, the painting will indeed seem neutral in color, an effect that disturbed many contemporary writers. Or, if one stands so close that the individual colors may be discerned, then the picture will appear rough and spotty, and none of the intended qualities of modeling and luminosity will be evident to the observer. However, if one assumes a station point between five and seven feet from *Les Poseuses*, most of the individual spots of color discernible at the close view fuse into a variety of indefinable tones that sparkle with a subtle warmth; atmosphere seems to permeate the picture; and the abrupt contrasts of value and color seen at the close view give way to smooth transitions in modeling in which effects of chiaroscuro are reinforced by warm lights and luminous, transparent half-tones and shadows.[103]

Such effects of luminosity and lustre were described eloquently by Fénéon, as we saw in an excerpt from one of his articles cited in our discussion of lustre in *La Grande Jatte*. Closely related in content to Fénéon's observations and especially significant in the light of Seurat's perfected chromo-luminarist technique in *Les Poseuses* is Rood's discussion of partial fusion of color through optical mixture. The following passage, quoted previously, is particularly relevant to this picture:

> If the coloured lines or dots are quite distant from the eye, the mixture is of course perfect, and presents nothing remarkable in its appearance; but before this distance is reached there is a stage in which the colours are blended, though somewhat imperfectly, so that the surface seems to flicker or glimmer — an effect that no doubt arises from a faint perception from time to time of its constituents. This communicates a soft and peculiar brilliancy to the surface, and gives it a certain appearance of transparency; we seem to see into it and below it.[104]

Thus Rood and Fénéon give us the necessary hints concerning the distance from which we should view Seurat's paintings. It is reasonable to assume, in view of the foregoing discussion, that Seurat sought just such effects as those described by the American scientist; and we have seen that these effects can be perceived only if one stands in the appropriate viewing range. Hence the arguments among Seurat's critics between the group who felt that his pictures were truly luminous, and those who thought they were dull, gray, and colorless, must be resolved in favor of the former group. The latter evidently stood too far away from the paintings to experience the beneficial effects of partial fusion and lustre.[105]

If *Les Poseuses* was Seurat's first major painting that exemplified his fully developed chromo-luminarist technique, in his next important picture, *La Parade*, this language was employed in solving an even more difficult artistic problem. In many ways, *La Parade* represents the ultimate conclusion of Seurat's interest in depicting light, and for this reason a brief discussion of several aspects of the technique and method used in this picture will occupy us in the following pages.

### *Light and Color in* La Parade

Seurat obtained a degree of luminosity in *La Parade* (1887–1888; Figure 49) surpassing that of any of his previous major paintings. This is due, in large part, to the character of the subject — a nocturnal scene illuminated by gas jets — which lends itself to effects of mysterious, shimmering light. The method by which Seurat created such effects is of particular interest to us here. As far as this writer can determine, the basic system governing the color technique of *La Parade* is the same as that used in *La Grande Jatte* and *Les Poseuses*, the theoretical basis of which has already been discussed. But in *La Parade* Seurat derived every possible advantage from this system to create effects of muted, glowing light emanating from the picture. While orange and yellow-orange dots, corresponding to the color of the gaslight, and blue

Figure 49. *La Parade de cirque*, The Metropolitan Museum of Art, New York, Bequest of Stephen C. Clark, 1960.

dots for the shadow color were used to model the forms, these colors were also scattered freely throughout *La Parade*, irrespective of any function they might have in modeling. Since, in any given area, these hues usually intermingle, they tend to neutralize one another by optical mixture, thus creating an effect of light-charged atmosphere that permeates the whole canvas. Often, in fact, underlying local colors are almost nonexistent, as in the open space behind the musicians at the left; here Seurat simply inundated the area with yellow-orange, orange, and blue dots that, through their optical mixture, convey a sense of impalpable, luminous shadow.

The local colors become somewhat more pronounced in the foreground, especially in the two-fifths of the painting at the right. However, almost all of the local colors are selected from a narrow range of hues in the violet and yellow-green sectors of the chromatic circle (violet and yellow-green, for example, are the dominant colors, respectively, of the upper and lower portions of the background at the right). It should be noted that in some instances the local colors do not appear alone, but are modified by the application of a few dots corresponding to their complementary, which tend to neutralize them. Thus in any given area of the picture the component colors will ordinarily be the following: the local color; a small quantity of its complementary; yellow-orange and orange, representing light; and blue, for shadow. What is unusual, as already suggested, is the fact that Seurat often allowed the last-mentioned pair to dominate the local colors, as frequently happens in the left-hand side of the painting.

The methods Seurat used in painting *La Parade* are admirably suited to the creation of neutral color effects. When viewed at a distance of thirty feet, only a few areas of the picture, such as the yellow-green background at the right and the red and orange surrounding the central trombone player, appear as intense colors; the remaining parts would best be described as warm and cool neutrals. It is extremely difficult to identify some of these tones specifically, particularly in the upper-left quarter of the picture, because their components have almost completely neutralized each other. In such areas as the jacket of the stage manager at the right, for example, four major hues — purple, green, yellow-orange, and blue — have been used in almost equal doses, and the result is an indescribable neutral tone that, as one follows the modeling of the form, shifts back and forth between warm and cool. (For a diagram of the color relationships in *La Parade* see Figure 50.) Thus, Seurat once more used the division of tone and optical mixture not only as a means of obtaining greater intensity of color but also to create a wide range of luminous neutrals that appear frequently in our experience of nature and which are, of course, even more pronounced in such a nocturnal setting.

When compared to *Les Poseuses* and *La Grande Jatte*, the surface of *La Parade* is even more abstract in relation to the subject matter depicted in the painting. As before, the pigments are applied in small, almost uniform dots, and the brushwork is completely un-related to the actual texture of the objects represented. But for the

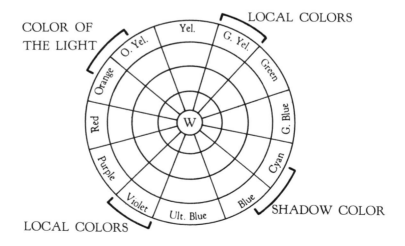

Figure 50. Diagram of Color Relationships in
*La Parade de cirque.*

first time in a major picture the canvas sometimes shows through the paint layer, again suggesting that Seurat was not thinking of the surface as a means of conveying the tactile reality of things but rather as an undifferentiated screen that yields the desired resultant color only when one is far enough away from it that the execution is invisible. The small spots of white canvas in *La Parade* play a very important role here: as in the conté crayon drawings, they reinforce the effects of lustre when one steps back from the painting and views it at a distance of thirteen to fifteen feet. That is, speaking in terms of the optical mixture of *values*, as well as of color, partial mixture takes place, which makes the surface seem to sparkle with light.

While Seurat carried his technique of chromo-luminarism to its ultimate conclusion in *La Parade*, in his last two major paintings, *Le Chahut* and *Le Cirque*, his interest in equaling nature's luminosity waned in favor of achieving emotional expression through different configurations of formal elements. Although Seurat continued to use a similar color technique in these later pictures, his esthetic theories and their mode of application changed considerably. The following chapter will be devoted to a discussion of the nature of these changes.

# 4

# Seurat's Theories of Expression, Their Sources and Application (1887—1891)

### THE CHANGE IN SEURAT'S INTERESTS AFTER 1886

AFTER THE COMPLETION OF *La Grande Jatte*, Seurat became increasingly concerned with the problem of expressing specific emotions through various combinations of color, value, and line. As a result, the emergence of a second phase of Neo-Impressionist art and theory may be discerned between 1887 and 1891. The tenets of his new theory are reflected in his well-known letter to Maurice Beaubourg of August 28, 1890, where, in addition to explaining his chromoluminarist technique, Seurat outlined concrete pictorial methods of invoking gaiety, calmness, and sadness. In this letter a statement of his technique of achieving luminosity through optical mixture and his ideas about harmony that were formulated by 1886 serve as a foundation for his later esthetic, in which "dominants" of color, value, and line are used to control the emotional content of the work of art.

The general direction of the change in Seurat's interests was outlined in an important article by Gustave Kahn, who, after discussing the development of his friend's theories up to and including the year 1886, wrote: "Seurat's anxiety was caused by the following reflections: 'If I have been able to find scientifically and through the experience of art the law of pictorial color, can I not discover an equally logical, scientific, and pictorial system which will permit me to coordinate the lines of the painting towards harmony as I am able to coordinate colors?'[1] The shift in Seurat's interests from rationalized color-practice to the concordance of color and line for expressive purposes was also documented by his friend Teodor de Wyzewa in an article published shortly after the artist's death:

> First of all, he analyzed color: he searched for diverse means of rendering it, tried to discover the way which rendered it with the most accuracy and variety. Then, it was the expression of colors which attracted him. He wanted to know why certain combinations of tones produced an impression of sadness, certain others, an impression of gaiety; and, from this point of view, he made a sort of catalogue for himself, where each nuance of color was associated with the emotion which it suggested. Next in turn, expression through lines seemed to him a problem capable of a definite solution, for lines also have an innate, secret power of joy or melancholy. . . .[2]

Although no reason for the change in Seurat's theories is proposed in the previous passages, we have ample evidence indicating that the artist had come under the influence of Charles Henry, a young scientist and esthetician whom he had met in 1886, after the opening of the eighth Impressionist exhibition.[3] Henry, about whom more will be said shortly, had published in 1885 an elaborate theory of art[4] in which he had stressed the idea that colors and linear directions must be unified in their expressive purpose.

Furthermore, he believed that certain configurations of line, as reinforced by color, could convey specific emotional states, namely, happiness (or as he called it, *dynamogénie*), calmness, and sadness.

While the excerpts from Kahn's and de Wyzewa's articles already cited outline the nature of the changes in Seurat's theories, no indication was given as to when they took place or in which paintings we may expect to find the influence of his new theories. However, valuable information on this subject was supplied by his friends and critics who noted most of the important changes in his art and theory between 1886 and 1891.

One of the first indications that Charles Henry was to influence Seurat may be found in an article of Fénéon's published on September 19, 1886. Here the critic wrote: "Professor O. N. Rood has furnished them [the Neo-Impressionists] with precious facts. Soon the general theory of contrast, rhythm, and measure of Charles Henry, will provide them with new and very certain information."[5] The "*théorie générale du contraste, du rythme, et de la mesure*" to which Fénéon referred was the subtitle of one of Henry's books, *Cercle chromatique*, which he was preparing in 1886 (it was not published until 1888–1889).[6] At this time Seurat could have become acquainted with the scientist's theories through personal contact or by reading his "Introduction à une esthétique scientifique," published in *La Revue contemporaine*, August, 1885, which also dealt with questions of contrast, rhythm, and measure.

Fénéon again hinted at the increasing application of Henry's theories by the Neo-Impressionists in a review published on May 1, 1887, where he used, probably for the first time, a term dear to the scientist — "*dynamogénie*"[7] — in referring to the sensation of gaiety or happiness in landscape paintings by Signac. Unfortunately, this mention cannot be interpreted positively as giving evidence of the application of Henry's theories by a painter of the Neo-Impressionist group at this time, because Fénéon may well have been using the term "*dynamogénie*" for its verbal color rather than in any scientific context.

Mention of Henry's theories in relation to a specific painting by Seurat, *Les Poseuses* (D.-R. 178; 1886–1888), was finally made by Fénéon in a review of April 15, 1888, in which he wrote: "By a pseudo-scientific fantasy, the red umbrella, the straw umbrella, and the green stocking are oriented toward the directions of red, yellow, and green on Henry's chromatic circle." [8] The correspondence between the three colors noted by Fénéon and the directions that match them on Henry's chromatic circle is indeed close, and we shall have occasion to refer again to these relationships later in this chapter.

In another painting, *La Parade de Cirque* (1887–1888; Figure 49, page 176) exhibited at the same time as *Les Poseuses*, Seurat also appears to have relied on Henry's theories, although Fénéon did not mention the scientist's influence on this work in the review quoted. But in an unpublished preparatory drawing for *La Parade* Seurat divided up the architectural background according to a numerical system of proportions that Herbert has identified with Henry's theories and accompanied the sketch with quotations from his "Introduction à une esthétique scientifique." [9] Although this observation is not of particular relevance to the content of the present study, it helps us to determine when Seurat became interested in Henry's ideas.

In April, 1888, Gustave Kahn, too, commented on the newly formulated theories of Seurat and his friends: "The tendencies of the group are known: to paint in order to obtain the vibration of light by superimposing clean tones, to study the exact value of luminous contrasts in their manifold influences upon objects, to simplify and schematize the slightest details, and *to consider the picture as a harmony of lines effected by the direction of colors*" [italics mine]. [10] As far as this writer can determine, this is the first published statement that clearly reflects some of the esthetic concepts that appear in Seurat's letter written sixteen months later to Maurice Beaubourg. This passage, along with the data cited in the preceding two paragraphs, indicates that at least as early as the spring of 1888 Seurat had become involved with the problem of interrelating the expression of color and linear directions, probably under Henry's influence. However, while new ideas about the concordance between line and color were articulated in Kahn's article, harmony in painting, rather than specific emotional valence, still seems to have been Seurat's chief interest at this time.

In 1889 and 1890, Fénéon and other critics close to Seurat joined company in explaining in detail the artist's new theories, their sources, and their application in his paintings. In an article published in September, 1889, Fénéon outlined even more precisely than before his friend's beliefs about the relationship between line and color: "Seurat knows quite well that line, independent of its topographical role, possesses an appraisable abstract value. In each of his landscapes, the forms are governed by one or two directions matched to dominant colors and with which the accessory lines are obliged to contrast." [11] The paintings referred to in illustration of these ideas were *Le Crotoy, après-midi* (D.-R. 193), and *Le Crotoy, matin* (D.-R. 192), both dating from the summer of 1889. Later in the year, Fénéon again reflected the theoretical position maintained at this time by Seurat and Signac: "For several years, the anarchic forces of Impressionism have been uniting to produce definitive works, which will be executed, should they not meet too much resistance, by young painters of hyperacute vision and lucid intelligence, served by a superior technique (scientific division of tone) and *capable of wilfully uniting directions of colors and lines*" [italics mine].[12] In the two preceding excerpts we now find additional evidence concerning Seurat's interest in using the concordance of color and line for expressive purposes, rather than merely to augment the harmony of his paintings.

One of the best contemporary statements of Seurat's fully developed theories governing these concordances was published by Georges Lecomte, a mutual friend of Fénéon, Pissarro, and Seurat:

Georges Seurat is no longer solely concerned with irradiating his canvases with intense light and free harmonies of astral brightness, for he is also trying to make the directions of lines and their intersection in certain angles coincide with the dominant idea of the picture. A sensation of gaiety will not only be expressed by vermilions, oranges, and greens, etc. . . . but also by lines moving from bottom to top and by angles whose apex is turned downward. Everything will be calculated with this concern in mind: inflexion of the eyelids, position of the arms and legs, carriage of the head, and folds of the garments. His *Le Chahut* is, in this sense, a first conclusive theoretical realization. . . . This search for the harmony of lines and colors and the clear expression, even to the point of exaggeration, of the dominant idea of the picture will result in powerful effects of decorative painting, if ever one succeeds in concealing the unduly obvious method.[13]

This passage is of special importance for two reasons: it is a lucid summary of Seurat's latest theories; and the first major canvas that manifested these ideas is here identified — *Le Chahut* (Figure 64, page 221). Gustave Kahn, too, confirmed the fact that *Le Chahut* and the marines done at Le Crotoy had been conceived under the influence of Henry's theories of color and line; and he added *Le Cirque* (Figure 65, page 222) to the group of paintings so influenced.[14]

Finally, in March or April, 1890, Seurat's own formulation of his theory of art was published. It was, as he wrote to Fénéon, "a simple note of an esthetic, followed by a general line on technique (what I regard as the spirit and the [illegible word] of art)."[15] It appeared at the end of a short biography that Jules Christophe, another of the artist's friends, had written for the periodical *Les Hommes d'aujourd'hui* and follows here in its entirety:

Art is harmony; harmony is the analogy of opposites, the analogy of similar elements — of value, of hue, of line; value, that is, light and dark; hue, that is, red and its complementary green, orange and its complementary blue, yellow and its complementary violet; line, that is, directions from the horizontal. These diverse harmonies are combined into calm, gay, and sad ones; gaiety of value is the light dominant; of hue, the warm dominant; of line, lines rising above the horizontal; calmness of value is the equality of light and dark, of warm and cool for hue, and the horizontal for line. Sadness of value is the dark dominant; of hue, the cool dominant; and of line, downward directions. Now, the means of expression of this technique is the optical mixture of values, of hues, and their reactions (shadows), following very fixed laws, and the frame is no longer simply white, as in the beginning, but opposed to the values, hues, and lines of the motif.[16]

Christophe did not say where he obtained this theoretical statement, but in a letter to Fénéon Seurat identified himself as its author.[17]

The artist, however, was dissatisfied with the statement published by Christophe, allegedly because the printer did not understand it clearly, and in a letter to Maurice Beaubourg of August 28, 1890, wrote out his theories in greater detail. Although we referred consistently to the latter statement earlier in this study, it was not published until long after Seurat's death; apparently only the shorter one included in Christophe's biography of the artist was known to his contemporaries. It was reprinted several times in articles on Seurat that appeared during his lifetime and served until the early 1920s as the definitive formulation of his theory. With the publication of the Beaubourg letter by Coquiot and Pach,[18] the earlier statement was abandoned in most writings on the artist in favor of the more complete one. Although parts of it have already been referred to, it will now be quoted in its entirety:

ESTHETIC

Art is harmony.
Harmony is the analogy of opposites, the analogy of similar elements, of *value*, *hue*, and *line*, considered according to their dominants and under the influence of lighting, in gay, calm, or sad combinations.

The opposites are:
For value, a more $\left\{\begin{array}{l}\text{luminous}\\\text{light}\end{array}\right\}$ for a darker one.
For hue, the complementaries, i.e., a certain red opposed to its complementary, etc.
$\left\{\begin{array}{l}\text{red-green}\\\text{orange-blue}\\\text{yellow-violet}\end{array}\right.$

For line, those forming a right angle.

*Gaiety of value* is the light dominant; of *hue*, the warm dominant; of *line*, lines above the horizontal.

Calmness of value is the equality of dark and light; of hue, of warm and cool; and the horizontal for line.

Sadness of value is the dark dominant; of hue, the cool dominant; and of line, downward directions.

## TECHNIQUE

Granting the phenomena of the duration of the light-impression on the retina, synthesis necessarily follows as a resultant. The means of expression is the optical mixture of values, of hues (of the local color and the color of the illuminating light: sun, oil lamp, gas, etc.), that is to say, of the lights and their reactions (shadows), in accordance with the laws of *contrast*, gradation, and irradiation.

The frame is in a harmony opposed to that of the values, hues, and lines of the picture.[19]

It should be observed that Seurat did not allow his ideas on painting to be published until relatively late in his career; his statement to Christophe and his letter to Beaubourg both date from 1890, and he died in March, 1891. Significantly, in the following month Émile Verhaeren referred to the earlier of these — the statement published by Christophe — as a résumé of "all of his [Seurat's] new theory."[20] Kahn, too, pointed out that Christophe's résumé of the artist's theories concerned his "final evolution."[21] Such evidence from two writers who knew Seurat personally suggests that this theoretical statement from the artist's own hand was the embodiment of his newest and latest ideas on painting that had been formulated not long before his death. For this reason, it would seem unwise to attempt to relate the whole of this statement to paintings Seurat did before 1887.

In the foregoing account of the changes in Seurat's theories, as described by his friends and as witnessed by his own writings, we have seen that from 1886 to 1891 he became increasingly interested in the expressive possibilities of line as well as of color and value, and that these pictorial elements could be combined in different ways to convey definite emotions. And we have suggested that his new theory of expression, which his friends pointed out was based largely on the research of Charles Henry, was not formulated completely until at least 1888–1889, though inklings of it can be detected as early as 1887. A verbal statement of his theory, in turn, was published only in 1890 and was applied, according to the evidence cited here, in paintings done at Le Crotoy (1889), in *Le Chahut* (1889–1890), *Le Cirque* (1890–1891), and to a lesser degree in *Les Poseuses* and *La Parade*.

## CHARLES HENRY AND SEURAT'S LATER THEORY OF ART

Little attention in previous studies has been devoted to the relationship of Seurat's theories to the paintings he did during the last four years of his life. Nor has much been written about the sources of these theories as they appear in the artist's statement quoted by Christophe and in corrected form in his letter to Maurice Beaubourg. And thus far, the relationship between Henry's discoveries and Seurat's theory and practice has been explored only superficially. It will be our aim here to examine the connection between the artist and scientist in greater detail and to answer, as completely as possible, these questions: To what degree was Seurat's approach to painting in 1887–1891 influenced by Henry's ideas? What were the sources of Seurat's newly developed theories? And how closely did he follow his own theories in his later paintings?

### The Life and Writings of Charles Henry

Because of Charles Henry's importance in our answers to these questions, let us begin with a brief account of his life and work.[22] He was born in Bollweiler, Alsace, in 1859, and in 1875 came to Paris, where he audited courses at the Sorbonne and at the Collège de France. Henry worked briefly as preparator in the laboratories of Claude Bernard and Paul Bert, and in 1881 was appointed as librarian at the Sorbonne. (In 1892, after Seurat's death, he became *maitre de conférences* at the École Pratique des Hautes—Études, and in 1897 became director of the Laboratoire de Physiologie des Sensations at the Sorbonne.) Henry was admired by his friends as a universal genius who worked with equal brilliance in the fields of mathematics, chemistry, physics, psychology, esthetics, and the history of science. Although he seems to have exerted little influence in English-speaking countries, he was considered by some of his French contemporaries in the world of science and the arts as an important, if somewhat bizarre, figure.

Henry's first publications appeared in 1878, and between that year and 1885 he wrote prolifically about the great rational minds of the past, the history of science, and mathematical theory. During this period, he became acquainted with a group of talented young writers, some of whom were shortly to emerge as leading figures in the Symbolist movement in literature.[23] Among them was Gustave Kahn, whom he met in 1879, and who, in turn, introduced him to the poet and critic Jules Laforgue. Henry was also acquainted with Charles Cros, another of Kahn's friends, who in addition to being a poet and painter, was one of the inventors of color photography. And Henry collaborated with Charles' brother, Henri Cros, a sculptor, in writing a book on the history and technique of painting in encaustic. Its publication in 1884 marked the beginning of Henry's increasing interest in art, especially in the problem of formulating a scientifically valid system of esthetics. His first definitive statement of the theory of expression that was to occupy him for the next decade was the article entitled "Introduction à une esthétique scientifique," which appeared in *La Revue contemporaine*, August, 1885.

Before 1886, Henry's contact with the world of art had been limited largely to the group of Symbolist poets, to whose publications he contributed, but in that year he was introduced to Seurat, probably through Fénéon. As a result of this meeting, the artist was brought into direct contact with the young scientist, and their association continued until Seurat's death in 1891. Signac, too, was close to Henry after 1886 and contributed the illustrations for several of his publications.[24] Another point of contact between Henry and the Neo-Impressionists can be found in the public lectures given by the scientist, which were attended by some of the artists. We know that Seurat had to explain Henry's complex mathematical reasoning to Camille Pissarro, who had heard one of these lectures but apparently could not understand it without the young artist's help.[25] Furthermore, we have reports from Seurat's friends that he was influenced by Henry's theories, particularly those embodied in his *Cercle chromatique* and *Rapporteur esthétique*.[26]

Having noted which of Henry's writings interested Seurat, we must now investigate their contents briefly in order to determine their relevance for the artist's theory and practice. No attempt will be made here, however, to discuss Henry's theories in their entirety: his remarks on composition and on ways of obtaining harmonious outlines will be passed over in favor of his ideas on expression and harmony through the elements of color and line.

In the first of Henry's important articles — his "Introduction à une esthétique scientifique" — he stated that while the role of art was to pursue the expression of the physiognomy of things, the discipline of esthetics was concerned with "the conditions which they satisfy when they are represented as gay or sad, pleasing or displeasing, beautiful or ugly."[27] This discipline, as practiced up until the last quarter of the nineteenth century had, in Henry's opinion, been much too metaphysical in character. In its place, he recommended the adoption of a scientific approach. While science cannot create beauty, it could fulfill the following role: "It is to spread pleasure within us and without, and, from this point of view, its social function is immense in these times of oppression and muted collisions. It must spare the artist useless hesitations and attempts in pointing out the path by which he can find richer and richer esthetic elements. It must furnish the critics with rapid means of discerning ugliness, which is sensed but often in-expressible." [28]

After defining the prerogatives of a scientific esthetic, Henry briefly sketched the progress made toward this end in earlier periods; the ancient Greeks, Leonardo da Vinci, Rameau, Michel-angelo, and Hogarth are praised because in one way or another they guided their art through the use of precise rules and theories. More significant for our purposes is the fact that he singled out a book by Humbert de Superville, *Essai sur les signes inconditionnels dans l'art* (Leyden, 1827–1832), as representing the growth of scientific tendencies in esthetics in the early nineteenth century; this volume, which Seurat undoubtedly knew, was important to Henry because Humbert de Superville linked the directions of lines in the human face — horizontal, slanting upward or down-ward — with emotions of calmness, joy, and sadness. Further evidence of the emergence of scientific esthetics in the nineteenth century was to be found in the work of a number of German and French scientists, estheticians, and writers on art theory, such as Fechner, Wundt, Lévèque, Sully-Prudhomme, and Taine, all of whom attacked problems similar to those that interested Henry. These problems were divided into two categories: the esthetics of lines and the esthetics of colors. In the first category the major questions to be answered were: "Which are the pleasing direc-tions? Which are the displeasing directions? In other words: which directions do we associate with pleasure and sorrow?" [29]

After presenting various arguments based on physiological findings, Henry concluded that "gestures directed in the direction of weight affirm sadness; gestures directed in the opposite direction affirm joy." [30] Or, expressed schematically on the basis of a circular form: "The diagram of the expression of sorrow presents us with a rotation in the direction of weight; the diagram of the expression of pleasure, a rotation in the opposite direction." [31] Henry justified these assertions by observing that in the case of sadness we tend to place our body in a position that demands the least effort, and in the case of pleasure, in a position that involves the most effort.

The foregoing observations were summarized in the following proposition: "The direction from bottom to top corresponds to pleasure. . . . The direction from top to bottom corresponds to sorrow."[32] To these Henry added a second pair of directions: movements from left to right tend to be agreeable, and movements from right to left, disagreeable; however, the sensations resulting from these movements are not as clearly predictable as are those for the first pair.[33]

Henry also proposed an algebraic formula based on Gauss's theory that would enable one to determine which changes in the direction of lines, expressed as radii extending from the center of a circle to its circumference, would be rhythmical:

> A change in direction determining on a circumference whose center is itself the center of the change, a possible geometric division, i.e., a division of $M$ into a number of parts which may be: 2, $2^n$, or a prime number of the form $2^n + 1$, or the product of a power of 2 by one or several different numbers of that form. For example, only the following values of $M$ within the first hundred will be rhythmical: 2, 3, 4, 5, 6, 8, 10, 12, 15, 16, 17 20, 24, 30, 32, 34, 40, 48, 51, 60, 64, 68, 80, 85, 96.[34]

It follows that each of the reciprocals of these numbers, expressed as fractions (that is, $\frac{1}{2}$, $\frac{1}{3}$, $\frac{1}{4}$, $\frac{1}{5}$, $\frac{1}{6}$, $\frac{1}{8}$, $\frac{1}{10}$, and so on), will, according to Henry, represent a harmonious division of the circle.[35] For the convenience of measuring the angles between the radii dividing the circle, these fractions may be converted into degrees; for example, one-quarter of the circle equals 90 degrees, one-eighth equals 45 degrees, one-tenth equals 36 degrees, and so on. In 1888, Henry published a device which he called an "esthetic protractor," or *rapporteur esthétique* (Figure 51), which would enable one to determine with a minimum of mathematical effort whether or not such angular relationships between straight lines originating from a single point were rhythmical.

Turning to the esthetics of color, Henry first attacked Chevreul's system of arranging hues as being completely arbitrary. The latter was vulnerable because he did not carefully calculate the angles separating the radii representing the different colors of

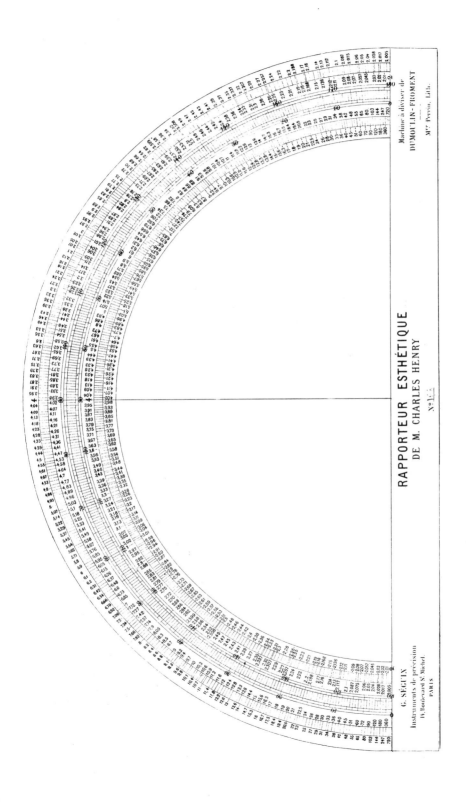

# RAPPORTEUR ESTHÉTIQUE
## DE M. CHARLES HENRY

G. SÉGUIN
Instruments de précision
9, Boulevard St-Michel
PARIS

Machine à diviser de
DUMOULIN-FROMENT
Mᵐᵉ Perrin, Lith.

the chromatic circle (Figure 7, page 22). According to Henry: "It is evident that these angular distances should be determined if one wishes to arrive at a rational classification of colors and a knowledge of the laws of their harmony."[36] After discussing Chevreul's shortcomings, he presented the idea that colors have certain precise expressive values. In their simplest terms: "Red, orange, and yellow are gay colors; green, blue, and violet are sad colors; with the former we associate light, with the latter dark."[37] Having observed that there are gay and sad colors and values, as well as gay and sad lines, Henry concluded that "as one cannot suppose a color without direction, there is only one suitable direction for a color, i.e., of identical expression."[38]

According to Henry, the relationships between color and linear directions may be plotted conveniently in circular form, with the gay colors (red, orange, and yellow) corresponding to directions moving from low to high and left to right, and the saddest colors (blue-green, blue, and blue-violet) corresponding to directions moving from top to bottom and right to left. Although these relationships were described verbally in the article, there were no illustrations; for this reason, we shall refer to the diagram of the chromatic circle and a reproduction of it (published in full color) in Henry's *Cercle chromatique* (Paris, 1889) in order to point out the exact location of hues and linear directions (Figure 52).

Red, the most dynamogenous color, corresponds to the direction of low to high on Henry's circle; yellow, being less dynamogenous, is associated with the direction of left to right. Blue, which is relatively inhibitory, corresponds to the directions of top to bottom and right to left. The eight colors of the circle, which are situated on radii separated from each other by 45 degrees are, beginning at the top and moving clockwise, red, orange, yellow, green, blue-green, blue, blue-violet, and violet. They pass gradually from one to the next throughout the circle, and in its center, a small spot of white appears. These eight hues are found at full intensity at a point midway between the center of the circle and the circumference. Between this point and the center, they are

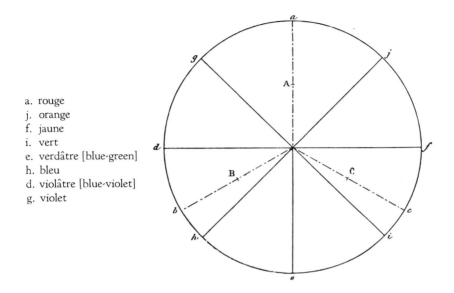

a. rouge
j. orange
f. jaune
i. vert
e. verdâtre [blue-green]
h. bleu
d. violâtre [blue-violet]
g. violet

Figure 52. Illustration of Chromatic Circle (from Henry, *Cercle chromatique*).

gradated by the addition of white; between this point and the circumference they are gradated by the addition of black.

According to Henry, this chromatic circle is valuable because it can serve as a device by which colors may be related to each other according to rational principles. He summarized the possibilities of its application as follows:

> There is no one single appropriate color for a given definite direction; there are all the rhythmical colors with it (which permit the creation of a new industrial art) and all the complementary colors (which promise maxima of intensity of excitation). It is clear that in assigning to each direction a color separated by a variable rhythmic interval on the chromatic circle, one will obtain simultaneously with linear rhythms virtual melodies and consequently harmonies of a totally musical power of expression.[39]

How can one establish these harmonious, rhythmical intervals between colors? The answer is similar to that which applies to the relationship between linear directions: "All other conditions being satisfied, contrasts of colors separated on the rational chromatic circle by a section of the circumference expressed by a number of the forms $2^n$, $2^n + 1$ prime, or of their product, are pleasing."[40] In order to find harmonious relationships of color on the chromatic circle accompanying the text of Henry's *Cercle chromatique*, he suggested that a screen exactly its size be made out of cardboard, in which small apertures corresponding to the harmonious divisions of the circle could be cut, their placement to be determined by following the series of rhythmic fractions derived from the formula cited in the preceding excerpt. That is to say, angles separating the radii corresponding to harmonious colors will be determined in the same way as were rhythmical changes in direction. When the perforated cardboard circle is superimposed over the chromatic circle, the colors that show through the apertures will, according to Henry, harmonize with each other.[41] (Such a screen was constructed by the writer, following Henry's instructions; it is reproduced as Figure 53).[42] Again, the esthetic protractor, or *rapporteur esthétique* (Figure 51, page 193), could be used to determine the rhythmical angles separating the radii corresponding to each color of the circle. Because it will prove to be important in Seurat's work, let us examine this protractor in greater detail.

In each copy of the *Rapporteur esthétique* (Paris, 1888), one of the esthetic protractors, printed on translucent fabric, was included. Like an ordinary protractor, it is in the shape of a half-circle and is marked off in degrees from 0 to 180. In a scale adjoining this is another series of numbers, the reciprocals of which correspond to fractional divisions of the circle. The latter scale permits one, with the aid of tables supplied by Henry, to locate rhythmical numbers easily and to convert them into degrees immediately. Angles that are rhythmical may be found directly on the protractor, thus eliminating mathematical calculations. This device had a dual value: it permitted the artist to determine whether the angular distances between lines radiating in different directions from a

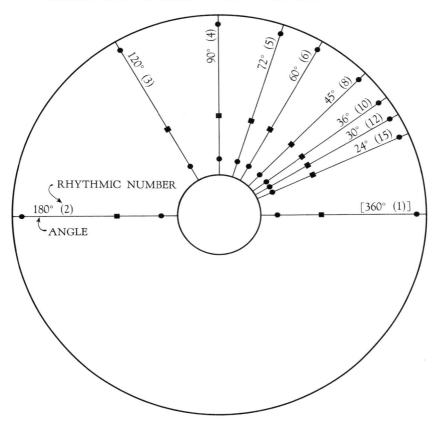

Figure 53. Screen Marked Off in Harmonious Intervals.

single point were harmonious; and it enabled him to create, or to analyze, rhythmical changes of direction in linear contours.[43]

In summary, the key points of Henry's theories as expressed in his "Introduction à une esthétique scientifique," *Cercle chromatique*, and *Rapporteur esthétique* are the following: for every direction, there is a corresponding color that is exactly matched to it. Together, colors and directions have intrinsic expressive value, the extremes of which Henry termed *dynamogénie* and *inhibition*. Directions moving from low to high and left to right are dynamogenous, or pleasing, while those from high to low and right to left are inhibitory, or sad. To these directions correspond gay and sad colors. The relationship between color and linear directions, in turn, may be plotted on a chromatic circle. Harmonious, rhythmical intervals between colors or between linear directions may be obtained by separating the radii of the circle by angles determined by Henry's formula cited above. Instead of following this formula, however, the *rapporteur esthétique* with its corresponding tables could be used to achieve the same end. With this summary of Henry's theories of harmony and expression in mind, let us now pass to the question of how much Seurat's paintings and theories were determined by the scientist's ideas.

## Henry and the Sources of Seurat's Later Theory of Art

With the increasing interest on the part of some scholars in the impact of Henry's ideas on Seurat, there has been a tendency to overestimate the scientist's influence on the artist's best known theoretical statement, which appears in his letter to Beaubourg.[44] If, however, this statement is analyzed carefully, much of its content will be found to be based on writings other than Henry's. In the following pages we shall identify and discuss the sources of the concepts expressed in the letter, and in so doing shall try to place Henry's influence on it in proper perspective.

Before proceeding, it should be noted that Henry and Seurat read many of the same books independently of each other before their meeting in 1886, and for this reason some of the ideas that they hold in common may be traced to the same sources. Henry, for example, referred to the work of Blanc, Chevreul, and Rood in his "Introduction à une esthétique scientifique" of 1885; and writings by these three authors, as we have seen, were also known by Seurat before 1885. Thus, when Seurat met Henry, he had already formulated a scientifically inspired esthetic under his own initiative; Henry, too, had followed a similar course but reached a point somewhat in advance of Seurat's progress as of 1885–1886. It is natural, then, that the painter should turn to Henry for guidance in the matter of the expression of emotions through color and line. Yet many of the similarities between Seurat's esthetic and Henry's theories still must be regarded as coincidental, rather than the result of direct influence of the scientist on the artist.

Turning to Seurat's theory of painting, as written down in his letter to Beaubourg, we find as its keynote the statement: "Art is harmony." The sources of this concept, of course, are manifold. Harmony, in general, had been cited as one of the chief ends of art by several nineteenth-century figures who were closely associated with the academic tradition and whose writings Seurat had read: in different ways, Chevreul, Sutter, Blanc, and Couture all championed this idea. Henry, too, believed in the importance of social and artistic harmony, man's destiny being "the creation of universal harmony." [45]

While these authors were concerned with the general idea of harmony, we must identify more specifically the sources of Seurat's special definition of it: "Harmony is the analogy of opposites, the analogy of similar elements of *value*, *hue*, and *line*, considered according to their dominants and under the influence of lighting, in gay, calm, or sad combinations." We have already traced the origins of Seurat's conviction that harmony is based on the analogy of contrary and similar elements to Chevreul's *De la loi du contraste simultané*, to the writings of Charles Blanc, and to the paintings of Delacroix. But it should be emphasized that in Seurat's view, harmony and expression are closely interrelated. Harmony by analogy and contrast is the prime desideratum, but this type of harmony should, at the same time, serve specific expressive ends through being governed by gay, calm, or sad "dominants":

Gaiety of value is the light dominant; of *hue*, the warm dominant; of *line*, lines above the horizontal.
Calmness of value is the equality of dark and light; of hue, of warm and cool; and the horizontal for line.
Sadness of value is the dark dominant; of hue, the cool dominant; and of line, downward directions.

The ideas expressed in this excerpt clearly have much in common with Charles Henry's theories. It will be recalled that in his "Introduction à une esthétique scientifique" the scientist associated gaiety with ascending lines and sadness with descending lines. And he linked the emotion of gaiety with red, orange, and yellow (warm colors) and sadness with green, blue, and violet (cool colors); light values were associated with the former group of colors, while dark values corresponded to the latter. Moreover, Henry insisted that color and line be rationally conjoined in expressing the emotions of gaiety or sadness, and turned to evidence provided by a wide variety of scientific disciplines to confirm his theories.

In spite of the similarities between Seurat's esthetic and the scientist's ideas, there are several important differences between their views, which may be accounted for, in part, by Seurat's reliance on several other sources, in addition to Henry's writings, in formulating the theory of expression that appears in his letter to Beaubourg. One of these sources is the *Essai sur les signes inconditionnels dans l'art* (Leyden, 1827–1832) by the Dutch painter-theorist David Pierre Giottino Humbert de Superville (1770–1849),[46] who, like Henry, had emphasized the concordance of color and line for expressive purposes. (Henry, the reader will recall, had recognized the importance of this book in foretelling the emergence of a scientific system of esthetics later in the nineteenth century.) Humbert found three types of lines constituting the basis of our experience of nature: those slanting

Figure 54. Diagrams of Linear Directions (from Humbert de Superville, *Essai sur les signes inconditionnels dans l'art*).

upward [*directions obliques expansives*], downward [*directions obliques convergentes*], and horizontals.[47] These he illustrated in a group of linear diagrams (Figures 54 and 55) and in three schematized drawings of the human face (Figure 56). He maintained that such

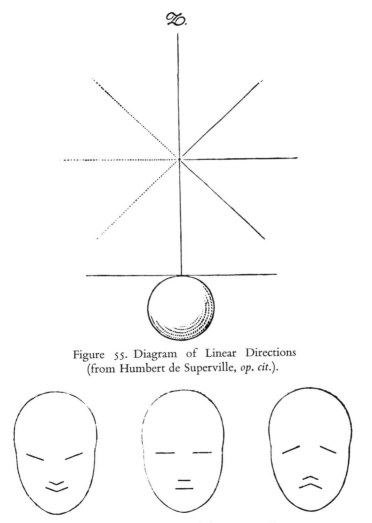

Figure 55. Diagram of Linear Directions
(from Humbert de Superville, *op. cit.*).

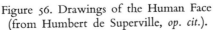

Figure 56. Drawings of the Human Face
(from Humbert de Superville, *op. cit.*).

lines conveyed emotion not only through association with the act of smiling or weeping, but also by virtue of the abstract evocative value "attached not at all to the facial organs as such, but to their *directions* as *esthetic signs*, that is to say, as visible and constant elements of all the non-convulsive action of the physiognomy, from its *minimum* in infantile expression to its *maximum* in calm, expansive, or contemplative expression. . . ."[48]

In addition to affirming the value of linear directions as vehicles of expression, Humbert also considered colors as an equally abstract means of conveying feeling. As he said: "The whole question would be reduced to the simplest terms, if it were possible for us to consider color *abstractly*, just as we have considered and interpreted simple linear patterns up till now, independently of any idea of accident or of concrete quality."[49] His next step was to unite, as Henry later did, the elements of line and color, allowing them to reinforce each other in the expression of any given emotion. Red was associated with lines slanting upward from the horizontal; white, with an equivalence of horizontal and vertical lines; and black with lines slanting below the horizontal.[50] (Between the extremes of red and black, orange, yellow, straw-color, pearl-color, blue, and indigo were ranged consecutively.)[51] The expressive values of these combinations are as follows: for upward-turned lines and red, "vacillation, agitation, dispersion, explosion, *éclat*"; for the horizontal and white, "equilibrium, calmness, order, clarity, light"; and for descending lines and black, "concentration, contemplation, solemnity, profoundness, gloom." (These relationships were outlined by Humbert in the synoptic table reproduced as Figure 57.)[52]

In some respects, Humbert de Superville's theory is closer to Seurat's ideas than are Henry's concepts, but in other ways it is quite different. The diagrams of lines spreading diagonally upward or downward from a central vertical axis (Figures 54 and 55) are closer in appearance to the sketches with which Seurat illustrated his letter to Beaubourg (Figure 58) than are any of Henry's diagrams published before 1892; and Humbert's general principle

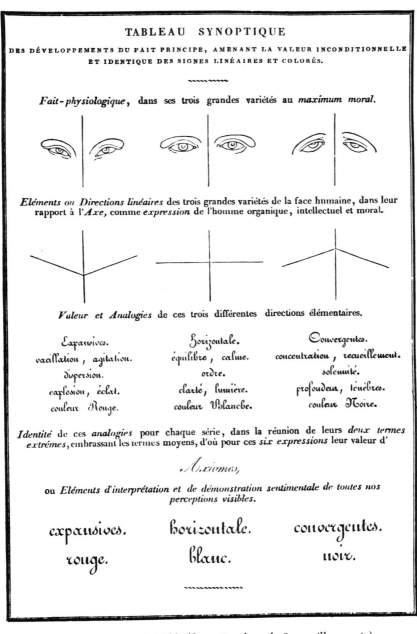

Figure 57. Synoptic Table (from Humbert de Superville, *op. cit.*).

of the concordance of line and color as abstract elements that can evoke predictable emotions was certainly followed explicitly by Seurat. Moreover, the Dutch theorist devoted much more attention to the intermediary state of calmness, as expressed through horizontal lines, than did Henry, who was more concerned with the two opposed poles of dynamogeny and inhibition.

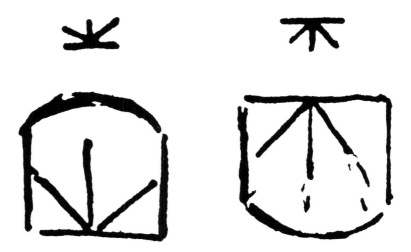

Figure 58. Diagrams of Linear Directions (from Seurat's Letter to Maurice Beaubourg, August 28, 1890).

But the three tones (red, white, and black) associated with Humbert's linear configurations have little counterpart in Seurat's theory, and the emotion invoked by the three chief combinations of color and line were far more complex and "literary" than those referred to by Seurat, or for that matter, Henry. These two preferred to condense the sentiments in question into simple, all-encompassing terms, such as gaiety or sadness, dynamogeny or inhibition.

It should be noted that the *Essai sur les signes inconditionnels dans l'art* demonstrated clearly the relationship between the elements of color and line and the physiognomic characteristics of the human countenance. The lessons Seurat learned from Humbert de Superville on this subject, as we shall show later, will be reflected in *Le Chahut* and *Le Cirque*. Also, in several unpublished schematic drawings of the human face Seurat tried to work out a system of expression that was apparently based on Humbert's study of the association of states of feeling with the linear directions of the eyes and mouth. Unfortunately, these sketches have not yet been made available for publication.[53]

We have seen that Henry was much more rigorous in his approach to the problem of expression in painting than was Humbert, and that he based his theories on scientifically determined principles of psychology, physiology, and mathematics. Yet, we must repeat that Seurat's explanation of, and diagrams illustrating, his own ideas about linear directions are closer in many respects to Humbert de Superville than they are to Henry. While the latter asserted that dynamogenous colors and lines occupy the upper right-hand quarter of a circular diagram and inhibitory ones fall in the lower left-hand quarter, Seurat began with a horizontal line and ascribed qualities of gaiety to lines rising above it, and sadness to lines falling below it (for comparative purposes, the relationships described by Henry and Seurat have been illustrated here in schematic diagrams, Figures 59 and 60). In his own words: "Gaiety . . . of line, lines above the horizontal; calmness . . . the horizontal for line; sadness . . . of line, downward directions." Still, Seurat followed Henry's general principle that ascending lines are gay and descending ones sad, the difference being that the painter's theory ignores the inhibitory and dynamogenous qualities that Henry said were also associated with directional movements from right to left and left to right, respectively. But obviously dependent on Henry's theories is Seurat's insistence on the unity of color, value, and line for the purpose of expressing the emotions of gaiety, calmness, and sadness. And these emotions — particularly gaiety and sadness — are those referred to repeatedly by Henry in the three texts reviewed earlier in this chapter.

SEURAT'S THEORIES OF EXPRESSION

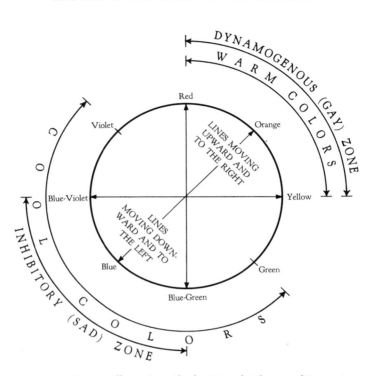

Figure 59. Diagram Illustrating Charles Henry's Theory of Expression.

Seurat may also have derived some of his ideas about the concordance of color and line from Delacroix. Although Seurat's notes of 1881 on paintings by Delacroix do not reflect any such interests (indeed, we should not expect them to at this early date), Signac stated that his friend saw in Delacroix's work "the application of traditional laws, as much in color *as in line*" [italics mine].[54] Delacroix was also cited by Signac as a progenitor of the Neo-Impressionist approach to painting because he favored the union of line and color in expressing the emotion inherent in his subject:

Once his linear composition is determined, the Neo-Impressionist will think of completing it with a combination of directions and colors appropriate to the subject and to his conception, whose "dominants" will vary according to whether he wants to express joy, calmness, sadness, or intermediate sensations. Thus concerning himself with the moral effect of lines and colors, he [the Neo-Impressionist painter] will only be following once more the teaching of Delacroix.[55]

Similar ideas were also voiced by David Sutter, whose "Phénomènes de la vision" Seurat studied. Although Sutter's theory of expression was not particularly scientific in origin, he established many principles that Seurat appears to have followed. Briefly, Sutter's thesis was that harmony is an essential requisite in works of art, but that the goal of pure harmony should not overshadow the expression of the sentiments and moral character of the subject through "esthetic lines" [lignes esthétiques], chiaroscuro, and color.[56] In this respect the connection between Sutter's view of the role of harmony and expression and Seurat's is remarkably close, particularly when it is noted that Sutter also believed in the

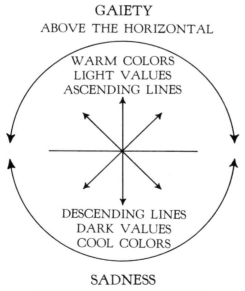

GAIETY
ABOVE THE HORIZONTAL

WARM COLORS
LIGHT VALUES
ASCENDING LINES

DESCENDING LINES
DARK VALUES
COOL COLORS

SADNESS
BELOW THE HORIZONTAL

Figure 60. Diagram Illustrating Seurat's Theory
of Expression.

efficacy of formal elements in conveying specific emotional and moral states. Sutter saw the intrinsic power of lines as follows:

> The vertical line is the line of nobility, of grandeur, majesty, and authority. . . . One will give nobility to a subject, then, by affirming the vertical.
> The horizontal line is that of great expanses, of vast scenes from nature, and of large gatherings; it is the line of matter.
> The diagonal line is the consequence of the contradiction between the vertical and the horizontal. It separates oblique lines from the vertical harmony and from the horizontal harmony.[57]

While the qualities conveyed by horizontal, vertical, and diagonal lines are associative, as well as intrinsic, the belief that abstract elements such as these have fixed expressive value was certainly shared by Seurat.

Views similar to these were elucidated by still another author whose writings Seurat studied: Charles Blanc. While he served earlier in Seurat's career as one of the sources for his theory of chromo-luminarism, the artist may well have reassessed Blanc's value later in the 1880s, regarding him now as a proponent of the intrinsic expressive value of esthetic elements. In his *Grammaire des arts du dessin*, Blanc had reviewed Humbert de Superville's ideas on this subject and reproduced the three schematic drawings of the human face (Figure 56, page 201) that had appeared in the latter's *Essai sur les signes inconditionnels dans l'art*.[58] He also reproduced in slightly modified form, Humbert's abstract diagram showing the three main expressive linear directions: vertical, diagonal, and horizontal (Figure 61; cf. Figure 55, page 201).

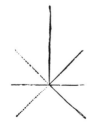

Figure 61. Diagram of Linear Directions (from Blanc, *op. cit.*).

Their value, according to Blanc, is as follows: "These three great lines, the horizontal and the two slanting ones, besides their mathematical value, have a moral meaning, that is, they have a secret rapport with feeling."[59] Here, once more, the evocative power of simple linear elements was affirmed, in this case by a writer whom we know Seurat admired.

Statements similar to the one just quoted — apropos of color and chiaroscuro — were repeated throughout Blanc's *Grammaire*. About color, for example, he wrote: "In its variety, charming or pathetic, gay or sombre, it expresses only the variable shades of sentiment or sensation."[60] And about the power of chiaroscuro, as discovered by Leonardo, Blanc wrote: "The first of the great modern geniuses, Leonardo da Vinci, brought into painting a new light, and, finding the eloquence of the shadow, made it apparent that chiaro'scuro could express the depths of reverie as well as those of space, and, with all the reliefs of the body, all the emotions of the soul."[61] Although Blanc believed that color, chiaroscuro, and line could, through their arrangement, evoke any desired sentiment in the spectator, he did not devise a system like Henry's or Humbert de Superville's whereby these three elements could be united in arriving at the expression of a single emotion. Yet he did touch upon the idea of "dominants" and their relation to the over-all unity of the painting:

> Unity, that is the true secret of all composition. But what is unity with respect to arrangement? It signifies that in the choice of the great lines a certain character should govern, that in the disposition of the parts there should be a dominant.... Straight or curved, horizontal or vertical, parallel or divergent, all the lines have a secret relation to the sentiment.[62]

In brief, Blanc's thesis was that the dominant character of the formal elements should be adjusted to match the sentiments the artist wished to evoke in the spectator.[63] Those painters who compose according to predetermined, *a priori* conceptions of unity are chastised by Blanc, who felt that while unity was important to the work of art, the expression of the dominant idea of the picture should not be sacrificed to it:

Two things are to be observed and reconciled in the arrangement, — its optical beauty, that which responds to the pleasure of the eyes, and its moral or poetical beauty, that which touches the feelings. The first of these would be the most important, and might almost suffice if the composition were purely decorative, as would be, for instance, a painting representing the pleasures of the harvest or the vintage. But if the picture appeals to the mind or heart, if it aims to excite the passions, the moral character of the arrangement should take precedence of the picturesque, which ought pitilessly to be sacrificed to the expression if it is impossible to obtain both, to strengthen one by the other.[64]

The relationship between the harmony of the picture and its expressive content, as explained by Blanc in this passage, is almost identical to that voiced by Seurat in his letter to Beaubourg where he implied that, while the aim of art should be harmony, this harmony must be ruled by "dominants" of line, color, and value that correspond to the feelings of gaiety, calm, or sadness. It is on this level, then, that Blanc's chief contribution to Seurat's later esthetic lies; although he wrote on the expressive value of formal elements, he did not relate them systematically to each other, nor did he base his theories on scientific evidence.

The belief that specific arrangements of pictorial elements can induce definite states of feeling in the viewer, and that these arrangements may be classed as "modes," prevailed in the Académie Royale de Peinture et de Sculpture during the second half of the seventeenth century and became part of the academic credo that persisted well into the nineteenth century.[65] The conception of modes as understood in French art theory was articulated by Nicolas Poussin in a letter to Paul de Fréart, Sieur de Chantelou (November 24, 1647). Basing his remarks almost exactly on a passage from Gioseffo Zarlino's *Istitutioni Harmoniche* (Venice, 1558), he wrote:

The Modes of the ancients were a combination of several things put together; from their variety was born a certain difference of Mode whereby one was able to understand that each one of them retained in itself a subtle variation; particularly when all the things which entered into combination were put together in such a proportion that it was made possible to arouse the soul of the spectator to various passions. Hence the fact that the ancient sages attributed to each style its own effects. Because of this they called the Dorian Mode stable, grave and severe, and applied it to subjects which are grave, and severe and full of wisdom.

And proceeding thence to pleasant and joyous things, they used the Phrygian Mode, in which there are more minute modulations than in any other mode, and a more clear-cut aspect. These two styles and no others were praised and approved of by Plato and Aristotle, who deemed the others superfluous; they considered this [Phrygian Mode] intense, vehement, violent, and very severe, and capable of astonishing people.[66]

Such ideas were soon popularized by Charles le Brun and André Félibien and became the subject of *conférences* in the Academy and of several seventeenth-century treatises on the theory of painting.[67] Writing in the early nineteenth century and basing his remarks largely on Félibien's preface to the *Conférences*, Paillot de Montabert revived the doctrine and terminology of the modes in his *Traité complet de la peinture* (Paris, 1829). Significantly, about this time Humbert de Superville published his influential *Essai sur les signes inconditionnels dans l'art* (Leyden, 1827–1832) which, like Paillot's treatise, associated predictable expressive values with abstract configurations of colors and lines. (It is difficult to ascertain whether these two theorists influenced each other or arrived at their conclusions independently; whatever the case may be, both texts stand as conclusive evidence of the continuing interest in expression through pictorial modes in the nineteenth century.)

Seurat linked his theory of art to this long tradition by studying not only Humbert de Superville's *Essai* but also Blanc's and Sutter's writings. Blanc, as we saw, popularized some of Humbert's ideas and illustrations in the *Grammaire des arts du dessin*; and equally important, he also knew Paillot de Montabert personally and was influenced by his *Traité complet de la peinture*, to which he referred in his book. David Sutter, whose writings affected Seurat's theory of art, also participated in the nineteenth-century revival of interest in the modes. Such doctrines were incorporated in his "Les Phénomènes de la vision," but his specific debt to Poussin and Félibien is even more obvious in his *Philosophie des beaux-arts*, where he wrote:

> In his *Pyrrhus*, Poussin represented the subject in a lively, animated mode; the disposition of the lines gives vivacity to the expression, the movement has animation, and the style is quite in keeping with the scene which he represents. When this great master treated solemn subjects, he never departed from the serious and tranquil character which was proper to the lines. Each subject or scene in nature has its own special mode, and, consequently a determined character. Now the disposition of lines, of shadows, of light, and of coloring will be in harmony with the mode adopted, from which one must not depart.[68]

Seurat's awareness of such academic concepts of pictorial expression was attested by Signac in a discussion of Puvis de Chavannes' esthetic, where he compared his means of conveying precise sentiments in painting to Seurat's and observed that Puvis had derived his ideas on this subject from Poussin.[69] In illustration of these points, he wrote the following about Puvis' *Le Pauvre pêcheur* (d. 1881, Louvre, Paris; Figure 62):

> However sad the subject chosen, however lamentable the pictorial components which make it up may be, the painting will never give — except to insensitive viewers — the expression of sadness if the "dominant" of lines, hues, and values is not in plastic concordance with the feelings which the artist wishes to express. If the mast of the boat in Puvis de Chavannes' *Le Pauvre pêcheur* were not slanted in an inhibitory direction (in a counterclockwise direction), this picture would not suggest sadness.[70]

In this light, the theory of expression that appears in Seurat's letter to Beaubourg may be regarded as a modernized version of the academic concept of communication through rationally determined pictorial modes. Seurat, of course, avoided literary overtones and analogies to the musical modes of ancient Greece, preferring to limit his three sets of abstract visual configurations to universal states of feeling: gaiety, calmness, and sadness.

In the foregoing account of the basis of the first part of Seurat's letter to Beaubourg — entitled "*esthétique*" — we have seen that

Figure 62. Pierre Puvis de Chavannes, *Le Pauvre pêcheur*, Louvre, Paris.
(Photo Giraudon.)

Henry exerted considerable influence on it. But he was by no means the only source for Seurat's theories. Before meeting Henry in 1886, Seurat had formulated under his own initiative a rational esthetic based largely on ideas of harmony through contrast and analogy gleaned from Chevreul, Blanc, and Delacroix. After establishing contact with Henry in 1886 his interest in the expressive value of linear directions and their relation to color and value was kindled, but not at the expense of his earlier theories of harmony. Following Blanc's example, rather than Henry's ideas,

Seurat considered the general harmony of the work of art and its expression of sentiment through one "dominant" or another as being of equal importance. However, Henry, along with Humbert de Superville and Sutter, did provide the artist with the fundamentals of a theory of expression based on the concordance between line and color. In composing the Beaubourg letter, Seurat fused this concept of expression with the theory of harmony that he had already formulated — and embodied in two major paintings — by 1886.

Another reason why Henry's ideas should not be considered the chief source of Seurat's theory of art is that his influence on the second part of the Beaubourg letter, entitled "*technique*," is negligible. As indicated previously, the artist's conception of color technique was formulated as early as 1885, that is, before Henry influenced him. Although the scientist dealt with many of the same problems in his *Rapporteur esthétique* (1888) and *Cercle chromatique* (1889), these books appeared after Seurat had independently worked out many of the solutions contained in their pages. We may suggest, then, that the artist's remarks on technique appearing in the latter half of the Beaubourg letter were confirmed but not determined by Charles Henry's ideas.

Having traced the origins of Seurat's theories of harmony and expression embodied in the first part of the Beaubourg letter [*esthétique*], it would be well at this point to review briefly the sources of the second part [*technique*], which were analyzed at greater length in Chapters 2 and 3. The portion of the letter concerning technique reads as follows:

> Granting the phenomena of the duration of the light-impression on the retina, synthesis necessarily follows as a resultant. The means of expression is the optical mixture of values, of hues (of the local color and the illuminating light: sun, oil lamp, gas, etc.), that is to say, of the lights and their reactions (shadows), in accordance with the laws of *contrast*, gradation, and irradiation.

We observed earlier that Seurat was influenced by Rood's chapter "On the Duration of the Impression on the Retina," and saw that the idea of synthesizing color and value through optical mixture could be traced to the writings of Rood, Blanc, and Chevreul. Rood also advocated the separation of the local colors and illuminating light, and both he and Chevreul noted that the "reactions" of the light (that is, the hue of shadow) should be colored by its complementary. These different elements, Seurat wrote, should be synthesized according to the laws of contrast, gradation, and irradiation.

By contrast he meant, of course, the principle of simultaneous contrast formulated by Chevreul and put on a more scientific basis by Rood; and, as we have seen, this principle had also been utilized by Delacroix and the Impressionists, whose paintings Seurat studied. Gradation, too, had been employed by these artists, among others, and its use in painting had been recommended by Blanc, Rood, and Ruskin; moreover, the laws of gradation, as Blanc pointed out, had been formulated by the "orientals," from whom Delacroix presumably had learned them.

The principle of irradiation, which we have mentioned only briefly, was discussed by Helmholtz, Sutter, and Henry.[71] Its operation was defined in the following way by Hermann von Helmholtz:

> To the series of subjective phenomena, which artists are compelled to represent objectively in their pictures, must be associated certain phenomena of *irradiation*. By this is understood cases in which any bright object in the field spreads its light or colour over the neighbourhood. The phenomena are the more marked the brighter is the radiating object, and the halo is brightest in the immediate neighbourhood of the bright object, but diminishes at a greater distance.[72]

Believing in the importance of such effects — which Fénéon called "*normales irradiations de complémentaires*"[73] — Seurat painted them into his canvases.[74]

To conclude: we have seen that Seurat's theory of painting was eclectic in nature and was based on a number of different sources rather than on the ideas of a single writer or painter. These sources include texts by Henry, Blanc, Humbert de Superville, Sutter,

Chevreul, Rood, and Helmholtz,[75] as well as lessons derived from the study of Delacroix's paintings and the methods of the "oriental tradition." We have already found that these verbal and pictorial sources cannot be regarded as equally "scientific" in content. Although highly rational in approach, Sutter's and Blanc's texts were usually not guided by the most advanced findings of nineteenth-century physics and optics. True, Blanc had referred to the scientific studies of Bourgeois and Chevreul, and Sutter had known the discoveries of the latter, as well as of Augustin-Jean Fresnel; but at the time of Blanc's and Sutter's writing, the data provided by their scientific sources had been challenged by more recent advances, of which they did not take advantage. In addition to knowing the work of the aforementioned writers, Seurat also turned to three of the more advanced scientists of his day: Helmholtz, Henry, and Rood. And through his study of Rood's *Text-Book of Color* (*Théorie scientifique des couleurs*), Seurat became familiar with the work of several other important nineteenth-century scientists, such as Maxwell, Mile, and Dove. Furthermore, through personal contact with Henry, Seurat was undoubtedly kept abreast of the most recent discoveries not only in physics and optics, but in the fields of physiology and experimental psychology as well.

Thus Seurat drew both on traditional art theory and modern science in formulating his artistic credo. Many of his earlier ideas were suggested by the less scientific authors he read, but they were corrected and given consistency through his acquaintance with more advanced currents of nineteenth-century science. As witnessed by his letter to Beaubourg, he drew upon more than one kind of "science": on one hand, he relied largely on physicists' discoveries in his remarks on *technique*, where optical mixture, division of color, contrast, and irradiation constitute a language of representation that follows the accepted optical and physical principles of his day. On the other hand, much of the first part of the letter — in which he defines his *esthetic* — is based on another kind of discipline: the recently developed branch of psychology known as experimental esthetics. The aims of this discipline, as practiced by Henry and his contemporaries, were to determine through controlled laboratory experiments which forms were harmonious and to discover which emotions were associated with given configurations of line and color. As we have seen, Seurat took advantage of Henry's research in this field. But at the same time he drew many similar ideas from writers close to the academic tradition, who likewise were concerned with the power of visual elements in conveying predictable emotions, "passions," and subjective sentiments.[76]

## THE THEORETICAL BASIS OF SEURAT'S LATER PAINTINGS

### Les Poseuses

With the foregoing survey of Seurat's theories in mind, we shall now try to determine the degree to which he followed his own verbal pronouncements, as well as Henry's ideas, in planning and executing his later paintings. The first canvas found to be linked with Henry's theories is *Les Poseuses* (D.-R. 178; 1886–1888), about which Fénéon wrote: "By a pseudo-scientific fantasy, the red umbrella, the straw umbrella, and the green stocking are oriented toward the directions of red, yellow, and green on Henry's chromatic circle."[77] If the painting is examined with these relationships of color and direction in mind, a very close correlation will indeed be found between the directions of the two umbrellas and the leg of the model at the right with their corresponding colors on Henry's chromatic circle (see Figure 63).[78] Such correlations, however, are limited to these incidental details in the painting. Further examination discloses no more relationships of the type described by Fénéon; this is undoubtedly because the painting lacks the large areas of saturated color necessary to the operation of Henry's theories of correspondence between hues and linear directions.

SEURAT'S THEORIES OF EXPRESSION

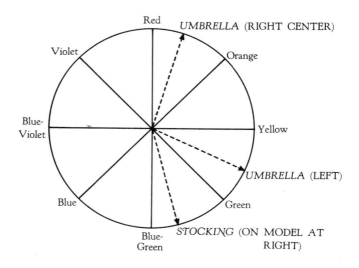

Figure 63. Diagram Illustrating Correlation of Colors and Linear
Directions in *Les Poseuses*.

Actually, the system of color harmony Seurat used in *Les Poseuses* is similar to that found in *La Grande Jatte*, part of which appears as a painting within a painting on the wall at the left. We recall that Seurat grouped the chief hues of *La Grande Jatte* around four points on the chromatic circle separated from each other by 90 degrees, following Rood's principles of color harmony, rather than Henry's theories. By virtue of its presence in the painting, *La Grande Jatte* sets the color scheme for *Les Poseuses*, which repeats in smaller doses almost all of the major hues in that canvas. *Les Poseuses*, however, incorporates fewer large areas of intense color than *La Grande Jatte*, and thus it is primarily accessories and details that are governed by a definite system of color harmony; the three figures, the floor, and the wall tend to read as warm or cool neutrals when viewed at the appropriate distance.

We may also ask whether Seurat, in order to express some definite emotional state, followed in *Les Poseuses* the system of creating "dominants" of color, value, and line articulated in the

Beaubourg letter. Evidence from the picture itself, as well as critical estimates of it, suggests a negative answer. Apparently his chief aim, in addition to establishing pleasing color harmonies, was to record as accurately as possible the effects of studio lighting on the three nude figures and to model them convincingly. According to Arsène Alexandre, who knew Seurat personally, "He wanted at this moment to prove that his very interesting theory for outdoor subjects was applicable to large figures in interiors; and he painted his *Poseuses*."[79] Henry van de Velde, in a similar vein, suggested that because some writers criticized the hieratic, rigid poses of the figures in *La Grande Jatte*, Seurat painted *Les Poseuses* to show that he was capable of representing the human body realistically.[80] Thus Seurat's aims here may be regarded as being chiefly naturalistic — aims that are inconsistent with the stylization and abstraction necessary to the effective expression of feeling through "dominants." The three nudes in the studio appear to have served as inert subject matter of what might be regarded as a large-scale study piece in which the artist concerned himself with the effects of light falling on the human form, rather than the expression of a definite emotional valence.

## La Parade

We must ask once again whether Seurat regulated the color, value, and linear directions of his next major painting, *La Parade* (1887–1888; Figure 49, page 176), according to a system of "dominants," partially under Henry's influence.[81] Clearly, horizontals and verticals predominate in its linear organization; there are no major diagonals. The verticals are distributed almost equally above and below the horizontals, so that neither a gay nor sad "dominant" of lines is permitted to govern the picture. However, horizontal lines predominate over verticals; this is because there are many more of them, and because the format of the canvas is horizontal, which also emphasizes the emotion of calmness.

In terms of color, there is a balance between warm and cool in *La Parade*. If Rood's definition of warm and cool hues is followed,[82] the major pair of local colors, violet and yellow-green, will be seen to fall directly on the warm-cool axis of the color wheel and thus are neither pronouncedly warm nor cool in tone. However, the color of the light, ranging from orange to yellow-orange, falls on the warm side of Rood's chromatic circle, while that of shadow, blue, is situated on the cool side. As far as this writer can determine from direct study of the picture, warm and cool tones are distributed about equally throughout the painting, and thus its color "dominant" is calm, because, in Seurat's words, it is based on "the equality . . . of warm and cool." Moreover, if the chief local colors (violet and yellow-green) are plotted on Henry's chromatic circle, they will fall in "neutral" zones, that is, in the upper left and lower right quarters of the circle, which are neither pronouncedly gay nor sad in character (cf. Figure 59, page 206).

So far we have suggested that the emotion of calmness in this painting is conveyed through color and line. Seurat's handling of value, too, contributes to the accord between all three elements — color, line, and value — in arriving at a common expressive goal. The value scheme is based on "the equality of dark and light"; that is, in terms of the area they occupy, light and dark values are distributed about equally throughout the painting. Furthermore, many of the tones Seurat used are concentrated around the middle of the value scale, again reinforcing the impression of calmness based on an equivalence of light and dark. It is thus apparent that in *La Parade* Seurat systematically practiced, for the first time in a major work, a rationalized method of uniting color, line, and value in expressing a single state of feeling — in this case, calmness. In so doing, he followed an esthetic theory similar to the one he wrote out in his letter to Beaubourg, which, in turn, was based partly on Henry's research.

Concerning *Le Chahut* (1889–1890; D.-R. 199; Figure 64) and *Le Cirque* (1890–1891; D.-R. 211; Figure 65), Seurat's last two major paintings, we are fortunate in having considerable evidence from his friends and critics, already cited, confirming our thesis

Figure 64. *Le Chahut*, Rijksmuseum Kröller-Müller, Otterlo.

Figure 65. *Le Cirque*, Louvre, Paris. (Photo Giraudon.)

that in conceiving them he applied theories of expression inspired largely by Henry. As Signac said: "If Seurat's *Le Chahut* and *Le Cirque* were not composed of dynamogenic lines, hues, and values, they would not be, in spite of their titles, paintings of movement and joy."[83]

## Le Chahut

What are the elements of "dynamogeny" in *Le Chahut*? In hue, local colors ranging from red-orange to yellow (with heavy concentration in the orange sector of the color circle) dominate the picture. These tones, in turn, are inundated by a shower of yellow-orange and orange dots, corresponding to the color of the gaslight. In much smaller quantity, the complementaries of these colors (hues ranging from ultramarine through blue to blue-green) also contribute to the chromatic composition of the painting; but their role is minor, and they are included undoubtedly because they strengthen their opposites by contrast. Also, blue, the complementary of the color of the light, is, as usual, found on the shadowed side of objects and, as in *La Parade*, is distributed arbitrarily throughout the picture. But unlike *La Parade*, there is relatively little blue when compared to the quantity of red-orange, orange, and yellow-orange in the painting. Seurat also assured the presence of a warm dominant by a very generous dosage of yellow-orange and orange dots almost everywhere in the canvas, thus illustrating the way in which pictorial harmony may come "under the influence of lighting," to use his own words. Moreover, these warm colors are located in the upper right-hand quarter of Henry's chromatic circle, which is the most dynamogenous, or gay, zone (for a diagram of the hue relationships in *Le Chahut* see Figure 66).[84]

The main linear directions in *Le Chahut*, however, do not entirely correspond to the positions of the major colors on Henry's chromatic circle. (For a diagram of the linear structure of the painting, see Figure 67.) While the torsos of the dancers lean

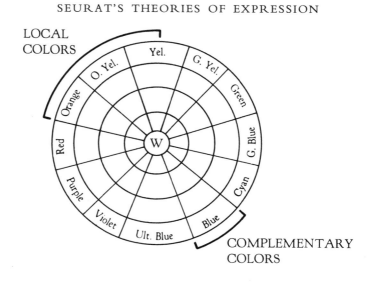

Figure 66. Diagram of Color Relationships in *Le Chahut*.

from lower left to upper right (that is, in a dynamogenous direction corresponding to warm, orange-dominated colors), their upward-thrust legs point toward the direction occupied by purple-violet on Henry's circle. But purple and violet, which, according to Henry's theories, should match the direction of the legs, play a relatively small role in the picture. Apparently, then, Seurat was not following closely Henry's system of correspondences between color and linear directions as illustrated in Figure 59, page 206, but, rather, his own more general theory as outlined in his letter to Beaubourg. (The color-value-line relationships that the artist described have been diagrammed in Figure 63, page 218.) We will recall that in this letter Seurat postulated the idea that *all* lines above the horizontal, regardless of whether they fall in the dynamogenous zone of Henry's circle, are gay. In *Le Chahut*, these upward-moving diagonals are distributed about equally to the left and right of an implied vertical between them, thus creating a series of slightly canted "V"s as the dominant scheme of lines in the dancing figures (see Figure 67).

Figure 67. Linear Structure of *Le Chahut*.

Seurat also achieved an effect of gaiety by tilting upward the eyebrows, eyes, and mouths in the faces of the dancers on the stage. By regulating the facial features in this way he almost certainly applied lessons learned from Humbert de Superville's *Essai sur les signes inconditionnels dans l'art*. We recall that the Dutch writer had proposed the idea that, in addition to representing the emotion of happiness in the human face by showing it in its smiling or laughing aspect, the artist could strengthen the desired emotion by arranging the features in upward-slanting lines, which, he felt, would reinforce the feeling of gaiety conveyed to the viewer through their abstract evocative power.

One way in which *Le Chahut* reflects Henry's theory of dynamogeny should be mentioned here: the action of the figures themselves, as distinct from the abstract, schematic lines of force discussed previously, requires a maximum expenditure of energy. The dancers' legs kick upward, their right arms are raised, and their heads are tilted back; even the conductor lifts his baton high in the air. In drawing the figures, Seurat was undoubtedly following Henry's ideas concerning the position of the human body and expenditure of energy as outlined in his "Introduction à une esthétique scientifique":

> It is scarcely necessary to speak of *dejected, prostrated, concentrated* attitudes of sorrow, of the *active, exultant, radiant* attitudes of pleasure: these metaphors clearly tell us that gestures in the direction of weight affirm sadness, gestures in the opposite direction affirm joy.... We find in the expression of the physiognomy the law of gesture: it is evident that the goal of these movements is, in the case of sorrow, a tendency to place the body in a position which demands the least work to produce; in the case of pleasure, in a position which demands the most work to produce....[85]

Seurat also appears to have followed Henry's system of obtaining rhythmical angles, as outlined in his *Rapporteur esthétique*, by measuring the inclination of the main lines of the painting with the "esthetic protractor." The present writer tested these angles with the protractor and found them to be almost always in accord with Henry's precepts on rhythmical relationship between lines.[86]

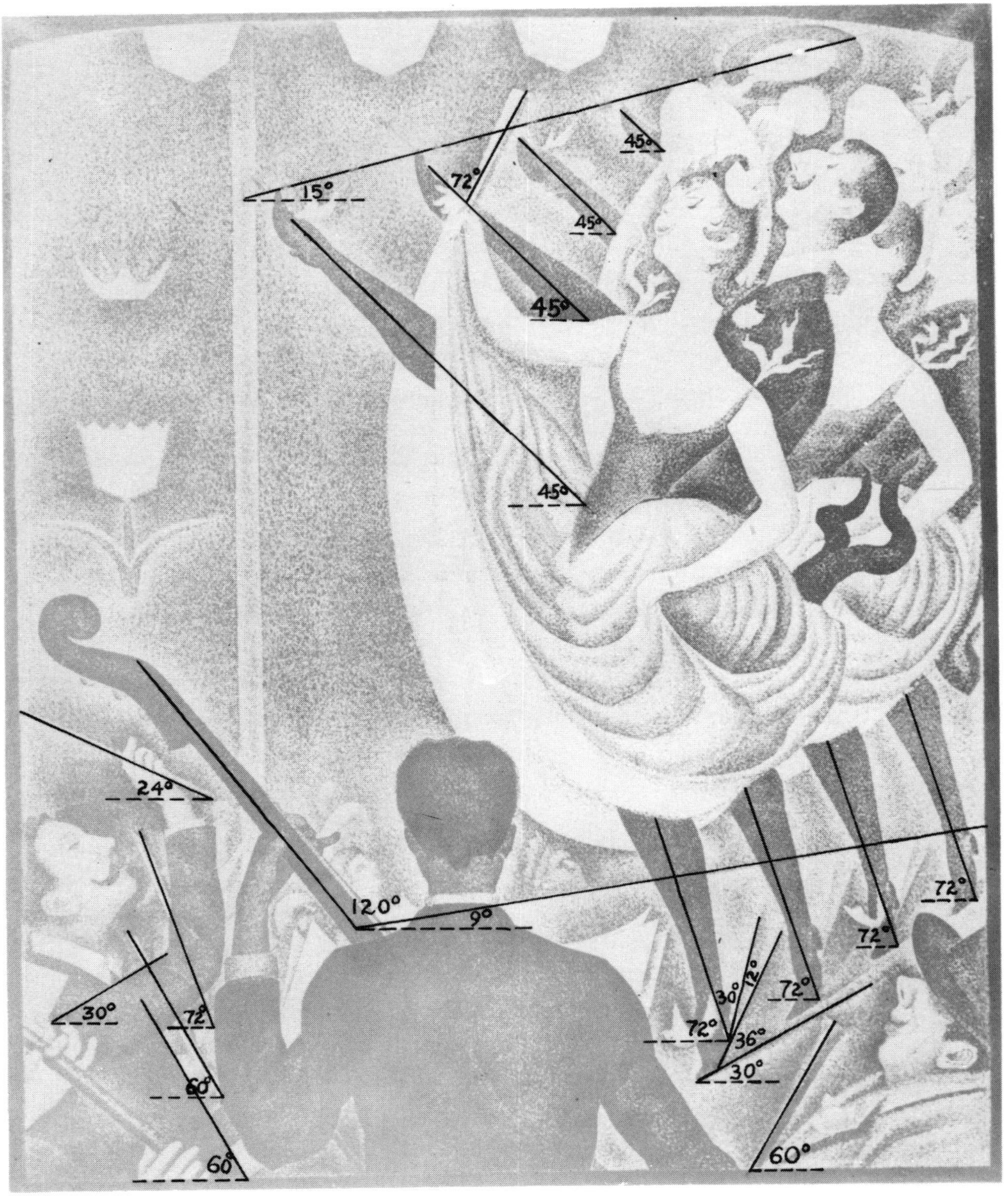

Figure 68. Angular Measurements in *Le Chahut*.

This aspect of Seurat's art has also been studied by Dorra, who observed that the raised legs of the dancers were parallel to a set of 45-degree diagonal axes extending from lower right to upper left, and that parts of the figures were parallel to diagonals of the same angle extending from lower left to upper right.[87] However, there are many angles other than 45 degrees that occur in *Le Chahut*, and when measured with the esthetic protractor, they too will be found to be harmonious. These have been diagrammed in Figure 68, which shows that angles of 72 degrees (rhythmic number of 5), 60 degrees (rhythmic number of 6), and 30 degrees (rhythmic number of 12) appear frequently. In addition, some of the smaller angles in the painting, of 24, 15, 12, and 9 degrees, are equally rhythmical according to Henry's theories.

To the characteristic gaiety of the color and linear directions in *Le Chahut*, Seurat added a corresponding treatment of value in which, quantitatively, more tones are taken from the upper end of the value scale than from the middle or lower end, thus creating a light "dominant." This effect occurs partly because the chief hues of the painting — pink, orange, and yellow-orange — are intrinsically quite light in tone when plotted on the value scale (cf. Figure 2, page 7). True, there are some medium and dark values, but these do not seriously threaten the dominance of the lighter tones.

In sum, Seurat appears to have followed in *Le Chahut* Henry's formulae for obtaining rhythmical relationships between colors and lines, but applied the theory of expression based on the correspondence between color, line, and value that he (Seurat) had articulated in his letter to Beaubourg. The painting corresponds much more closely to the principles of matching colors and linear directions proposed by the artist in this letter than it does to the theory of correspondences devised by Henry.

## Le Cirque

In his next, and last, major painting, *Le Cirque* (Figure 65, page 222), Seurat repeated many of the same expressive devices used in *Le Chahut*, but in some ways, as we shall see, he followed Henry's ideas more explicitly. The major local colors of *Le Cirque* are taken from the dynamogenous zone of Henry's color circle: they are red, red-orange, orange, yellow-orange and yellow. While the first two colors are used here and there, yellow and yellow-orange are actually the dominant hues of the picture. The color of the light, yellow-orange, also falls in the dynamogenous zone, and, as in *Le Chahut*, ensures the presence of a warm, gay tonality. The only other hue that contributes to the general color harmony is blue, which serves as the local color of the clothing of many of the male figures. In addition, blue dots are scattered rather freely throughout the composition, especially in parts that recede into depth, and thus (as in *Les Poseuses* and *La Parade*) aid in creating the effect of atmosphere and function decoratively in the color harmony of the painting. And, as we might expect, blue is also used in the shadows and serves as a complementary "reaction" of the yellow-orange light. (For a diagram of the hue relationships in *Le Cirque*, see Figure 69.)

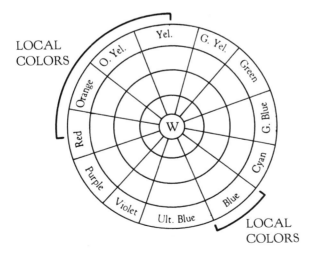

Figure 69. Diagram of Color Relationships in *Le Cirque*.

In addition, there are many diagonals and verticals placed above horizontals, as well as "V"-shaped configurations, which contribute to the gaiety of the painting. Rather than attempt to point them out verbally, the writer has represented the upward-moving lines on a schematic diagram of the linear structure of *Le Cirque* (Figure 70). It should be observed that very few lines — for example, those described by the ringmaster at the right — contradict the "dominant" of ascending lines by falling below the horizontal.

Seurat used upward-slanting lines once again in the faces of the spectators and performers to accentuate the gay mood of the scene, thus reflecting in *Le Cirque*, as in *Le Chahut*, the influence of Humbert de Superville's theories. If the faces of the audience are examined carefully, a close correlation between their physiognomy and Humbert's drawings (Figure 56, page 201) will be found: from an implied central axis bisecting the front view of the face, short diagonal lines corresponding to the eyes, nose, and mouth rise obliquely to the left and right, creating an undeniable effect of gaiety. And as in *Le Chahut*, Seurat reinforced the effect of gaiety, or dynamogeny, by placing three of the four main performers in positions requiring a maximum expenditure of energy: the arms of the clown in the foreground are lifted upward; the arms of the *equestrienne* are raised; and even the tumbler in his upside-down position flings his legs upward, defying gravity. Only in the ringmaster at the far right are the limbs placed in a downward position, thus serving as an element of contrast to the three figures at the left.

Finally, it should be noted that the value scheme of *Le Cirque* is also gay, following Seurat's theories: that is, there is a dominance of light tones over dark ones. The light "dominant" here is even more pronounced than in *Le Chahut* because Seurat added large quantities of white to the painting, particularly in the horse, the wide curve describing the edge of the ring, and the horizontal bands of the grandstands.

In *Le Cirque*, even more than *Le Chahut*, Seurat distributed his colors so that they correspond to the scheme of linear directions in

Figure 70. Linear Structure of *Le Cirque*.

the painting. The dominant hues, which range from red to yellow, clearly fall in the dynamogenous zone (the upper right-hand quarter) of Henry's chromatic circle (cf. Figure 59, page 206). The picture, too, is dominated by linear movements from lower left to upper right, such as the axis of the *équestrienne* and the curtain at the doorway at the right. Even the band representing the edge of the circus ring rises from lower left to upper right, thus reinforcing the dynamogenous character of the painting. The chief hues of *Le Cirque*, then, correspond rather closely to the direction of most of the lines, as plotted on Henry's circle, though they are not matched to specific colors as they were in parts of *Les Poseuses*.

Henry's impact may also be felt in the angular relationships between the major axes of the painting. Dorra has pointed out that, if the surface of *Le Cirque* is examined closely, an underlying compositional grid of horizontal, vertical, and diagonal lines may be detected.[88] Many of the forms in the painting are parallel to the network of diagonal guide lines that, as in *Le Chahut*, are consistently tilted at angles of 45 degrees, which the scientist said were harmonious.[89] Dorra also observed that several of the major axes were canted at 30- and 60-degree angles (which again are rhythmical according to Henry), and cited as examples the tangent to the parapet at the far left and the figure of the *équestrienne*.[90] In addition, many of the smaller angles appear to have been determined by Henry's system, as tested by the esthetic protractor in combination with his tables of rhythmic numbers. For the sake of convenience, our measurements of these smaller angles, along with the major ones, have been recorded in Figure 71. While some of our results duplicate Dorra's findings, we have been able to point out the exact location of these angles in the painting, and additional harmonious angles of 6, 9, 18, 36, and 72 degrees have been discovered. (These are based, respectively, on the following rhythmic numbers established by Henry: 60, 40, 20, 10, and 5.)

Because of the close correspondence between linear directions, colors, and values in arriving at a common goal — the expression of gaiety — *Le Cirque* is a better example than *Le Chahut* of the

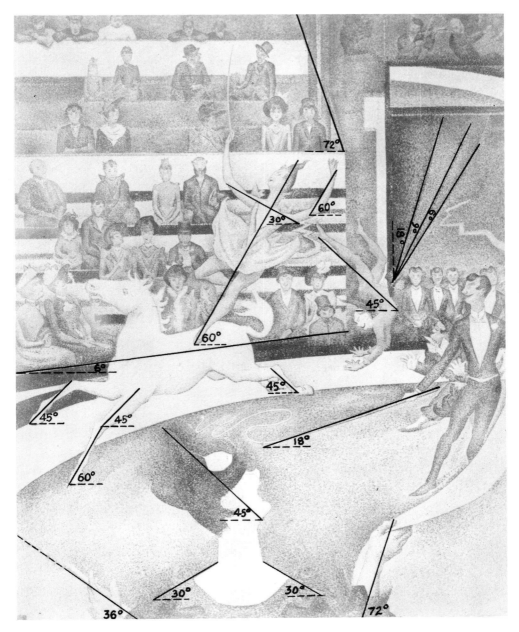

Figure 71. Angular Measurements in *Le Cirque*.

strict application of Charles Henry's precepts. Considering that Seurat's initial presentation of his theory by Christophe and the artist's letter to Beaubourg were the products, respectively, of the spring and summer of 1890, we must admit the possibility that he may have begun to develop new esthetic ideas in *Le Cirque* that had not yet been committed to writing — ideas that were more directly inspired by Henry. It may be suggested here that, while the Beaubourg letter coincides in content and date with *Le Chahut* (which was executed in 1889–1890), the esthetic theories that Seurat followed in *Le Cirque* had not yet been fully articulated because the artist's career was terminated suddenly by his death on March 29, 1891. But if we can agree with reports from his friends, we may assume that his theories were in a state of constant change.[91] Thus even the Beaubourg letter, which we have shown to be especially applicable to his work of 1888–1890, may already have become somewhat obsolete by 1891 as a result of Seurat's development of new esthetic concepts during the last few months of his life.

In the foregoing analysis of Seurat's later theories, their sources, and their application in painting we have, by choice, stressed the scientific and mathematical aspects of his thought. The writer realizes that to emphasize these elements, at the expense of Seurat's intuitive side, is to do the painter an injustice. To compensate in part for this imbalance we shall attempt, in the first part of the next chapter, to reconstruct his attitude toward the roles he believed scientific theories, vision, and intuition should play in the creative process. The latter part of the following chapter will be devoted to a summary of the nature of Seurat's "science" and its contribution to his art.

# 5

# Seurat and Science

THE NEO-IMPRESSIONIST STYLE
Seurat created in 1884–1886 was not, as some writers have
assumed, the result of slavishly following scientific treatises at the
expense of the visual perception of nature. We have seen that his
optical sensibilities were highly developed and that such texts
served primarily to guide him in making his pictures operate
according to the laws governing light and color in the physical
world. Because Seurat distrusted the instinctive, "romantic"
elements of the Impressionists' approach, he turned for assistance
to scientific studies of the very phenomena these painters had
examined perceptually. The scientists, of course, did not confine
themselves exclusively to observation but attempted to arrive at
general laws, the validity of which they demonstrated through
controlled laboratory experiments. In this connection, one of the
most perplexing questions facing contemporary critics of Seurat's
work concerned the degree to which he subordinated art to
science. As a result of exhibiting *La Grande Jatte* before the public
in 1886 and 1887, he was attacked by many writers for relying
unduly on scientific formulae in the conception and execution of
the painting. This was certainly an understandable reaction, if one

considers the apparent mechanical quality of his technique and the aura of scientific certitude about his theories, as publicized by Fénéon's articles and his booklet *Les Impressionnistes en 1886*. Indeed, we discovered in our analysis of *La Grande Jatte* — not to mention *Une Baignade* — that the artist did in fact rely, to a considerable degree, on scientific and semiscientific sources at this time. Thus the following central question must be posed: what was the relationship between scientific theories, vision, and intuition in Seurat's creative process during the first, or chromo-luminarist, phase of Neo-Impressionism?

From writings by his close friends, especially Fénéon, we hear repeatedly that science was used primarily as a means of guiding and controlling his highly developed optical sensibilities. In the course of this study, too, it has been found that, rather than closeting himself in his studio and working according to some mathematical or chemical formula, Seurat often painted out of doors and recorded his sensations spontaneously almost in an Impressionist manner in 1884–1885. And from some of the witness accounts cited earlier, we know that the artist was capable of acute perception of nature's phenomena. Further evidence of his optical sensitivity to the world surrounding him may be found in several of his letters to Signac.

From Honfleur, where he had gone to paint during the summer of 1886, Seurat wrote the following to Signac on June 25: "If you find Les Andelys colored, I see the Seine — gray water, almost undefinable, even in brightest sun with blue sky, at least during the last few days."[1] This brief excerpt certainly hints at his consciousness of the character of light and color as perceived in nature and suggests, too, that he was aware of changes in the weather. At the beginning of the summer at Honfleur, Seurat appears to have worked freely from nature in order to acquaint himself with his subject, inasmuch as he stated in the same letter: "The weather has been good for five days. . . . Up to now I have only done [oil] sketches in order to acclimatize myself."[2] On July 5, 1886, he wrote again to Signac: "The wind and consequently the clouds have bothered me these last few days. The stability of the first days surely ought to return." [3] To anyone familiar with the letters of Monet and Pissarro of the late seventies and early eighties, this complaint about the troublesome instability of the weather may sound as though it could have been written by either of these Impressionist painters; it is certainly not the statement of a "scientific" artist who evolved his style only by consulting treatises on physics and optics. And in closing this same letter Seurat wrote: "Let's go get drunk on light *once more, it's consoling*." [4] In this enthusiastic outburst we have in concise form Seurat's dominating interest at this time — to go outside and become immersed in light.

In these excerpts, there is considerable evidence testifying to Seurat's well-developed optical sensibilities, the importance of which his friend Fénéon pointed out in his remarks on the Neo-Impressionists' method:

> These painters are accused of subordinating art to science. They only make use of scientific facts to direct and perfect the education of their eye and to control the exactness of their vision. Professor O. N. Rood has furnished them with precious discoveries. . . . But Mr. X can read optical treatises forever and he will never paint *La Grande Jatte*. Between his courses at Columbia College, Mr. Rood, whose artistic acumen and erudition seem nil to us, paints: it must be wretched. The truth of the matter is that the Neo-Impressionist method demands an exceptionally delicate eye: all those clever people, who hide their visual incompetency with dexterous niceties, will flee, frightened, from its dangerous integrity. This kind of painting is accessible only to *painters*. [5]

In the same vein, Seurat's friend Émile Verhaeren wrote: "Seurat is depicted as a scholar, an alchemist, etc., and what more I wonder? However, he only makes use of scientific experiments for controlling his vision. Once the painting is finished, one does the proof, as for a problem. What's wrong with this?" [6] Here again we have a statement to the effect that the artist was not being carried away by scientific theories, but that they were used merely to guide his vision. And on the Neo-Impressionists' derivation of principles of color from Chevreul and Rood, Signac observed: "There is indeed a science of color, easy and simple, which all should learn and the knowledge of which would do away with so many foolish judgments. . . . These laws of color can be learned in several hours. They are contained in a few pages by Chevreul and Rood. The eye, guided by them, has only to perfect itself." [7] Although he underestimated the extent of Seurat's debt to Chevreul and Rood, Signac, like Fénéon and Verhaeren, regarded scientific laws of color as a means of perfecting the artist's vision, not as a substitute for optical sensibility.

During the first, or chromo-luminarist, phase of Neo-Impressionism Seurat and his friends believed that if they studied the laws governing the behavior of color proposed by modern physics and at the same time observed their subject closely, they could produce pictures that actually duplicated nature's mode of operation and would thus automatically surpass the Impressionists at their avowed purpose. But between 1887 and 1891, Seurat became much less concerned with naturalistic values and turned increasingly to the problem of conveying emotions through more abstract pictorial means. At this time, as we have seen, the artist directed his interest to theoretical sources dealing with questions of harmony, rhythm, and expression, and had succeeded in incorporating ideas derived from them in such paintings as *Le Chahut* and *Le Cirque*. This brings us to a second question: to what extent was Seurat ruled by the theoretical texts discussed in the preceding chapter, and to what degree did he transcend them?

Some critics who did not know him well complained that he went too far in regulating his later works through didactic "scientific" formulae. However, several friends of the artist who had discussed with him the role he thought scientific theories (especially those of Henry) should play provide a more reasonable answer to this question. Apropos of the influence of Henry's ideas on Seurat, Kahn wrote: "This furnished Seurat with only the basis, the exact and demonstrated basis that he needed, permitting him to arrive at his final synthesis, which became apparent from his Crotoy marines and was affirmed in his canvases *Le Chahut* and *Le Cirque*."[8] The notion that Henry's scientific theories of expression were not followed slavishly by the artist was also echoed by Fénéon: "Seurat, who was acquainted with the works of Charles Henry, took pleasure in formulating a philosophy of concordances between the character of tones (dark, light . . .), of hues (cool, warm . . .), and of lines (descending, ascending . . .); and his theories were always subject to the finest painterly genius."[9] The same writer, in an important article about Signac, discussed the impact of Henry's ideas in terms that might apply equally well to Seurat, considering the congruity of the artistic aims of the two painters between 1886 and 1891:

> From the start he has subordinated each of his compositions to the charac-
> ter of a dominant direction and accentuates the supremacy of the latter by
> the contrast of accessory lines: more by intuition than by principle.
> Having collaborated on [Henry's] *L'Éducation du sens des formes* (in press),
> *L'Éducation du sens des couleurs* (in press), he is certainly acquainted with the
> flourishing theory of living reactions, and knows, as everyone does, the
> close bond which unites angles and rhythmic measurements to the numbers
> $2^n$, to the prime numbers of the form $2^n + 1$, and to the products of these
> numbers. But he has not become slave to these engaging mathematics;
> he knows well that a work of art is inextricable. Moreover, nowhere did
> Henry claim to furnish artists with the means of mechanically creating a
> somewhat complex beauty. He said: every direction is symbolic.[10]

In this passage we find, again, that the mathematical formulae and theory of linear directions proposed by Henry cannot produce beauty by themselves; they serve merely as the "basis" through which the artist can insure the expression of certain specific emotional states or create pictorial harmony.

Furthermore, if Henry's ideas about esthetics and Seurat's letter to Beaubourg are examined, both will readily be seen to be couched in the most general terms: they deal essentially with *principles* of expression and harmony rather than with any concrete and specific instructions about producing works of art.

Even Henry's most mathematical pronouncements are geared to the measurement of intervals between lines and colors on an abstract level; he provided no instructions about the way in which these principles should be applied in paintings. The same may be said about the contents of Seurat's letter to Beaubourg: it merely deals with the raw materials, so to speak, of pictorial expression and harmony; no specific rules for the actual construction of the work of art are proposed.

Seurat's later theory of painting, as we tried to show in the previous chapter, was followed in determining the resultant emotional tone of *La Parade*, *Le Chahut*, and, to some degree, *Le Cirque*. At the same time, under Henry's influence, he also designed the compositional framework of these paintings according to the golden section ratio and arrived at rhythmic relationships between linear directions in *Le Chahut* and *Le Cirque* by measuring their angles with the *rapporteur esthétique*. But a glance at the diagrams made by the present writer to illustrate these elements will show that, taken by themselves, they are not works of art: they merely act, in Kahn's words, as "the exact and demonstrated basis" to ensure a specific expressive result or to guarantee pictorial harmony.

Fortunately, we have several important contemporary accounts of Seurat's personality and aims that shed further light on his attitude toward the role of theory in art. One of the most perceptive reports on the interaction between artistic intuition and scientific theory in his creative process was furnished by his friend Gustave Kahn, who wrote:

If he believed that a scientific esthetic cannot be entirely imposed upon a painter because there are intimate questions of art and even of artistic technique which the painter alone can evoke and resolve, he experienced the absolute need to found his theories on scientific truths. His intellect was not absolutely that of a born painter, a painter like Corot, happy to place pretty tones on a canvas. He had a mathematical and philosophic bent of mind, adapted to conceiving art in a form other than painting.

I will explain myself more clearly in saying that if certain painters and even good painters give the impression that they could be nothing but painters, Seurat was of those who give the impression, in short, of a more developed aptitude which leads them to devote themselves to the plastic arts, other cycles of human intelligence being reabsorbed in their faculties.[11]

In a similar vein, the Belgian poet Émile Verhaeren, who knew Seurat personally, wrote the following recollections shortly after the artist's death: "To hear Seurat explaining his work, confessing in front of his yearly exhibitions, was to follow a person of sincerity and to allow oneself to be won over by his persuasiveness. Calmly, with cautious gestures, his gaze never leaving you and his slow and uniform voice searching for slightly preceptorial words, he pointed out the results obtained, the clear certainties, what he called 'the basis.'"[12] Here the underlying foundation of Seurat's art is again referred to, recalling the term used by Kahn, as the "basis" — "*la base.*" Continuing on this subject, Verhaeren remarked:

> Not only did he never begin his paintings without knowing where he was going, but his concern went even beyond their success as individual works. They had no great meaning for him if they did not prove some rule, some truth of art, or some conquest of the unknown. . . . Perhaps he thought that the scientific and positivist spirit of his time demanded within the realm of the imagination a more clear and solid tactic for the conquest of beauty. He wanted to inscribe this tactic point by point at the bottom of each of his paintings, and he often succeeded. And that is why each year a great work appeared, more theoretical perhaps than simply beautiful, but magnificent in truth sought out and victorious will![13]

It is interesting to note that Seurat's conception of method, or theoretical "basis," described in Verhaeren's account was one that could be reduced to terms so simple that they might be inscribed at the bottom of each canvas, again confirming our hypothesis that Seurat's "science" involved the application of general guiding principles, not elaborate formulae governing the total creative process.

Finally, on a more personal level, de Wyzewa's recollections provide a picture of the artist's temperament close to that found in the accounts just quoted:

> From the first evening I met him, I discovered that his soul was also one of times past. . . . He believed in the power of theories, in the absolute value of methods, and in the continuance of revolutions. I was very happy to find in a corner of Montmartre such an admirable example of a race which I had supposed extinct, a race of painter-theorists who combine idea and practice, unconscious fantasy and deliberate effort. Yes, I very clearly felt Seurat's kinship with the Leonardos, the Dürers, the Poussins. . . . I add that his research dealt with the same matters, in my opinion, that can occupy an artist. He wanted to make a more logical art out of painting, more systematic, where less room would be left for chance effect. Just as there are rules of technique, he also wanted there to be [rules] for the conception, composition, and expression of subjects, understanding well that personal inspiration would suffer no more from these rules than from others.[14]

De Wyzewa understood better than most of his contemporaries the image in which Seurat probably saw himself: that of a painter-theorist like Leonardo da Vinci or Poussin — both of whom, significantly, played major roles as progenitors of the academic tradition in France, and whose achievements were admired by several of the authors Seurat read. And, like these two masters, he relied on carefully formulated theories to guide his artistic imagination.

Seurat's allegiance to the academic tradition, as manifested in the early nineteenth century by Ingres, was also observed by Verhaeren: "As he appeared to us, he most often brought Ingres to mind. He had already molded certain of his ideas into axioms, he theorized willingly and loved doctrines, fixed precepts, and sure and indisputable means. But he was colder and more austere than the author of the *Odalisque*."[15] The connection established here between Seurat and Ingres on the basis of their devotion to rational laws and theories in art is all the more significant when we consider that at the École des Beaux-Arts Seurat had been a devoted admirer of Ingres and had studied under one of the master's pupils, Heinrich Lehmann. Indeed, it may be that Seurat's devotion to an approach in painting that owes much to the academic point of view prompted his friend Pissarro to write: "Seurat is of the École des Beaux-Arts; he is impregnated by it." [16]

During the last three or four years of his life, Seurat did, in fact, revive some of the tenets of the academic tradition against which he had rebelled between 1880 and 1886. In resurrecting these tenets he turned, as Sutter had urged,[17] to some of the sources that remained undefiled by the corrupt teachings of the École des Beaux-Arts. But, in addition to following the original academic conception of the role of discipline and law in painting, Seurat also took advantage in a nonacademic way of many of the discoveries made by his contemporaries in the physics of light and color, visual perception, and the psychology of the affective value of color, tone, and line. In realizing that it was imperative to turn to the science of his own day rather than merely imitating the methods inherited from the distant past, he probably saw his own position, as de Wyzewa suggested, as being analogous to that of the painter-theorists of the Renaissance and Baroque periods who used — or occasionally originated — the most advanced "science" of their time.

The observations that we have made concerning Seurat's application of scientific and semiscientific laws and principles to his paintings, along with the foregoing remarks by his friends, bring us to the conclusion that instinct and intuition, on one hand, and a highly rationalized theory of art on the other, were balanced in his creative process from 1886 to 1891, the year of his death. Significantly, just such a relationship was advocated by Sutter, Blanc, and Delacroix, who, in different ways, believed in regulating instinct through proven theories but who, at the same time, favored the independence of the artist's imagination and creative genius. Even Henry, the most scientific of all the writers read by Seurat, admitted the limitations of his own discipline and in the concluding paragraph of his *Rapporteur esthétique* stated: "It is not to be asserted that I wish to substitute the mechanism of an instrument for the creation of the artist. Genius is inimitable, for it is expressed not only by visible rhythms but by an infinite number of more or less invisible rhythms. . . ." [18]

In the course of this study we have seen that Seurat conceived of science in several different ways and that he continually sought to improve it, with the result that he turned to a number of different texts at various stages in his development. It will be appropriate, therefore, to conclude with a summary of his changing conceptions of science and their sources. At the beginning of his career, he studied carefully Charles Blanc's *Grammaire des arts du dessin* and Chevreul's *De la loi du contraste simultané*, both of which dealt with the problems of obtaining harmony through contrast and analogy, and demonstrated ways in which colors could be made to appear more intense by juxtaposition to their complementaries. Blanc also enunciated two principles that were to be of paramount importance for Seurat's art: gradation and optical mixture. His "science," however, was based mainly on his knowledge of Delacroix, Chevreul, and the "oriental" rules of coloring that had been handed down by artists and craftsmen from generation to generation. In short, though Blanc's book was published in 1867, it was based more on painters' recipes than on recent developments in physics and optics.

Unlike Blanc, Chevreul was trained as a chemist and was generally respected in scientific circles. But though he lived until 1889, his *De la loi du contraste simultané*, which was published early in his career — in 1839 — was never revised by its author. From the standpoint of new developments in physics in the 1860s and 1870s, Chevreul's book was antiquated as a scientific treatise; yet he was still hailed widely in the 1880s for discovering a number of important principles governing color behavior. It should be kept in mind, too, that the book was not conceived as a contribution to the discipline of physics or chemistry, but rather was designed as a manual for painters, designers, and decorators.

The systems of color harmony advocated by Chevreul and Blanc, while proposed as general laws, cannot be regarded as entirely scientific in origin, in the sense of being derived exclusively from the disciplines of physics or optics. As we have seen, both authors shared the idea that complementary colors, as well as those close to each other on the chromatic circle (analogous colors), were harmonious. This concept of harmony, however, had been understood instinctively by artists since the Renaissance. In the nineteenth century, as Blanc pointed out, Delacroix brought this system to a high point of development, first by studying the principles of coloring utilized by "oriental" artists and then by following Chevreul's precepts. Thus the laws of color harmony proposed by Chevreul and Blanc, while rigorous in nature, tend to be codifications of principles already discovered independently by painters and decorators. Moreover, neither Chevreul nor Blanc used the scientific instruments available in their day to investigate the phenomena of color and light, but instead relied on empirical observation — called the "experimental method" by Chevreul — in arriving at their conclusions. There is, particularly in Chevreul's system of arranging colors, a predetermined, "classical" quality that may be seen in the regularity of subdivisions of the chromatic circle and its radii (Figure 7, page 22) that resulted from a dogmatic and overly arbitrary approach to the problem of color on the author's part.

While Seurat based much of his early color technique on the principles set forth by Blanc and Chevreul, their errors were pointed out in the writings of Rood and Henry. Chevreul, in particular, came under attack by Rood for arranging colors in an *a priori* fashion rather than placing them carefully on the color circle on the basis of data provided by physicists' instruments of measurement. Henry, too, insisted that the angular relationships between the radii of the color circle be determined with great care. Moreover, Rood and Henry demonstrated the incorrectness of Chevreul's and Blanc's conception of the mixture of colored light and countered with a definition of the difference between additive and subtractive mixture based on the experiments of Helmholtz and Maxwell — a definition that in its essentials is still accepted by color scientists today. We have seen that Seurat understood these principles of additive mixture of colored light as a result of studying Rood's *Théorie scientifique des couleurs* and applied them rigorously in *La Grande Jatte*, *Les Poseuses*, and *La Parade*.

With his discovery of Rood's book, Seurat's theory took on an increasingly scientific character. The American scientist approached many of the same matters discussed by Chevreul and Blanc — division of color, optical mixture, contrast, gradation, and color harmony — but based his conclusions on the rigorous measurements of color phenomena with instruments developed by the disciplines of physics and optics. Thus, while Chevreul and Blanc proposed a number of general principles of color behavior, Rood gave more specific instructions to artists about how color should be handled, particularly with the aim of achieving a high degree of luminosity. And in addition to basing his book on color theories current in his day, he performed a valuable service for Seurat in demonstrating precisely how modern physics could — and should — be applied in the art of painting.

We have also seen that Rood was concerned with the question of color harmony and that in *Une Baignade* and *La Grande Jatte* Seurat followed some of his recommendations. But in this matter Rood was far less scientific in approach than he was elsewhere in his *Text-Book of Color*. The chapter on color combinations, for example, is comprised largely of a summary of agreeable arrangements proposed by Chevreul and the Viennese physiologist Ernst Wilhelm von Brücke (the latter's suggestions, in turn, were not based on any system of physical measurement, but again on personal choice). Rood's own suggestions for harmony stem from his observation of nature and an analysis of colors used by the old masters. Thus as one of the major influences on Seurat between

1883 and 1886, Rood advocated a system of color harmony based on esthetic judgments that he and several other writers had formulated in a rather arbitrary fashion. This point is mentioned here in order to underline our conclusion that, while many aspects of Seurat's technique were grounded in modern physics, his conception of harmony can hardly be called scientific, in the strict sense of the word, stemming as it does from a wide variety of traditional artistic and theoretical sources. In one respect, however, Rood's advice on the subject of color harmony may be regarded as scientific: he provided Seurat with a contrast-diagram (Figures 14 and 15, pages 40 and 41, respectively) on which the placement of complementary colors that harmonized with each other had been determined by controlled laboratory experiments.

So far we have found that two rather different types of "science" were studied by the artist: the first, as exemplified by Chevreul's work, was a result of abstracting general laws from a large number of experiences of color behavior as observed in nature and in the composition of tapestries; Blanc's writings, too, fall in this category, with the difference that through personal contact with Delacroix he had based some of his theories on color recipes that the artist had pointed out to him. While Chevreul and Blanc exerted a strong influence on Seurat's early work, he entered a second, more rigorously scientific phase in his painting and theory between 1884 and 1886, largely through the application of the principles presented in Rood's *Théorie scientifique des couleurs*. This book, as we have indicated, was a compendium of most of the important recent developments in the physics of light and color, and it provided Seurat with a theoretical and technical foundation for the style that is best described as "chromo-luminarism."

Between 1887 and 1891, however, he adopted another type of science, partly as a result of his contact with Charles Henry. While the latter's writings indicate that he was conversant with most of the sources on which Seurat's theory of chromo-luminarism was based, Henry's major contribution was in stimulating the artist's interest in the expressive possibilities of color and line. Henry's theories, in turn, were based on several different scientific disciplines. First, he attempted to prove his hypothesis that different sensations produce measurable physiological reactions in the human organism by citing experiments conducted by such pioneers in psychology as Féré, Wundt, Fechner, and Helmholtz. Second, he relied on Rood and Helmholtz, among others, for their discoveries relating to the physical laws of color and light. Equally important, however, was Henry's use of algebra and geometry: he recommended the use of a formula based on Gauss's theory, and the golden section, as devices that would enable artists to guarantee harmonious results in any given visual configuration. Thus, experimental psychology, physiology, mathematics, and physics were all drawn upon by Henry's encyclopedic mind in creating a universal system of harmony based on the achievements of modern science.

We have seen that, in the matter of expression through formal elements, Seurat's theory and practice were heavily influenced by Henry, whose writings synthesized the four disciplines just enumerated; but as far as we can determine, Seurat did not, except in the case of physics, turn directly to the sources upon which Henry based his theories. Thus, the scientist undoubtedly opened new horizons for the artist, particularly by embodying in his books and demonstrations the discoveries made by the nascent discipline of experimental psychology, which proved scientifically the propositions that Seurat had studied in the less rigorous theories of expression formulated by Humbert de Superville, Blanc, and Sutter. These three writers, however, did provide valuable lessons for Seurat and contributed in part to his esthetic, as stated in his letter to Beaubourg. This third type of "science" — geared to the expression of specific feelings through configurations of color, value, and line — may thus be added to the two already mentioned. It should be kept in mind that the first and second phases of Seurat's use of science, which resulted in his chromo-luminarist style, were not *replaced* by the third; rather, this was added as a modifying element that further enriched his total theory of art.

Seurat's belief that the underlying basis of painting should be a configuration of abstract elements that might convey a variety of emotions became increasingly popular among artists in the late 1880s and early 1890s and in essence parallels the theories developed at this time by the Symbolist painters. There are, of course, important differences between Seurat's later views and those held by the Symbolists, but they have in common the conviction that a painting is essentially an abstraction that can communicate feelings through the inherent evocative power of visual forms. In his concern with specific emotional states and the pictorial means by which they could be conveyed, Seurat entered a phase of his development that, in spite of the name of the movement he instituted — Neo-Impressionism — had little to do with Impressionism in theory or practice. From a scientific "reform" of Impressionism, his major interest from 1884 to 1887, he gradually devised a more conceptual, schematic, and symbolic art that, with its accompanying theory of expression, was to have many implications for twentieth-century painting. In the first stage of his career, then, Seurat brought to a final point of development the artistic innovations of the Impressionists; in the second phase, which was cut short in 1891 by his fatal illness, his art and theory pointed prophetically to the future.

# Epilogue

This book was limited purposely to a discussion of Seurat's art and theories. No attempt was made in the text to view his achievements in the light of art contemporary with him or to assess his influence on later painting. To have done so would have required the writing of another book. Still, in the following pages we might try to hint at some of the wider implications of Seurat's art and theories for his own time and for subsequent generations.

In his own time, the work of Paul Cézanne immediately suggests itself for comparison. An artist who shared Seurat's dissatisfaction with Impressionism during the 1880s, Cézanne wished to reassert in his paintings the geometric structure that he found implicit in nature. This he did by organizing his pictorial designs with the utmost rigor and by accentuating the geometric form of solid objects. Yet like the Seurat of *La Grande Jatte* and *Les Poseuses*, he also insisted on the importance of the artist's immediate sensations of the visual world. Both painters, then, imposed a new sense of order over an Impressionist framework, though they differed in the way they conceived of this order.

Between 1884 and 1891, Seurat, too, consciously structured his paintings far more than had the Impressionists. As we have seen, he constantly refined them in the studio; their final form was not dictated solely by the visual data presented by nature. And as Dorra has pointed out, the compositions of his major paintings were based, in varying degrees, on the golden section ratio, a geometric system of proportion that was anathema to the Impressionists. Significantly, Seurat's rigorously planned designs, like Cézanne's, were to influence profoundly the Cubist and abstract art of the twentieth century.

Seurat also effected a reform of the Impressionists' method of representing color and light. Like Cézanne, he first passed through an Impressionist phase in which a premium was placed on accumulating a multitude of color sensations and recording them on canvas. We might regard this as part of an "analytical" stage in his art, where repeated observation and experiment were performed as a means of reaching some valid generalizations about the behavior of color and light in nature. In his search for "a formula for optical painting" and, later, for an all-encompassing theory of art, Seurat subscribed to the methods of inductive reasoning, a mainstay of so much nineteenth-century scientific thought. But once he had developed a theory of art based on continued observation of nature, of paintings, and the study of theoretical texts, his method became more deductive in character. That is, he began to approach the matter of picture making with a hypothesis already in hand, which he developed into a theory that could be applied to a variety of individual cases or problems ranging from indoor subjects under artificial light to quiet evening landscapes along the Channel coast.

By 1887, Seurat had formulated a large part of his theory of painting, which liberated him from continual reference to nature's data. By applying this theory, he was able to create light and color on the canvas synthetically, according to a system he had found at work consistently in nature. In terms of color, then, his later canvases are similar to nature primarily in their mode of operation;

they are no longer a record of a total visual impression received by the artist's eye, as was the case with the Impressionists. In his later paintings, Seurat also turned to arbitrarily chosen hues that were close enough to nature in their appearance but which were abstractly related to each other according to the logic of his system of harmony. And as we have seen in his work after 1887, the surfaces of his canvases become more and more detached from the anatomy of his subject matter; they seem to be impartial screens or grids whose transmission of light and color depends on their own internal laws. In this context, the painter's brushwork becomes decorative and patternistic; it does not function any longer as a bridge between the tactile experience of the subject and the work of art.

We have also seen that, just as Seurat earlier had formulated a major set of principles or laws for dealing with color and light, he later formulated another set which he could use to guide the expressive content of a number of specific paintings executed after 1887. By working in this way his method once again echoed that of the deductive approach in the physical sciences. Passing thus from analytical, inductive procedures in the earlier part of his career to a more deductive method after completing *La Grande Jatte*, Seurat mirrored an important change in scientific methodology in France that began to take place during the last third of the nineteenth century. This change was due largely to the influence of the noted physiologist Claude Bernard, whose pioneering *Introduction à l'étude de la médecine expérimentale* (Paris, 1865) proclaimed the advantages of the deductive method in scientific reasoning. Perhaps it is no accident that Seurat's "deductive" approach to artistic problems matured after he became a friend of Charles Henry, who had served earlier as preparator in Claude Bernard's laboratory.

More can be said, too, about the relationship of Seurat's ideas to those of the Symbolists, particularly during the late 1880s and early 1890s. Although alienated from the leading Symbolist painter, Paul Gauguin, after 1886, Seurat was in close touch with many of the Symbolist writers as well as with Charles Henry, who influenced their literary techniques. Indeed, several Symbolist authors regarded his achievement in painting as being quite close to their aims in literature. It is not surprising, then, to find that Seurat's theories have something in common with Symbolist views on the nature and role of artistic creation. In his later work, he, like the Symbolists, liberated himself from natural appearances in favor of the expression of interior states of feeling. And like the Symbolists, Seurat tried to devise for these feelings pictorial equivalents that would communicate them directly to the spectator. These interests are clearly parallel to the "theory of correspondences" that fascinated the Symbolist painters Gauguin, Sérusier, Denis, and their literary spokesman, Albert Aurier. As Sérusier wrote in his *ABC de la peinture* (Paris, 1921, p. 21): "Thoughts and moral qualities can only be represented by formal equivalents. It is the faculty of perceiving these correspondences which makes the artist."

Seurat and the Symbolists, however, disagreed about the way in which one should determine these "correspondences." The former remained scientific in approach, relying largely on the authority of experimental psychology to confirm his theories; the Symbolists, on the other hand, almost always allowed their own intuition or subjective experience to suggest formal equivalents for their states of feeling. (Although they were undoubtedly aware of scientific theories of expression, such as those promulgated by Charles Henry, most of the Symbolist painters rejected scientific systems in determining their art and theory.) Yet, in spite of their differences in approach, Seurat and the Symbolists clearly foreshadow the subjective, psychological interests manifested in art after 1900.

Seurat's relationship to Van Gogh remains to be explored in depth. We might note here that before their meeting in 1888, they had both studied Delacroix's work and Charles Blanc's writings and had come to many of the same conclusions about the phenomena of color and its expressive possibilities. After they met in Paris, Van Gogh's style underwent marked influence from Seurat's and Signac's work, though he soon forged ahead in his own individual way. Van Gogh always maintained an interest in the progress of Seurat's art, and it seems fair to assume that, though they were obviously different in temperament, Seurat and Van Gogh shared many of the same esthetic theories. Both, for example, were interested in pictorial means of intensifying and harmonizing hues and were concerned with the symbolism of color and line in their late work. And, like Van Gogh, Seurat discovered the artistic value of treating the canvas as an abstract pattern in its own right.

With Seurat's death in 1891, the inspiring force of the Neo-Impressionist movement was gone. Paul Signac tried to take his place and carry the burden of leadership alone; but without Seurat's genius, as theorist and painter, the movement could not maintain its initial momentum. Several members drifted away from the group in the 1890s, and the premises of Neo-Impressionism were increasingly challenged by the Symbolist painters. Perhaps the greatest loss was Camille Pissarro, who became disenchanted with the methods of Neo-Impressionism and attempted to return to his previous style of painting, so that he was no longer in a position to continue as a major supporter of the movement. In the early 1890s, then, the prospects for Neo-Impressionism looked rather bleak.

Some of the painters who had come under Seurat's influence in the 1880s, such as Van Rysselberghe and Petitjean, continued to pursue optical effects of light in a pointillist technique. Others — Lemmen and Luce, for example — modified this technique in favor of a looser, more Impressionist execution. It was Signac and Cross, however, who most successfully worked out the implications of Seurat's discoveries in the realm of color without merely imitating his style. In the 1890s and early 1900s, both painters enlarged the size of their brushstrokes and at the same time made their colors much purer and more intense than Seurat's. And in surface pattern and design they carried even further the abstraction implicit in his later paintings. Intuition and freedom from scientific laws, too, played a greater part in their creative process. As Signac wrote in his diary on September 1, 1895: "We leave the hard and useful period of analysis, when all our studies resembled one another, to enter into that of personal and varied creation."

Although eclipsed temporarily by other currents in painting during the 1890s, the freer and more personal Neo-Impressionism that Signac and Cross developed after Seurat's death became one of the leading *avant-garde* styles in the opening years of the twentieth century. Its popularity was undoubtedly reinforced by the publication of Signac's book *D'Eugène Delacroix au néo-impressionnisme* in 1899. Of the painters who were briefly influenced by Neo-Impressionism — Matisse, Kandinsky, Mondrian, and Braque (to mention only a few) — Matisse seems to have adopted the style most profitably. He had read Signac's book, which appeared serially in *La Revue blanche* in 1898. But more important, he worked with Signac and Cross at Saint Tropez in 1904, an experience that contributed significantly to the style that established his reputation as leader of Les Fauves in 1905.

Aspects of Seurat's achievement were carried further by still another *avant-garde* group of painters: the Italian Futurists. Prior to the advent of the Futurist movement, a version of Neo-Impressionism, called Divisionism, had grown up in Italy in the late 1880s and 1890s. Among its chief practitioners we may count Segantini, Previati, and Pellizza da Volpedo, who were kept in touch with Parisian developments by the painter and dealer Vittore Grubicy. The dynamic, pulsating side of Italian Divisionism, along with direct influence from Seurat's work, in turn served as the basis of the "first" style of Futurism about 1908–

1910. Practiced by Severini, Boccioni, Russolo, and Balla, this style was modified and partly supplanted around 1911 by Cubist influences and the expression of rapid movement.

What about the implications of Seurat's theories for later art? There is no evidence to indicate that any of his followers in the Neo-Impressionist group continued to develop his theories in their totality. True, a few of his former associates carried on experiments with certain specialized aspects of these theories: Petitjean studied optical effects; Hayet worked on the problem of color contrasts, making innumerable chromatic charts based on Chevreul; and Signac and Cross pursued a search for greater intensity and harmony of color. But few, if any, of Seurat's former colleagues extended his research on the predictable expressive qualities of formal elements. It remained for such major twentieth-century painters as Mondrian, Klee, and Kandinsky to follow the course that Seurat had mapped out in the late 1880s. If these three were not directly influenced by Seurat's theories of harmony and expression, they certainly shared his view that a rationally determined set of pictorial principles could help the artist communicate universal states of thought or feeling.

By virtue of the magnitude of his contribution, Seurat may rightfully be regarded as a major progenitor of twentieth-century art. Almost every important movement owes something, directly or indirectly, to his achievement. It should be obvious that he is an ancestor of many varieties of abstract art. Yet in his concern for the expression of interior states of feeling, along with his departure from naturalistic representation, he also foreshadows several varieties of twentieth-century Expressionism. Even his research into the psychological and physiological effects of color was carried on by some American abstract painters in the period after the Second World War. The Dadaists and Surrealists, however, seem to have been immune to his influence, undoubtedly because they promoted the irrational in art so avidly, in contrast to

Seurat's overtly rational method of approach. In view of his contribution to so many facets of modern art, it is regrettable that Seurat should have died so young. Had he lived well into the twentieth century, European and American painting might have benefited all the more from the influence of his fertile mind and brush.

# Notes

## INTRODUCTION

1. The contents of this volume were published serially in *La Revue blanche* in 1898 and in the *Revue populaire des beaux-arts* in 1898–1899; the first edition of the book was issued in 1899 (Éditions de *La Revue blanche*). The 1939 edition (Librairie Floury, Paris) will be referred to in this book.
2. Fortunately, much of Signac's diary for the period during which he wrote this book has been published. Entries for the following dates testify to the changes in his esthetic theories and his partial disillusionment with the Neo-Impressionist style before 1892: August 23, 1894; September 1, 1895; December 28, 1897; January 3, 1898; and March 11, 1898 ("Extraits du journal inédit de Paul Signac," *Gazette des beaux-arts*, XXXVI, July–September, 1949, pp. 97–128; XXIX, April, 1952, pp. 265–284). In his diary Signac mentioned his work on Delacroix as early as June 2, 1897; the manuscript was finished as of March 7, 1898.
3. Closely related to the growing differences between Seurat's style and Signac's after 1891 is the latter's desire to carve a niche for himself as a major contributor to the development of the Neo-Impressionist movement. Between 1886 and 1891, while Seurat was still alive, the majority of the critics correctly recognized him as the leader of the movement and relegated Signac to a secondary position. Although he admitted that Seurat was the originator of Neo-Impressionism (*D'Eugène Delacroix au néo-impressionnisme*, Paris, 1939, p. 72; also "Le Néo-impressionnisme — Documents," *Gazette des beaux-arts*, XI, January, 1934, p. 54), Signac tried to confer on himself as much credit as possible as "co-founder" of the movement.
4. In addition to consulting published sources, the writer has studied and taken notes on the collection of Seurat and Signac documents in the hands of Mme. Ginette Signac, Paul Signac's daughter. These include unpublished letters by Signac and other members of the Neo-Impressionist group; Signac's diary (large parts of which have been published); an unpublished catalogue of his own paintings compiled by Signac; drafts of theoretical statements by Seurat; and letters from Seurat to Signac, many of which were published by Henri Dorra and John Rewald in *Seurat, l'œuvre peint; biographie et catalogue critique*, Paris, 1959; and Seurat's and Signac's palettes. Another group of Seurat

documents is in the collection of César de Hauke; many of them were published in his *Seurat et son œuvre*, I, Paris, 1961 [1962]. Through his kindness, the author was permitted to read the proofs of this book in the summer of 1962 and to consult several documents in his collection which have not yet been published. One reason for the paucity of documentary information about Seurat's life and work is the fact that many important personal papers were burned by his family.

5. Robert Rey, *La Renaissance du sentiment classique*, Paris, 1931, pp. 95–137.
6. "The Evolution of Seurat's Style" by Henri Dorra in his and John Rewald's *Seurat*, pp. lxxxix–cvii.
7. These are *Georges Seurat*, New York, 1943 and 1946; *Georges Seurat*, Paris, 1948; *The History of Impressionism*, New York, 1946, rev. ed., 1961; *Post-Impressionism — from Van Gogh to Gauguin*, New York, 1956, 2nd ed., 1962; "Seurat: the Meaning of the Dots," *Art News*, XLVIII, April, 1949, pp. 24–27, 61–63; "Félix Fénéon," *Gazette des beaux-arts*, XXXII, July–August, 1947, pp. 45–62, XXIV, February, 1948, pp. 107–126; the chapter "La Vie et l'œuvre de Georges Seurat," in Dorra and Rewald, *op. cit.*, pp. xxxiii–lxxviii.
8. Rewald acknowledged Fénéon's assistance in verifying the text of *Georges Seurat*, New York, 1943, p. xix.
9. These are pp. 161–167 in his *Georges Seurat*, Paris, 1948; pp. 583–591 in *Post-Impressionism*; and pp. 287–301 in his and Dorra's *Seurat*.
10. Robert L. Herbert, "Seurat in Chicago and New York," *The Burlington Magazine*, C, May, 1958, pp. 146–155; and "Seurat and Puvis de Chavannes," *Yale University Art Gallery Bulletin*, XXV, October, 1959, pp. 22–29. Mr. Herbert discussed Seurat's early work in his unpublished doctoral dissertation ("Seurat: Paintings, Drawings, and Theory, 1875–1886," Yale University, 1957), but this was not available to me during the writing of the present book.
11. Roland Rood, *Color and Light in Painting* (ed. by George L. Stout), New York, 1941.
12. Gaetano Previati, *I principii scientifici del divisionismo*, 2nd ed., Torino, 1929.
13. Édouard Fer, *Solfège de la couleur*, Paris, 1954.
14. Henry G. Keller and J. J. R. MacLeod," The Application of the Physiology of Color Vision in Modern Art," *The Popular Science Monthly*, LXXXIII, November, 1913, pp. 450–465.
15. Richard F. Brown, "The Color Technique of Camille Pissarro," unpublished Ph.D. dissertation, Harvard University, 1952.
16. Kurt Badt, *Die Farbenlehre Van Goghs*, Köln, 1961.

17. J. Carson Webster, "The Technique of Impressionism: A Reappraisal," *College Art Journal*, IV, November, 1944, pp. 3–22.

18. Brown, *op. cit.*, pp. 11–14.

19. George M. Richter, *Giorgio da Castelfranco*, Chicago, 1937.

20. Otto Grautoff, *Nicolas Poussin, sein Werk und sein Leben*, Munich, 1914.

21. Wilhelm Ostwald, *Color Science*, Parts I and II, London, n.d.

22. Arthur Pope, *The Language of Drawing and Painting*, Cambridge (Mass.), 1949, chapter I.

23. Pope, *op. cit.*, pp. 17–18.

24. The need for making this change in the placement of colors in the hue circle was suggested by Brown, *op. cit.*, p. 21. Because the Neo-Impressionists frequently visualized hue relationships according to the system embodied in Rood's chromatic circle (Figure 43, page 150), which was arranged according to the laws of additive mixture, this circle will serve as the basis for a number of color diagrams illustrating this book. The writer used Édouard Fer's excellent *diagramme des contrastes*, which is based on Rood's chromatic circle, as a means of identifying the hues in most of the paintings discussed in this study; it is reproduced in color as Plate XIII of his *Solfège de la couleur*.

25. The fundamental difference between the additive mixture of light and the subtractive mixture of pigments was articulated by Hermann von Helmholtz in his *Handbuch der physiologischen Optik*, Leipzig, 1867. Helmholtz's ideas on additive mixture, which were based in part on Thomas Young's theories, corrected the misconception held popularly until the latter part of the nineteenth century that red, yellow, and blue were the three original or fundamental kinds of *light* (that is, primaries), and that these could be mixed in various proportions to produce all other kinds of colored light. O. N. Rood complained as follows about the prevalence of this misconception (shared, incidentally, by Chevreul, Blanc, and Sutter): "This theory of the existence of three fundamental kinds of light, red, yellow, and blue, is found in all except the most recent text books on physics, and is almost universally believed by artists. Nevertheless, it will not be difficult to show that it is quite without foundation." (*Students' Text-Book of Color* [*Modern Chromatics*], New York, 1881, p. 109.) The erroneous conceptions held by some art historians concerning the nature of additive mixture have been pointed out by J. Carson Webster, *op. cit.*, pp. 3–6. For further discussion of the differences between additive and subtractive mixtures, see M. Luckiesh, *Color and its Applications*, New York, 1921, pp. 54–60; Ralph M. Evans, *An Introduction to Color*, New York, 1948, p. 64; James P. C. Southall,

*Introduction to Physiological Optics*, London, 1937, pp. 307–308; Maitland Graves, *Color Fundamentals*, New York, 1952, pp. 29–46; Pope, *op. cit.*, pp. 21–24; and Ostwald, *Colour Science*, II, pp. 32–35.

26. Graves (*op. cit.*, p. 29) has explained the use of the term "subtractive" as follows: "The subtractive method . . . is based on subtraction from white light of red, green, or blue light (the three component primaries of white light). This subtractive modification of white light is produced by two or more selectively absorbing light transmitters or light reflectors — called *colorants*. In this process the light-transmitting or light-reflecting colorants (that is, the transparent filters and dyes, or the opaque paints) are physically mixed by overlapping or by blending. Because one colorant cannot add to, but can only subtract from, the light transmitted or reflected by the other colorants, physical mixtures of colorants are called *subtractive light mixtures*."

27. Graves, *loc. cit.*, explained the term "additive" as follows: "The additive method is based on the addition of red, green, or blue light; but in the additive method the colorants themselves are not physically mixed — only the light that they transmit or reflect is mixed. That is, light is added to light."

28. There is some argument among scientists about the exact identity of the three additive primaries, but suffice it to say that they agree that the positions should be in the red, green, and blue-to-violet areas of the spectrum (cf. Rood, *op. cit.*, pp. 120–122). In this connection, it should be mentioned that the English physicist James Clerk Maxwell was the first to demonstrate experimentally the mixture of colored beams of light which correspond to the three additive primary hues. Thus he laid the foundation for modern three-color photography. (Cf. Ralph M. Evans, W. T. Hanson, Jr., and W. Lyle Brewer, *Principles of Color Photography*, New York and London, 1953, pp. 271–272; and Joseph S. Friedman, *History of Color Photography*, Boston, 1947, pp. 2–3.) In a series of recent articles and demonstrations, Dr. Edwin Land, of the Polaroid Corporation, has shown that fewer and/or different components, other than the traditional three additive primaries (red, green, and blue-violet), may be mixed to produce the full gamut of resultant colors. Dr. Land does not deny the validity of the trichromatic theory proposed by Helmholtz and Maxwell; he merely suggests at this point that combinations of color not mentioned by these two scientists may be used to obtain similar effects. Dr. Land's arguments appear to be directed against the theory of vision postulated by Thomas Young (and accepted by Helmholtz), which states that the eye contains three sets of receptors

corresponding to the three primary light sensations — red, green, and blue-violet; Land's demonstrations have shown convincingly that the eye can perceive full color when entirely different — and fewer — hues are used as the fundamental color stimuli. Although the present writer has not yet devoted further study to this subject, he feels that Land's ideas, while relevant to mixing beams of colored light, have no bearing on the basic theoretical presuppositions of the Neo-Impressionist painters. Cf. Edwin H. Land, "Color Vision and the Natural Image," *Proceedings of the National Academy of Sciences*, XLV, January, 1959, pp. 115–129, and April, 1959, pp. 636–644; and "Experiments in Color Vision," *Scientific American*, May, 1959, pp. 2–14.

29. Just as there is some argument about the exact identity of the additive primaries, so there will be some variation in the exact identification of their resultant mixtures. The resultants listed here are based on Luckiesh, *op. cit.*, p. 58, and Southall, *op. cit.*, p. 305.

30. The three additive primaries are closely related to Thomas Young's theory of vision. In 1802 and 1807 the English scientist postulated the idea that the eye was capable of receiving three primary sensations of color through three sets of receptors, which were sensitive to red, green, and violet. Through different combinations of these three color sensations, all the varieties of visible color could be produced. If, according to Young, the three sets of receptors are stimulated simultaneously, the sensation of white will occur (cf. Thomas Young, *A Course of Lectures on Natural Philosophy and the Mechanical Arts*, I, London, 1807, pp. 439–440).

31. A simple schematic diagram such as Figure 5 (page 10) will suffice for our purposes, since we are interested primarily in referring to color relationships in paintings, rather than establishing absolute color measurements. For the sake of convenience, Rood's color triangle (Figure 13, page 38), contrast-diagram (Figure 14, page 40), and chromatic circle (Figure 43, page 150), which Seurat knew, will be referred to in this book when discussing additive mixture. Modern color scientists have perfected diagrams of additive mixture such as Figure 13 through the rigorous measurement of color properties, but even today the relative positions of the primaries and their resultant mixtures are about the same as those postulated by Helmholtz and his followers (cf. Ralph M. Evans, *op. cit.*, p. 233, fig. 14-7).

32. Cf. Luckiesh, *op. cit.*, p. 60; Graves, *op. cit.*, p. 39; and Evans, *op. cit.*, p. 86.

33. The following experiment was reported by Luckiesh, *loc. cit.*: "If one

end of a pack of cards be painted red and the other end green, on reversing every other card and viewing an end of the pack at a distance of several feet, it will appear yellow in color." Cf. also Graves, *op. cit.*, p. 39: "Reflected light beams may be additively mixed either by pointillism or by rotating disks. Pointillism is the method whereby the chromatic light beams reflected by tiny, juxtaposed dots of paint . . . are additively mixed by the eye and fused into one solid color. This fusion occurs only when the chromatic dots are too small to be resolved by the eye, or when they are viewed at a sufficient distance."

34. Cf. Graves, *loc. cit.*: "The effects produced by additively mixing chromatic light beams reflected from opaque paints (chromatic reflectors) are essentially identical with those effects produced by additively mixing chromatic light beams transmitted by transparent filters (chromatic transmitters)."

35. Cf. Evans, *op. cit.*, pp. 86–87, and Graves, *loc. cit.*

36. This letter, dated August 28 [1890], is reproduced in Robert Rey, *La Renaissance du sentiment classique*, opp. p. 132. Formerly in the collections of Félix Fénéon and Robert Rey, this important document was sold at auction at the Hôtel Drouot, Paris, April 2, 1963. It is now in the Berès Collection, Paris.

2

# UNE BAIGNADE AND THE ORIGINS OF NEO-IMPRESSIONISM

1. Two of the most important biographies published before Rey's *La Renaissance du sentiment classique* and Rewald's writings on Seurat are Lucie Cousturier, *Seurat*, Paris, 1926 (originally issued in slightly different form in *L'Art décoratif*, June, 1912, and March, 1914) and Gustave Coquiot, *Georges Seurat*, Paris, 1924. Neither Cousturier nor Coquiot knew the artist personally; the former, however, based much of her book on Signac's recollections, while Coquiot had also consulted Signac, along with Seurat's friends Charles Angrand and Edmond Aman-Jean. While Coquiot was criticized by Fénéon for inaccuracies in his discussion of Seurat's work ("Précisions concernant Seurat," *Le Bulletin de la vie artistique*, August 15, 1924, pp. 358–360), his book still remains one of the most important single sources of information about the artist's life, and

it is particularly valuable for its publication of excerpts from letters by Seurat's friends. Important contemporary biographical accounts, which will be referred to in this and subsequent chapters, were furnished by Félix Fénéon, Gustave Kahn, Émile Verhaeren, Jules Christophe, Arsène Alexandre, Teodor de Wyzewa, and Paul Signac, all of whom were close to the artist. Unfortunately, there appear to be no witness accounts that deal with Seurat's life before about 1875. A few brief passages on this subject may be found in Coquiot, *Seurat*, chapter I.

2. Jules Christophe, "Georges Seurat," *Les Hommes d'aujourd'hui*, VIII, 368 [March–April, 1890], no pagination [pp. 1–2].

3. See Aman-Jean's recollections quoted in Coquiot, *op. cit.*, pp. 27, 28–29. (The school was the École Municipale de Dessin et de Sculpture du 10ème Arrondissement.)

4. The dates of Seurat's period of study at the École des Beaux-Arts are based on the records of the school, which were published by Rey, *op. cit.*, p. 101. He was admitted to the section of painting on March 19, 1878.

5. Archives of the École des Beaux-Arts, no. 4411 *du registre matricule*. Cf. Aman-Jean as quoted by Coquiot, *op. cit.*, p. 27; cf. also Émile Verhaeren, "Georges Seurat," *La Société nouvelle*, April, 1891, p. 432; and Christophe, *op. cit.* [p. 1].

6. Aman-Jean as quoted by Coquiot, *op. cit.*, p. 29.

7. Many of these drawings were reproduced in de Hauke, *Seurat et son œuvre*, II, pp. 5–31.

8. Paul Signac quoted in Coquiot, *op. cit.*, p. 30; Christophe, *op. cit.* [p. 2]. A number of Seurat's copies after earlier paintings, drawings, and sculptures were reproduced in de Hauke, *op. cit.*, I, pp. 3–5; II, pp. 5–15, 23–33, 37, 39. Many of these were identified by the present writer and R. Ross Holloway in "The Literature of Art: Seurat's Paintings and Drawings," *The Burlington Magazine*, CV, June, 1963, pp. 283–284.

9. For a description of the collections of the École, see Eugene Müntz, *Guide de l'École Nationale des Beaux-Arts*, Paris, 1889. For the holdings of the library, see Ernest Vinet, *Catalogue méthodique de la bibliothèque de l'École Nationale des Beaux-Arts*, Paris, 1873.

10. Cf. Signac, *Delacroix au néo-impressionnisme*, p. 80; Verhaeren, *loc. cit.*; and Arsène Alexandre, "Chronique d'aujourd'hui: un vaillant," *Paris*, April 1, 1891.

11. Léon Rosenthal, "Ernest Laurent," *Art et décoration*, XXIV, March, 1911, pp. 65–66; Paul Jamot, "Ernest Laurent," *Gazette des beaux-arts*, V, March, 1911, p. 177.

12. Seurat served with a regiment at Brest from November 8, 1879, to November 8, 1880 (information courtesy of Dr. Jean Sutter, Paris). His name does not appear in the records of the École des Beaux-Arts after March 22, 1879.

13. Signac, *Delacroix au néo-impressionnisme*, p. 83; Coquiot, *op. cit.*, p. 141. A brief account of the early career of Paul Signac is in order here, considering the importance of his role in the subsequent development of Neo-Impressionism. He was born in Paris on November 11, 1863; but little is known about his life before 1880, because neither his own recollections nor his biographers have devoted much attention to this period. We know, however, that his parents wanted him to become an architect and that he became interested in drawing and painting at an early age. He was educated at the Collège Rollin, but did not take a degree there. One account indicates that he entered the École Nationale Supérieure des Arts Décoratifs in 1882, but the length of his stay is not known. Also, he is said to have been enrolled in 1883 in the Atelier libre de Bin, a school run by a minor academician who offered training to men who did not care to go to the École des Beaux-Arts. As early as 1880 Signac had seen Monet's work in an exhibition sponsored by the magazine *La Vie Moderne* — an exhibition that determined his allegiance to Impressionism. From this time to 1884, according to his own report, his idols were Monet, Pissarro, Renoir, and Guillaumin. On occasion, he worked side by side with Guillaumin, whom he met painting on the *quais* of the Seine. And, so interested was Signac in Monet that in 1884 he wrote to him for advice and, according to his biographer, Georges Besson, later paid him a visit. During his Impressionist period, Signac painted chiefly in Paris, often working along the *quais* or in Montmartre, where he was in touch with some of the artists and writers who congregated at Rodolphe Salis' Chat Noir café (in 1882 he contributed to Salis' magazine *Le Chat Noir*). In the summers of 1882, 1883, and 1884, he traveled to Port-en-Bessin, where he painted landscapes and seascapes in an Impressionist manner. In search of a place to exhibit, Signac sent some paintings in the spring of 1884 to the newly founded Salon of the Groupe des Artistes Indépendants, at which Seurat showed *Une Baignade* for the first time. When the two artists met here, an exchange of theoretical and technical ideas took place, a discussion of which will be postponed until Chapter 3. But it should be noted that from 1884 to 1891 Seurat and Signac were in close touch with each other personally and through correspondence. For details about Signac's life, we are fortunate in being able to turn to several reliable autobiographical accounts, for example, his *Delacroix au néo-impressionnisme*, pp. 82–85;

"Le Néo-impressionnisme — Documents," pp. 50–52; "Extraits du journal inédit de Paul Signac," *Gazette des beaux-arts*, XXXVI, July–September, 1949, pp. 97–128; XXIX, April, 1952, pp. 265–284; XLII, July–August, 1953, pp. 27–57. Signac also related considerable material about his life to his pupil Lucie Cousturier, author of *Paul Signac*, Paris, 1922, and to Georges Besson (now his executor), author of *Paul Signac*, Paris, 1935. Valuable information may be found, too, in articles written about Signac during his lifetime by Félix Fénéon, Antoine de la Rochefoucauld, Jacques Guenne, Claude Roger-Marx, and Arsène Alexandre (see Selected Bibliography).

14. These notes were published in *Le Bulletin de la vie artistique*, April 1, 1922, pp. 154–158.

15. Christophe, *loc. cit.*; Signac as quoted in Coquiot, *op. cit.*, p. 30; Gustave Kahn, "Seurat," *L'Art moderne*, April 5, 1891, p. 108, and *Les Dessins de Georges Seurat*, I, Paris, n.d., n.p. On the basis of information provided by Signac, Arsène Alexandre also wrote that "Georges Seurat . . . conjointly began with his friend Signac, by minute analysis and in patient application, to take up again what Delacroix had synthesized by impulse and genius." (*Exposition d'œuvres de Paul Signac* [exhibition catalogue], Paris, 1902, p. 4.)

16. No extended discussion of the stylistic influences on Seurat's early paintings has yet been published, but the following studies have suggested that between 1881 and 1884 he was well acquainted with the paintings of the Barbizon School and Impressionism: Henri Dorra, "The Evolution of Seurat's Style," in his and Rewald's *Seurat*; Daniel Catton Rich's essay "Seurat's Paintings" in *Seurat: Paintings and Drawings* (exhibition catalogue), Chicago, 1958; Robert L. Herbert, "Seurat in Chicago and New York," *The Burlington Magazine*, C. May, 1958, pp. 146–155; and my "Seurat's Formative Period, 1880–1884," *The Connoisseur*, CXLII, August–September, 1958, pp. 58–62. One of the first writers to recognize Seurat's debt to Impressionism in paintings done prior to 1884 was Professor Paul Bonnet; see his "Seurat et le néo-impressionnisme," *Le Crocodile*, October–December, 1957, pp. 8–10.

17. While he studied Impressionism in the early eighties, Seurat, along with his friends Aman-Jean and Laurent, seems not to have associated himself actually or in spirit with the Impressionists. On the contrary, these three artists still directed their efforts to the annual Salons and achieved some success there. In 1882, entries by Seurat's two friends were accepted (Seurat apparently did not submit anything in that year), and in 1883, all three showed their work at the Salon.

18. See Paul Jamot, "Une Étude pour le 'Dimanche à la Grande Jatte' de

Georges Seurat," *Bulletin des Musées de France*, March, 1930, p. 52; and R. H. Wilenski, *Modern French Painters*, New York, n.d. [1940], p. 68. Also, in the early 1880s, Seurat executed a free copy of Puvis' *Le Pauvre pêcheur* (D.-R. 4).

19. For a discussion of Puvis' influence on Seurat's early work, see Daniel Catton Rich, *Seurat and the Evolution of "La Grande Jatte,"* Chicago, 1935, pp. 47–48; and Robert L. Herbert, "Seurat and Puvis de Chavannes," *Yale University Art Gallery Bulletin*, XXV, October, 1959, pp. 23–29.

20. In three different versions of this letter (here designated as "A," "B," and "C") Seurat provided valuable data about the sources he studied between 1876 and 1884. The most complete of these is version "B," in the collection of César de Hauke, published in his *Seurat*, I, p. xxi, and quoted in the text of the present work. Version "A" is in the collection of John Rewald and was published in his and Dorra's *Seurat*, pp. xxvii–xxviii. Version "C," as yet unpublished, is in the collection of M. de Hauke. Drawing his information largely from these letters, Fénéon published the following summary of Seurat's sources: "The laws of Chevreul and Delacroix's precepts; Corot's ideas on the form, ensemble, and value of tones and on subordinating color to them, certain statements by Couture on the *finesse* of colors; the paintings of Camille Pissarro and Claude Monet; some remarks by Sutter on Greek art (*L'Art*, February and March, 1880); the book by Rood (1881) — were successively considered by him at the time that he was seeking (1876–1884) a formula for optical painting [*peinture optique*] based on the purity of the spectral elements" (*Le Chat noir*, April 2, 1892, p. 1932). Another important list of sources Seurat consulted was published by Signac: "The oriental tradition, the writings of Chevreul, Charles Blanc, Humbert de Superville, O. N. Rood, H. Helmholtz" (*Delacroix au néo-impressionnisme*, p. 80). Signac did not indicate when Seurat read works by these authors, but several of them are clearly more relevant to his later art and theory than they are to his formative period. On the basis of information supplied by Seurat's executors, and especially Fénéon, R. H. Wilenski stated that among the artist's papers were found excerpts from Chevreul's *De la loi du contraste simultané*, Blanc's *Grammaire des arts du dessin*, Charles Henry's *Cercle chromatique* and other works, and Sutter's "Les Phénomènes de la vision" (*Modern French Painters*, p. 108).

21. Although Seurat did not mention the title of Blanc's book in this letter, it was identified by Christophe, *op. cit.* [p. 2] and by Jules Antoine, "Les

Peintres néo-impressionnistes," *Art et critique*, August 9, 1890, p. 510. The *Grammaire des arts du dessin* was published serially in the *Gazette des beaux-arts* from April 1, 1860, to December 1, 1866. The section on color appeared in the issue of April 1, 1866, pp. 373–389. The following comments apropos of Seurat's knowledge of Blanc's writings are relevant here. Émile Verhaeren observed: "In Charles Blanc's *Grammaire des arts plastiques* [*sic*] a whole theory was formulated, which, in its fundamental ideas, seemed exact. This was his starting point." ("Georges Seurat," *La Société nouvelle*, April, 1891, p. 434.) Gustave Kahn, too, referred to Seurat's interest in Blanc: "[Seurat] was curious about any theoretical text and combed Charles Blanc as well as Roret." ("Au Temps du pointillisme," *Mercure de France*, April, 1924, p. 16.) Later the same author stated: "I realized that he knew his Charles Blanc better than anyone else...." (*Les Dessins de Georges Seurat*, no pagination.) Seurat must have communicated his views on the value of Blanc's book to Arsène Alexandre (with whom he was acquainted), who wrote: "The divided touch was rigorously founded on the principles of Chevreul. Delacroix had an inkling of its application, and Charles Blanc, albeit not a revolutionary, had affirmed the utility for art of the illustrious scholar's [Chevreul's] discoveries." ("Chroniques d'aujourd'hui: un vaillant.")

22. Charles Blanc, "Eugène Delacroix," *Gazette des beaux-arts*, XVI, January, 1864, pp. 5–6.

23. The title of Chevreul's book was mentioned by Christophe, "Georges Seurat" [p. 2]; Jules Antoine, *op. cit.*, p. 509; and Alphonse Germain, "Théorie chromo-luminariste," *La Plume*, September 1, 1891, p. 285. We know that Seurat copied excerpts from this volume because they were found among his effects after his death. Designated "*Réflexions sur la peinture*" by Fénéon, who apparently was unaware of their source, these notes were published in de Hauke, *op. cit.*, I, p. xxiv. That they were copied almost exactly from Chevreul's *De la loi du contraste simultané* (pp. 197–201 in the 1839 edition) was established by the present writer; see de Hauke, *loc. cit.*, p. xxiv [*bis*].

24. Seurat's friend Teodor de Wyzewa counted among the artist's sources "*les notes de Delacroix*" ("Une Critique," *La Revue indépendante*, November, 1886, p. 70). Signac, of course, was very much aware of the value of Delacroix's published remarks that were relevant to the Neo-Impressionists' esthetic and technique. Delacroix's articles, letters, and journals, according to Signac, show us that "the painters [the Neo-Impressionists] are only following the teachings of the master [Dela-

croix] and continuing his research." (*Delacroix au néo-impressionnisme*, p. 15.) While Signac frequently turned to excerpts from Delacroix's writings to defend his and Seurat's art, the latter, in his formative period, had studied such writings and had undoubtedly used them, among other sources, as part of the basis of his theory and color technique. By 1880, when Seurat began his independent study of painting and drawing, many of Delacroix's writings had been published. Although his journal did not appear in its entirety until 1893, two years after Seurat's death, excerpts from it had been included in Piron's *Eugène Delacroix, sa vie et ses œuvres* (Paris, 1865), where some of Delacroix's articles, too, were reprinted. Also, many of the artist's letters were collected and published by J.-J. Guiffrey in 1877 and Philippe Burty in 1878 and 1880. The articles, letters, and journals contain material on color practice and on the theory of art that surely would have interested Seurat, but the question of what he derived from them must remain unanswered for the present.

25. These excerpts were dictated by Seurat to Fénéon and were later found on leaves that Signac had pasted in his diary. (Extracts were published in "Extraits du journal inédit de Paul Signac, II, 1897–1898," *Gazette des beaux-arts*, XXIX, April, 1952, p. 284.)

26. As far as this writer can determine, no one other than Seurat mentioned Couture as being one of his sources. Several passages in Couture's *Méthode et entretiens d'atelier* specifically treat the problem of delicacy in color effects, and in the absence of further evidence these may be assumed tentatively to be the "precepts of Couture on the *finesse* of colors" mentioned by Seurat.

27. The dates of the six articles are: January 18 (pp. 74–76); February 1 (pp. 124–128); February 8 (pp. 147–149); February 22 (pp. 195–197); February 29 (pp. 216–220); March 14 (pp. 268–269), 1880. The fourth and sixth installments were found in Seurat's studio after his death. He must have had more than a passing interest in Sutter, because he cut out and preserved his obituary that appeared in *L'Art* in 1880.

28. Letter from Seurat to Fénéon (June 20, 1890), version "C."

29. *Ibid.*, version "A."

30. A native of Angers, Michel-Eugène Chevreul (1786–1889) studied chemistry in Paris under Vauquelin and rose rapidly in responsible scientific positions during the second and third decades of the nineteenth century. He was appointed in 1824 to the post for which he is best known: *directeur des teintures* of the Manufactures Royales des Gobelins — the royal tapestry workshop. For about sixty years he taught courses in chemistry there

and at the Muséum d'Histoire Naturelle. Chevreul was recognized by his countrymen as one of the most distinguished scientists of his era and was greatly admired for his versatility in different fields of investigation. In addition to his research on color theory, he made important contributions to the study of saponification and fats, among other subjects. For our purposes, his most significant work was his monumental book on color: *De la loi du contraste simultané des couleurs* (Paris, 1839). (This volume had actually been written by 1835, and some of its contents had been delivered in public lectures in 1836 and 1838; also, portions of his research on the subject were presented as lectures as early as 1828. But because of the great expense involved in printing the color plates, Chevreul did not find a publisher until 1839.) For Chevreul's biography see E. Chevreul, *Quelques notes et lettres de M. E. Chevreul*, Dijon, 1907; A. Riché, *Quelques pages intimes sur M. Chevreul*, Paris, 1889; Mme. de Champ, *Michel-Eugène Chevreul, vie intime*, Paris, 1930; Georges Bouchard, *Chevreul*, Paris, 1932; and M. Berthelot, "Michel-Eugène Chevreul," *Mémoires de l'Académie des Sciences de l'Institut de France*, XLVII, 1904, pp. ccclxxxvii–cdxxxiv.

31. Chevreul, pp. ix–x. References to Chevreul's *De la loi du contraste simultané* will be taken from the translation by Charles Martel published as *The Principles of Harmony and Contrast of Colours*, London, 1872.

32. *Ibid.*, pp. 37–41.

33. *Ibid.*, p. 11.

34. *Ibid.*, p. 55.

35. *Ibid.*, pp. 69–70.

36. *Ibid.*, pp. 98–112.

37. *Ibid.*, p. 117.

38. *Ibid.*, pp. 121–122.

39. *Ibid.*, p. 123.

40. *Ibid.*, p. 131.

41. *Ibid.*, p. 132.

42. *Ibid.*, p. 147.

43. *Ibid.*, p. 378.

44. *Ibid.*, p. 439.

45. *Ibid.*, p. 450.

46. Born in Castres, Charles Blanc (1813–1882) had reached his sixties and was an established editor, critic, and art historian at the time that Seurat first became interested in painting. When Blanc came to Paris as a young man, he studied etching and engraving, but by the 1840s had turned to writing, particularly on the arts. Eventually he rose to a position

of power in the official Parisian art world as an author, as founder and editor of the *Gazette des beaux-arts*, and as director of the Administration des Beaux-Arts in 1848–1850 and 1870. A member of the Académie des Beaux-Arts, he was appointed to a chair of esthetics and the history of art at the Collège de France, where he taught from 1878 to 1881 — significantly, during Seurat's student days at the École des Beaux-Arts. For Blanc's biography, see Louis Fiaux, *Portraits politiques contemporains, Charles Blanc* (III), Paris, 1881–1885; E. du Sommerard, *Notice sur M. Charles Blanc*, Paris, 1883; A. Soubies, *Les Membres de l'Académie des Beaux-Arts depuis la fondation de l'Institut, 1852–1876*, III, Paris, 1911, pp. 228–233; Tullio Maserani, *Charles Blanc et son œuvre*, Paris, 1884.

47. Blanc, *Grammar*, p. xix. We shall refer to the translation of Blanc's *Grammaire des arts du dessin* published as *The Grammar of Painting and Engraving* (trans. by Kate Newell Doggett), Chicago, 1879.

48. *Ibid.*, p. 146.

49. *Ibid.*

50. *Ibid.*, p. 149.

51. *Ibid.*, pp. 149–150. (Bourgeois' name was omitted in Doggett's translation of the *Grammaire*. It appears, however, on p. 561 of the original French text.)

52. Apparently Blanc's color diagram was not his own invention; it corresponds almost exactly to one devised by J. Ziegler, published in his *Traité de la couleur et de la lumière* (Paris, 1852), p. 16.

53. *Grammar*, p. 158.

54. *Ibid.*, p. 165.

55. *Ibid.*, p. 167.

56. Blanc, "Eugène Delacroix," *Gazette des beaux-arts*, XVI, February, 1864, p. 106.

57. *Ibid.*

58. *Ibid.*, p. 108.

59. Delacroix was undoubtedly very well acquainted with Chevreul's theories of color. Among the artist's papers was found a notebook, now preserved in the Cabinet des Dessins of the Louvre, comprised of fifty-three pages of notes and diagrams apparently taken from Chevreul's *De la loi du contraste simultané* (Paris, 1839) or from a series of lectures delivered by the scientist in 1848 (six of the leaves are dated January, 6, 13, 14, 18, 21, 25, 1848).

60. Blanc, "Eugène Delacroix," p. 109.

61. *Ibid.*, p. 110.

62. *Ibid.*, pp. 111–113.

63. Cf. Signac, *Delacroix au néo-impressionnisme*, pp. 45–48.
64. As evidence for Delacroix's belief in rational procedures, Blanc quoted the following from the painter's article on Charlet: "Great geniuses have rarely improvised.... So then, improvising means to sketch and finish at the same time, to satisfy imagination and reflection with the same effort, in the same breath; for a simple mortal this would be to speak the language of the gods, as though it were his native tongue! *Do we know well the resources which talent has to hide its efforts?* Who can say what this or that admirable passage has cost?... At the most what one may call improvisation in the painter would be the fiery spirit of execution with neither retouching nor repentance; but without both the quick sketch and the skillful and calculated sketch in view of the definitive finished work, this *tour-de-force* would be impossible, even for an artist like Tintoretto, who passes for the most impetuous of painters, and even for Rubens himself.... It is in the conception of the whole from the very first lineaments of the picture and in the arrangement of the parts that the most powerful of his faculties is exercised; that is where he has really worked." ("Eugène Delacroix," pp. 116–117.) This passage is from Delacroix's "Charlet," *Revue des deux mondes*, XXXVII, January 1, 1862.
65. Ogden N. Rood (1831–1902) was born in Danbury, Connecticut. After completing his undergraduate education at Princeton in 1852, he did graduate work at Yale University, and between 1854 and 1858 studied physics and chemistry in Berlin and Munich under Liebig, Magnus, and Dove. During his stay in Germany he also studied painting. Returning to the United States, he taught first at Troy University, but in 1864 was appointed to the faculty of Columbia College, New York, as professor of physics. At Columbia, where he remained for the rest of his life, Rood conducted an active program of research and publication and achieved a marked degree of fame as a scientist. His colleagues praised him as a gifted writer and teacher who was able to explain the intricacies of physics in simple, lucid terms. His greatest gifts, in their view, were shown in practical laboratory experiments, rather than in theoretical speculation. Throughout his career as a scientist, Rood painted as an avocation. He exhibited his work occasionally at the National Academy of Design and was an honorary member of the New York Water Color Society. Interestingly, he considered Turner the painter most worthy of study and emulation. And shortly after his return from Europe, Rood corresponded with John Ruskin, who sent him eight of his water colors and pastels. Because Chevreul and Blanc were well-known figures in

France, much biographical information about them was published during and after their lifetimes. Rood, though just as important as these two writers for the development of Neo-Impressionism, never equaled their fame; therefore far less material concerning his life and work is available. The following accounts have proved to be valuable: J. H. van Amringe, "Ogden N. Rood," *Columbia University Quarterly*, December, 1902, pp. 45–57; W. Le Conte Stevens, "Ogden N. Rood," *Science*, December 5, 1902, pp. 881–884; "Ogden N. Rood," *Popular Science Monthly*, January, 1903, pp. 284–286; Arthur W. Wright, "Ogden Nicholas Rood," *American Journal of Science*, January, 1903, pp. 73–77; Roland Rood, "Professor Rood's Theories on Color and Impressionism," *The Scrip*, April, 1906, pp. 215–219; Edward L. Nichols, "Ogden Nicholas Rood," *Biographical Memoirs, National Academy of Sciences*, VI, 1909, pp. 449–472.

66. Ogden N. Rood, *Students' Text-Book of Color*, New York, 1881, pp. 139–140. (We will refer consistently to the 1881 edition of Rood's book.) Mile's views are still supported by such modern scientists as Ralph M. Evans, W. T. Hanson, Jr., and W. Lyle Brewer, who have written: "All the mixture laws for superimposed projected colors, colors presented alternately in rapid succession, and colors simultaneously stimulating small adjacent areas of the retina can . . . be presumed to be the same." (*Principles of Color Photography*, New York and London, 1953, p. 25.)

67. Rood, *Text-Book*, p. 143.

68. On this subject, Rood declared: "Painters can not in many cases directly apply knowledge acquired from the palette to the interpretation of chromatic effects produced by nature, for these latter often depend to a considerable extent on the mixing of masses of differently coloured *light*. This fact is now admitted in a general way by intelligent artists, but probably few who have not made experiments in this direction fully realize how wide are the discrepancies which exist between the results given by the two different modes of mixture." (*Ibid.*)

69. *Ibid.*, p. 149, *et passim.*

70. *Ibid.*, p. 154.

71. *Ibid.*, p. 204.

72. Rood, however, did provide a formula for mixing additively any color in the spectrum with another, and it was probably of considerable interest to Seurat. Basing his remarks on a triangular color diagram devised by James Clerk Maxwell, the author explained: "Maxwell selected [as primaries] vermilion, emerald-green, and ultramarine-blue,

since according to his researches they approximately represent the three fundamental colours. These he placed at the three angles of an equilateral triangle and ascertained . . . the position of white (or grey) in the interior of the triangle. Every colour that can be obtained by mixing red with green will lie on the line joining red and green; it is the same with green and blue, also with red and blue. . . . These colours [are] disposed along the sides of the triangle; they are also so arranged that complementary colours are opposite each other; white is in the interior, and along the lines joining the sides with the centre are placed the various colours mixed with more and more white as they are situated nearer to the centre." (*Ibid.*, p. 220.) The color triangle which Rood described is reproduced as Figure 13 (page 38). Its chief value was in enabling one to visualize the hue that would result from the additive mixture of two colors — or, for that matter, any number of colors.

73. The contrast-diagram Seurat copied from the French edition of Rood's book is in the collection of Mme. Ginette Signac. It was first published by Rewald in *Art News*, XLVIII, April, 1949, p. 25, though it was associated there, incorrectly, with Chevreul's principles. Sven Lövgren has suggested erroneously that the diagram was based on Charles Henry's theories; on the contrary, it appears that the placement of hues on Henry's chromatic circle, published in 1889, was influenced by Rood's book (cf. Lövgren, *The Genesis of Modernism*, Stockholm, 1959, pp. 71–72). There also exists a copy of Rood's contrast diagram by Lucien Pissarro (in the collection of John Rewald).

74. Rood, *op. cit.*, pp. 279–280.

75. *Ibid.*, p. 280.

76. *Ibid.*, p. 314.

77. *Ibid.*, p. 306.

78. Rood wrote: "No rules will enable a painter coldly to construct chromatic compositions . . . ; the constant study of colour in nature and in the works of great colourists will do much, but even more important still is the possession of a natural feeling for what may be called the poetry of colour, which leads the artist almost instinctively to seize on colour-melodies as they occur in nature, and afterward to reproduce them on canvas, with such additions or modifications as his feeling for colour impels him to make." (*Ibid.*, p. 316.)

79. Born in Geneva, Switzerland, David Sutter (1811–1880) studied philosophy, mathematics, music, painting, and the physical sciences in that city. He came to Paris at the age of twenty-six and there wrote prolifically on art and music. Late in his career, he gave a course in esthetics at the

École des Beaux-Arts (1865–1870). His books included *Philosophie des beaux-arts* (Paris, 1858) and *L'Esthétique générale et appliquée* (Paris, 1865), which, in Rey's opinion, Seurat probably knew (Rey, *op. cit.*, p. 128), The answer to the question of whether he read Sutter's books is not exceedingly important here, since the articles in *L'Art* summarize many of the ideas contained in them. For Sutter's biography see Pierre Larousse, "David Sutter," *Grand dictionnaire universel*, XIV, Paris, n.d., pp. 1287–1288; Louis-Lucas, "M. Sutter," *L'Investigateur*, LI, 1880, pp. 111–115; and his obituary published in *L'Art*, XX, 1880, p. 272.

80. David Sutter, "Les Phénomènes de la vision," *L'Art*, XX, 1880, p. 216.

81. *Ibid.*

82. This color diagram was reproduced from Sutter's *Philosophie des beaux-arts*.

83. Sutter's statements on the nature of color are as follows: "White is the union of all colors. Black is the absence of all color. . . . There are three warm colors: red, orange, yellow. There are three cool colors: green, blue, violet. When the light is warm, the shadows are cool. When the light is cool, the shadows are warm. Colors in shadow always contain their complementary color." ("Les Phénomènes de la vision," p. 219.)

84. *Ibid.*

85. *Ibid.*

86. *Ibid.*, p. 268.

87. *Ibid.*

88. *Ibid.*

89. *Ibid.*

90. *Ibid.*

91. *Ibid.*

92. *Ibid.*, pp. 268–269.

93. *Ibid.*, p. 269.

94. *Ibid.*

95. These notes were published by Fénéon: "Notes inédites de Seurat sur Delacroix," *Le Bulletin de la vie artistique*, April 1, 1922, pp. 154–158. The earliest date appearing on the notes is February 23, 1881; the latest is November 11, 1881. Two pages of Seurat's manuscript have been published in de Hauke, *op. cit.*, II, p. 53. The three paintings on which Seurat took notes on February 23, 1881, were exhibited prior to their sale on the following day by MM. C. Pillet and Durand-Ruel (notice in *Le Figaro*, February 17, 1881, p. 1).

96. Signac, *Delacroix au néo-impressionnisme*, p. 38. Delacroix's *Massacre de Scio* is reproduced in color in Raymond Escholier, *Delacroix*, Paris, 1963, p. 21.

97. *Ibid.*, pp. 41–42.
98. *Ibid.*, p. 45.
99. *Ibid.*
100. *Ibid.*, p. 46. Delacroix's painting is reproduced in color in Escholier, *op. cit.*, p. 85.
101. *Ibid.*, pp. 45–46.
102. *Ibid.*, p. 46.
103. *Ibid.*, p. 52. These frescoes are reproduced in color in Escholier, *op. cit.*, pp. 153, 156.
104. *Ibid.*, pp. 81–82. Cf. also Signac as quoted in Coquiot, *Seurat*, p. 31.
105. R. Marx, "L'Exposition des Artistes-Indépendants," *Le Voltaire*, May 16, 1884, p. 2.
106. *Loc. cit.*
107. Gustave Kahn, "Seurat," *L'Art moderne*, April 5, 1891, p. 108.
108. *The Critic* (New York), April 17, 1886, p. 196 (quoted in Dorra and Rewald, *op. cit.*, p. 102).
109. Gustave Kahn, "Au Temps du pointillisme," p. 15. The Renoir portrait, *Mme. Charpentier and her Children* (d. 1878) is in the Metropolitan Museum of Art, New York. Seurat probably saw it at the Salon of 1879.
110. Kahn, "Seurat," p. 108.
111. *Ibid.*, p. 109.
112. Letter from Seurat to Fénéon (June 20, 1890), version "B."
113. For an account of Seurat's procedures in painting *Une Baignade*, see Benedict Nicolson, "Seurat's 'La Baignade,'" *The Burlington Magazine*, LXXIX, November, 1941, pp. 139–146; and Douglas Cooper, *Une Baignade, Asnières*, London, n.d.
114. This observation was made by Signac ("Journal inédit de Paul Signac, I, 1894–1895," *Gazette des beaux-arts*, XXXVI, July–September, 1949, p. 114). The additions may be found in the grass next to the straw hat and pile of clothing in the center of the picture; on the back of the seated boy in the center of the painting; in the hat of, and in the water to the left of, the boy at the far right; in the water at the left of the second figure from the right. Also, in 1928, Jacques-Émile Blanche observed that "*Une Baignade* has lost much of its light and resonance." (*De Gauguin à la Revue nègre*, Paris, 1928, p. 37.)
115. Lionello Venturi, "The Aesthetic Idea of Impressionism," *Journal of Aesthetics and Art Criticism*, no. 1, Spring, 1941, pp. 34–45. Venturi defined the period of "the real, the genuine Impressionism" as 1870–1880.

116. Meyer Schapiro, "Nature of Abstract Art," *Marxist Quarterly*, I, January–March, 1937, pp. 81–85.

117. Because the Impressionist group did not produce a manifesto, an understanding of their aims and theories must be gleaned from contemporary writings about their work, statements by the artists themselves, and evidence from their pictures. Actually, very few attempts have been made to analyze at length the techniques, methods, and theories of the Impressionist painters. The following texts have been particularly valuable in helping to define the specific character of their art and vision: Richard F. Brown, "The Color Technique of Camille Pissarro," unpublished Ph.D. dissertation, Harvard University, 1952; Paul de Lapparent, *La Logique des procédés impressionnistes*, Paris, 1926; William C. Seitz, *Claude Monet*, New York, n.d. [1960], and *Claude Monet, Seasons and Moments* (exhibition catalogue), New York, 1960; and J. Carson Webster, "The Technique of Impressionism: A Reappraisal," *College Art Journal*, IV, November, 1944, pp. 3–22.

118. Monet's conviction that nature should be approached without accumulated sense experiences was expressed concisely in a statement recorded by Lilla Cabot Perry (*American Magazine of Art*, XVIII, March, 1927, p. 120): "He [Monet] wished he had been born blind and then had suddenly gained his sight so that he could have begun to paint in this way without knowing what the objects were that he saw before him. He held that the first real look at the *motif* was likely to be the truest and most unprejudiced one. . . ." On the importance of the artist's sensations of nature, Monet said: "Impressionism is nothing but the immediate sensation. All the great painters were more or less impressionists. It is, above all, a question of instinct." (Monet quoted in Evan Charteris, *John Sargent*, New York, 1927, p. 129.) In a letter to Charteris (June 21, 1926) Monet denied using theories in his painting and again stressed the importance of the direct sensation of nature: "I am always horrified by theories other than those which I have only the merit of having painted directly from nature in trying to render my impressions in face of the most fugitive effects." (Charteris, *op. cit.*, p. 131.) Renoir's reliance on instinct and his distaste for theories are documented in some of his remarks addressed to Walter Pach in answer to the question of whether he (Renoir) followed some kind of special rational method: "No, I don't; that is the procedure of an apothecary, not of an artist. I arrange my subject as I want it, then I go ahead and paint it, like a child. . . . I am no cleverer than that. I have no rules and no methods; anyone can look over my materials

or watch how I paint — he will see that I have no secrets." (Walter Pach, *Queer Thing, Painting*, New York and London, 1938, p. 108.) In a similar vein, Renoir was quoted by Vollard as saying: "In painting as in the other arts, there is not one method, however insignificant it may be, which can be adapted to a formula. . . . There is something more to painting, which cannot be explained, yet which is essential. You come before nature with theories; nature throws them to the ground." (A. Vollard, *En Écoutant Cézanne, Degas, Renoir*, Paris, 1938, pp. 211–212.)

119. Theodore Duret, a close friend of Monet, Renoir, Sisley, and Pissarro, described the outdoor painting of the Impressionists as follows: "The landscape painters of the Impressionist group . . . not only made open-air painting a habitual practice, but also gave it the sanction of an absolute rule. Landscapes painted in the studio they eschewed altogether. They held that every landscape, whatever its importance, however much time was required for its execution, ought to be completed directly on the spot." (Duret, *Manet and the French Impressionists*, Philadelphia, 1910, pp. 71–72.)

120. See Laforgue's essay "L'Impressionnisme," *Oeuvres complètes de Jules Laforgue*, IV, Paris, n.d., p. 139. Several accounts of the amount of time Monet spent on his paintings are relevant here: according to L. C. Perry, *op. cit.*, p. 123, "He often said that no painter could paint more than one half hour on any outdoor effect and keep the picture true to nature, and remarked that in this respect he practiced what he preached." And "He told me that in one of his 'Peupliers' the effect lasted only seven minutes, or until the sunlight left a certain leaf, when he took out the next canvas and worked on that." (Perry, *op. cit.*, p. 121.) His American pupil Theodore Robinson noted that Monet worked on his canvases "at the same time of day and not too long, never for more than an hour." (*The Century Magazine*, XLIV, September, 1892, p. 696.)

121. For a general discussion of Monet's "series" method of painting, see W. C. Seitz, *Claude Monet, Seasons and Moments*.

122. Apropos of his method of viewing his subject, Monet gave the following advice to Lilla Cabot Perry: "When you go out to paint, try to forget what objects you have before you, a tree, a house, a field or whatever. Merely think, here is a little square of blue, here an oblong of pink, here a streak of yellow, and paint it just as it looks to you, the exact color and shape, until it gives your own naive impression of the scene before you." (Perry, *op. cit.*, p. 120.) Another valuable account

of Monet's struggle to capture nature's light and color in his canvases was recorded by René Gimpel: "I am lost if I am interrupted while I am at work. You understand, gentlemen, I pursue a patch of light. It is my fault, I want to seize the intangible. It's terrible, this light which escapes me, taking color with it. Color, any color, lasts but a second; sometimes three or four minutes, rarely as long as that." (*Art in America*, XV, June, 1927, p. 171.) An excellent account of Pissarro's Impressionist procedures and approach was given by Louis Le Bail: "When painting, make a choice of subject, see what is lying at the right and what at the left, and work on everything simultaneously. Don't work bit by bit but paint everything at once by placing tones everywhere, with brushstrokes of the right color and value, while noticing what is alongside. Use small brushstrokes and try to put down your perceptions immediately. The eye should not be fixed on one point, but should take in everything, while observing the reflections which the colors produce on their surroundings. Work at the same time upon sky, water, branches, ground, keeping everything going on an equal basis and unceasingly rework until you have got it. Cover the canvas at the first go, then work at it until you can see nothing more to add. Observe the aerial perspective well, from the foreground to the horizon, the reflections of sky, of foliage." (Le Bail quoted in Rewald, *The History of Impressionism*, pp. 356–358.) Monet's preoccupation with similar effects is reflected in a letter of October 7, 1890: "I'm grinding away, I've got it in my head to capture a series of different effects (some haystacks), but at this time of year the sun sets so fast that I can't follow it. . . . I'm becoming so slow in working that I'm in a state of despair, but the farther along I get, the more I see that much work is needed to succeed at rendering what I'm looking for: 'instantaneity,' above all, the *enveloppe*, the same light distributed everywhere. . . ." (Gustave Geffroy, *Claude Monet*, Paris, 1922, p. 189.) A valuable account of the Impressionists' attitude toward drawing was supplied by Louis Le Bail, who obtained the following ideas from Pissarro: "The motif should be observed more for shape and color than for drawing. There is no need to tighten the form which can be obtained without that. Precise drawing is dry and hampers the impression of the whole, it destroys all sensations. Do not define too closely the outlines of things: it is the brushstroke of the right value and color which should produce the drawing. In a mass, the greatest difficulty is not to give the contour in detail, but to paint what is within." (Le Bail quoted in Rewald, *The History of Impressionism*, p. 356.)

123. Almost all writings about and by the Impressionists insist on their subservience to the data supplied by nature and, at the same time, deny the value of training in art schools. Quoting Pissarro's teachings, Le Bail wrote: "Don't proceed according to rules and principles, but paint what you observe and feel. . . . One must have only one master — nature; she is the one always to be consulted." (Quoted in Rewald, *The History of Impressionism*, p. 358.) Monet, as quoted by Pach, echoed similar sentiments, adding his condemnation of schools: "The schools are no good. I am against teaching. It is from nature that we must study. . . . If a young man feels the sacred fire — let him work, let him study nature." (Pach, *op. cit.*, p. 100.)

124. Signac, *Delacroix au néo-impressionnisme*, p. 61. For a general discussion of the spectrum palette of the Impressionists see Brown, *op. cit.*, pp. 25–29. Monet's spectrum palette was described by R. Gimpel, *op. cit.*, p. 174. Renoir's palette, which included earth colors and black, was discussed by Rewald in *The History of Impressionism*, p. 433, note 52. A diagram of Pissarro's palette containing only spectral colors was illustrated by James W. Lane and Kate Steinitz in "Palette Index," *Art News*, XLI, December 1, 1942, p. 24. (On Pissarro's palette, cf. also the private notes of Louis Le Bail, cited in Rewald, *loc. cit.*; and Brown, *op. cit.*, p. 25.)

125. Webster, *op. cit.*, p. 4.

126. There are several exceptions to this method of handling the shadows. Seurat flecked some of the shadows with strokes of orange: the arm of the reclining man at the left; the shoulder and trousers of the figure wearing a straw hat seated behind him; and the top of the hat on the pile of clothes in the center of the picture.

127. Chevreul, p. 427.

128. *Ibid.*, p. 98.

129. *Ibid.*, p. 100.

130. Blanc, *Grammar*, pp. 165–166.

131. Rood, p. 273.

132. *Ibid.*, p. 141.

133. Delacroix described the means of obtaining such effects in one of his sketchbooks: "If you add the binary color to the primary color opposite it, you destroy it, that is to say, you produce the necessary half-tint" [*demi-teinte*]. (From a sketchbook in the Musée Condé, Chantilly.)

134. In the legs of the angel in *La Lutte de Jacob et de l'ange*, Saint-Sulpice, for example, the fundamental color is grayish-green. This tone is slashed over with strokes of soft red, reddish-tan, and red-orange, and

at a viewing distance of about sixteen feet these hues fuse into a magnificent, luminous optical gray, which — though generally neutral in tone — becomes cooler near the calf and warmer near the ankle. From such a technique of treating color Seurat undoubtedly drew many lessons.

135. Signac, *Delacroix au néo-impressionnisme*, p. 51.
136. Chevreul, p. 147.
137. *Ibid.*, p. 149.
138. Thomas Couture, *Conversations on Art Methods*, trans. by S. E. Stewart, New York, 1879, p. 144.
139. *Ibid.*, pp. 146–149.
140. *Ibid.*, p. 144.
141. *Ibid.*, pp. 151–152.
142. Rood, pp. 152–154.
143. *Ibid.*, p. 281.
144. *Ibid.*
145. *Ibid.*, p. 282.
146. Blanc, *Grammar*, p. 165.
147. Blanc, *Grammaire*, p. 570 (this passage was omitted from the English translation).
148. Rood, pp. 276–277.
149. Kahn, "Seurat," p. 108.
150. Blanc, "Eugène Delacroix," p. 117.
151. Signac, *Delacroix au néo-impressionnisme*, p. 77.
152. Chevreul, p. 9.
153. *Ibid.*, p. 10.
154. *Ibid.*, p. 11.
155. *Ibid.*, p. 16.
156. *Ibid.*, pp. 16–17.
157. *Ibid.*, p. 19.
158. *Ibid.*, pp. 123–124. After making this statement, Chevreul described the specific value of knowing the law of simultaneous contrast: "The first conclusion to be deduced from this is, that the painter will quickly appreciate in his model the colour peculiar to each part, and the modifications of tone and of colour which they may receive from contiguous colours. He will then be much better prepared to imitate what he sees, than if he was ignorant of this law. He will also perceive modifications which, if they had not always escaped him because of their feeble intensity, might have been disregarded because the eye is susceptible of fatigue, especially when it seeks to disentangle the modifications the

cause of which is unknown, and which are not very prominent."
(*Ibid.*, p. 124). Chevreul also recommended that the artist apply the
law of contrast in his paintings: "The painter, knowing that the impression of one colour beside another is the result of the mixture of the
first with the complementary of the second, has only to mentally esti-
mate the intensity of the influence of this complementary, to reproduce
faithfully in his imitation the complex effect which he has under his
eyes. After having placed upon his canvas the two colours he requires,
as they appear to him in the isolated state, he will see if the imitation
agrees with his model; and, if he is not satisfied, he must then recognize
the correction which has to be made." (*Ibid.*, p. 125.)

159. Blanc, *Grammar*, p. 156.
160. The *Trattato* was first translated into French by Roland Fréart Sieur de
    Chambray and was published in 1651. Another translation made by
    P. M. Gault de Saint-Germain was published in 1803. Both versions
    were reprinted frequently during the nineteenth century. Seurat's list
    of writers on the theory and practice of painting does not include the
    name of Leonardo da Vinci, nor is he mentioned as one of Seurat's
    sources by friends who met him after 1886. However, an article by
    Léon Rosenthal referring to Seurat's early association with Aman-Jean
    and Ernest Laurent stated that these artists studied Leonardo's *Traité
    de la peinture* ("Ernest Laurent," *Art et décoration*, XXIX, March, 1911,
    p. 66). If Seurat read this book, he probably would have done so before
    1884, since he saw little of these two friends after that year. We must,
    of course, accept Rosenthal's statement with caution, since we have no
    other indications that Seurat read Leonardo's treatise.
161. From the English translation, *A Treatise of Painting by Leonardo da
    Vinci*, London, 1721, pp. 140–141.
162. *Ibid.*, p. 87.
163. Blanc, *Grammar*, p. 135.
164. Rood, p. 244.
165. *Ibid.*, p. 246.
166. *Ibid.*
167. *Ibid.*, p. 249.
168. Signac, *Delacroix au néo-impressionnisme*, p. 52.
169. *Ibid.*, p. 83.
170. The trousers of the figures on the riverbank, the shoes, and the dark
    garments to their left were painted with mixtures in which black,
    umbers, and siennas figure prominently. The hair of the seated boy in
    the center is also dominated by ochres and siennas, as is the dog at the

lower left. Earth colors are used, too, in the tan wedge-shaped inden-
tation on the riverbank and in the grass.

171. Signac, *Delacroix au néo-impressionnisme*, pp. 83–84.

172. Reproduced in color in Escholier, *op. cit.*, p. 153. According to Théophile Silvestre (*Eugène Delacroix*, Paris, 1864, p. 17), Delacroix had
systematically arrived at such contrasts through the use of a device of
his own invention called a *chromomètre*. This was a circular color
diagram in the form of a clockface, in which, "at each of its degrees,
as around a palette, was placed a little mound of color, which had its
immediate neighbors and its diametrical opposites. . . . The intermediate
tones were subdivided step by step as half hours, quarter hours, minutes,
etc." The complementary pairs mentioned by Silvestre were red-green,
blue-orange, and yellow-violet. It may be suggested here that the source
of Delacroix's *chromomètre* was Chevreul's chromatic circle (Figure 7,
page 22) not only because Silvestre's account closely approximates it, but
also because we know that Delacroix owned a copy, in full color, of
Chevreul's circle; it is preserved in the notebook in the Cabinet des
Dessins of the Louvre, mentioned in note 59 of this chapter.

173. Chevreul, p. 70.

174. *Ibid.*, p. 69.

175. Rood, p. 292.

176. *Ibid.*, p. 299.

177. On this subject, Rood wrote: "In the employment of any of these
triads in painting or in ornament, the artist can, of course, vary the
hue of the three colours through the small interval without destroying
the definite character of the chromatic composition; and even small
quantities of foreign colours can also be added." (*Ibid.*, p. 300.)

178. *Ibid.*, p. 297.

179. *Ibid.*

180. Blanc, *Grammar*, p. 159.

181. *Ibid.*, p. 161.

182. *Ibid.*, p. 159.

183. *Ibid.*, p. 160.

184. Rood, p. 300.

185. *Gazette des beaux-arts*, XXIX, April, 1952, p. 304.

186. Cf. note 19 of this chapter.

187. According to one contemporary account, the custom at the École des
Beaux-Arts was for students to go out of doors and paint from nature —
often at Barbizon — from the end of the school's term in July to its
opening in October (Richard Whiteing, "The American Student at

the Beaux-Arts," *The Century Magazine*, XXIII, December, 1881, pp. 268–269). Jacques-Émile Blanche, a fellow student of Seurat's at the École des Beaux-Arts, stated that the fashion was to go to make sketches on the fortifications at the Suresnes factories, and at the island of La Grande Jatte. (*De Gauguin à la Revue nègre*, p. 37.)

188. Rood, p. 316.

189. *Ibid.*, p. 317.

190. *Ibid.*, p. 318.

191. *Gazette des beaux-arts*, XXIX, April, 1952, p. 304.

192. *Ibid.*

193. *Ibid.*

194. Rood, p. 319.

195. *Ibid.*

196. *Ibid.*, p. 320.

197. Although it would be possible to discuss at some length the stylistic sources for Seurat's drawings for *Une Baignade*, we shall limit our comments here to the relationship between the drawings and the final painting on the formal and technical level.

198. An interesting account of Rood's low opinion of Impressionism was published by his son, Roland Rood, in *The Scrip*, April, 1906, pp. 215–219. When told that the Impressionists had followed his theories, his reply was, "If that is all I have done for art I wish I had never written that book!" (p. 219).

3

# THE THEORY, TECHNIQUE, AND METHODS OF CHROMO-LUMINARISM (1884–1887)

1. Although the movement that grew up around Seurat came to be known as Neo-Impressionism, he preferred to be called a "chromo-luminarist." As Signac put it: "If these painters, better identified by the epithet *chromo-luminarists* — dear to Seurat — have adopted the title of *Neo-Impressionists*, it is to pay homage to their great precursors and to emphasize, even though divergent in technique, their common goal: light and color." ("Le Néo-impressionnisme — Documents," p. 58; cf. also Signac, *Delacroix au néo-impressionnisme*, p. 73.) Interestingly,

Seurat once referred to himself as an *impressionniste-luministe* (letter from Seurat to Signac, July 2, 1886, published in Dorra and Rewald, *Seurat*, p. lx). Also, he called his painting *"peinture optique"* in his letter to Fénéon of June 20, 1890 (version "A"); this term sometimes appears in the critical literature on Neo-Impressionism.

2. Camille Pissarro, *Letters to his son Lucien* (New York, 1943), p. 112. In October 1885, after Seurat returned to Paris, he met Camille Pissarro through Guillaumin or Signac (who had been introduced to the Impressionist master in Guillaumin's studio earlier in that year). Although Pissarro's paintings had influenced some of the work of Signac and Seurat before 1885, the latter's scientific refinements in color technique attracted the older artist, who had reached a crisis in his own style and in a less methodical way seems to have been working independently toward similar goals. Pissarro immediately recognized Seurat's leadership, and from the winter of 1885-1886 until about 1890, he was, in effect, a member of the Neo-Impressionist group, whose theories and technique he accepted during this period. On Pissarro's change in style, Signac wrote: "Pissarro became enthusiastic over the research of his young colleagues and encouraged them with his approval. Pressing further his study of passages and relationships, which had always tormented him, he courageously inaugurated a new technique akin to that of Seurat and his friends." ("Le Néo-impressionnisme — Documents," p. 52.) Pissarro was perfectly frank in acknowledging his debt to Seurat. In a letter to Durand-Ruel of November 6, 1886, he wrote: "It is Seurat, an artist of great merit, who was first to have the idea and to apply a scientific theory, after thorough study. Like my other colleagues (Signac, Dubois-Pillet), I have only followed Seurat's example." (Letter published in Lionello Venturi, *Les Archives de l'impressionnisme*, II, Paris, 1939, p. 24.)

3. Signac, "Le Néo-impressionnisme — Documents," p. 54.

4. *Ibid.* It should be noted that nearly all of Seurat's friends regarded him, not Signac or Pissarro, as the inventor and foremost exponent of the Neo-Impressionist style. But some writers, misled either by Signac's prominence as proselytizer or by Pissarro's previously established reputation, failed to acknowledge Seurat's leadership. As a result, he wrote several important letters to Fénéon in which he defended his position as innovator in 1885. In one of these letters, he pointed out that Pissarro's first canvases that were "divided in purity of hue" — following Seurat's example — dated from January or February 1886 (letter from Seurat to Fénéon [June 20, 1890] version "A"). Seurat also wrote that Signac modified his first major canvas, *Apprêteuse et garnisseuse (modes)*,

*rue du Caire* (dated 1885), at the time that he (Seurat) finished *La Grande Jatte* — the implication being that the younger artist became convinced of the value of his friend's technical innovations and applied them in this painting (letter from Seurat to Fénéon [June 20, 1890], version "B"). In version "A" of this letter, Seurat insisted that Signac's first paintings that were "divided without an achromatic underbody and pure in touch" (that is, following Seurat's new technique) were *Passage du Puits-Bertin, Clichy* (March–April, 1886) and *Les Gazomètres, Clichy* (March–April, 1886). Seurat's friends were admitted to his studio while work on *La Grande Jatte* was in progress, and it is here, presumably, that they received the necessary technical and theoretical information which enabled them to reflect his discoveries in their own canvases (Jules Christophe, "Albert Dubois-Pillet," *La Cravache*, September 15, 1888, no pagination).

5. For a discussion of Seurat's procedures in conceiving and executing *La Grande Jatte*, see Daniel C. Rich, *Seurat and the Evolution of "La Grande Jatte."*

6. Letter from Seurat to Fénéon (June 20, 1890), version "B."

7. *Ibid.*, version "A."

8. Dorra and Rewald, *op. cit.*, cat. nos. 108, 109, 110, 111, 112, 113, 114, 119, 120, 126, 127, 128.

9. *Loc. cit.*, cat. nos. 115, 116, 118, 122, 125, 134, 135, 136, 137.

10. The writer has discussed in this book only those paintings that he has studied personally or of which he has reliable color photographs. For this reason no attempt has been made to comment on all of the oil studies for *Une Baignade* and *La Grande Jatte*.

11. Paul Signac, "Les Besoins individuels et la peinture," *Encyclopédie française*, XVI, p. 16.84-89.

12. Letter from Charles Angrand to Gustave Coquiot, quoted in the latter's *Seurat*, pp. 40–41. In these remarks Angrand was referring to the years 1885–1886, when he was working with Seurat at the island of la Grande Jatte.

13. Dorra and Rewald, *op. cit.*, p. 151.

14. Letter from Seurat to Fénéon (June 20, 1890), version "A."

15. As in Dorra and Rewald, *op. cit.*, cat. nos. 133a, 133c, 134a, 134b, 134c, 134d, 138a, 138e, 138h, 138j.

16. As in *loc. cit.*, cat. nos. 131a, 133b, 138b, 138c, 138d, 138g, 138i.

17. Félix Fénéon, "Signac," *Les Hommes d'aujourd'hui*, VIII, 373 [1890], no pagination [p. 1].

18. As one of the few contemporary critics who understood the Neo-

Impressionists' aims and theories, Félix Fénéon (1861–1944) defended the group in a series of brilliant articles. As co-founder and editor of *La Revue indépendante*, he was responsible for introducing the painters to many of his literary colleagues — chiefly Symbolist poets — some of whom became close friends of Seurat, Signac, and Pissarro. The value of these contacts for the artists was twofold: they discussed mutual esthetic problems; but equally important, the literary group wrote at length about the achievements of the Neo-Impressionist painters, thus providing essential documentation for this period. Fénéon's article "Les Impressionnistes," written as a review of the eighth exhibition of Impressionist paintings, served almost as a manifesto for the first phase of Neo-Impressionism. The article first appeared in *La Vogue*, June 13–20, 1886, pp. 261–275, but was also published with minor changes as pp. 9–26 in a booklet entitled *Les Impressionnistes en 1886*, which also included reviews of the Fifth Exposition Internationale and the second exhibition of the Indépendants. This was sold at some of the Neo-Impressionists' exhibitions as well as through the principal booksellers; although the printing was completed on October 26, 1886, the booklet apparently was not distributed until December of that year. On Fénéon's role as critic and spokesman for the Neo-Impressionists, see John Rewald, "Félix Fénéon," *Gazette des beaux-arts*, XXXII, July–August, 1947, pp. 46–62, and XXXIV, February, 1948, pp. 107–126.

19. Fénéon, "Les Impressionnistes," *La Vogue*, June 13–20, 1886, p. 272.
20. *Loc. cit.*
21. Émile Hennequin, "Notes d'art — Exposition des Artistes Indépendants," *La Vie moderne*, September 11, 1886, p. 581.
22. This letter, which dates from November 6, 1886, was published in Venturi, *Les Archives de l'impressionnisme*, II, p. 24. In an unpublished letter by Pissarro, of September 19, 1886 (in the collection of Mme. Ginette Signac), he stated that Seurat was the first one to have the good sense to apply Chevreul's discoveries to painting.
23. A brief account of this meeting was given by Signac, *Delacroix au néo-impressionnisme*, p. 56. While it is usually assumed that Signac visited Chevreul without Seurat accompanying him, Signac later wrote to Édouard Fer: "I recall our visit to the Gobelins, *with Seurat* [italics mine], to see papa Chevreul" (letter reproduced in Édouard Fer, *Solfège de la couleur*, Paris, 1954, p. vii). Also, Jacques Guenne quoted Signac as saying: "Seurat and I followed the discoveries of Helmholtz and O. N. Rood, and the writings of Charles Blanc. *We went* [italics mine] to pay a visit to Chevreul" (*L'Art vivant*, I, March 20, 1925, p. 3).

24. Pierre Wolf, "Charles Angrand," *Par Chez nous*, February–March, 1921, pp. 2–3.
25. Signac, *Delacroix au néo-impressionnisme*, p. 56.
26. Wolf, *loc. cit.*
27. This text was mentioned in an article by Gustave Kahn: "Seurat was concerned about the so-called '*papier de Gauguin.*' He [Seurat] possessed a copy of it, for Gauguin did not hide the truth; it was an extract from an oriental text on the coloring of carpets and contained facts on the gradation of harmonies...." ("Au Temps du pointillisme," p. 16.) Excerpts from this text were published in translation by Van Wyck Brooks in *The Intimate Journals of Paul Gauguin*, London, 1923, pp. 31–33; Seurat's copy of it is in the collection of Mme. Ginette Signac. Cf. Robert L. Herbert, "Seurat in Chicago and New York," p. 151. H. R. Rookmaaker has suggested that the Zunbul-Zadé text may have been Gauguin's own creation, but cites no specific evidence to support this claim (*Synthetist Art Theories*, II [notes], Amsterdam, 1959, p. 37).
28. Kahn, *loc. cit.*
29. Several reliable accounts indicate that Seurat and the Neo-Impressionists knew the work of the German physicist Hermann von Helmholtz (1821–1894). Signac cited him in *Delacroix au néo-impressionnisme* (p. 80) as one of Seurat's sources and in a later account stated that he had followed the discoveries of Helmholtz (*L'Art vivant*, I, March 20, 1925, p. 3; cf. note 23 of this chapter). In an unpublished draft of some of his theories (in the collection of Mme. Ginette Signac) Seurat mentioned that they were drawn from, among other writers, "H. Helmholtz." Also, Octave Mirbeau cited Helmholtz as one of Pissarro's sources, presumably during the period when he was influenced by Seurat and Signac: "Pissarro wanted to adapt to the technique of his art the applications corresponding to science, in particular, Chevreul's theories and Helmholtz's discoveries on the nature of colors." (*Des Artistes*, I, Paris, 1924, p. 148, reprinted from *Le Figaro*, February 1, 1892.) While Seurat would have known Helmholtz's discoveries in the science of color through Rood's book, it is very probable that the artist was also familiar with Helmholtz's "L'Optique et la peinture," which appeared in the latter part of E. W. von Brücke's *Principes scientifiques des beaux-arts*, Paris, 1878 (the original German text, "Optisches über Malerei," was published in Helmholtz's *Populäre wissenschaftliche Vorträge*, II, Braunschweig, 1876). This popular essay drew heavily on the author's monumental *Handbuch der physiologischen Optik*, Leipzig, 1867 (translated into French and published in 1867 as *Optique physiologique*), a book on which Rood based

much of his *Text-Book of Color*. Because of the difficulties in determining which of Helmholtz's books Seurat studied and the period when he studied them, no attempt will be made here to discuss the direct influence of the German scientist's writings on Seurat's theories.

30. A valuable account of which writers and painters interested Seurat about 1886 was given by his friend Gustave Kahn: "What one may say here to characterize this epoch of the painter and his thought is that this technique had been revealed to him by two sources, the reading of books by Chevreul and Rood and also the knowledge of the prefiguring of this technique by earlier painters. He cited Delacroix's frescoes in Saint-Sulpice and declared that he had found division of tone in Veronese and Murillo." ("Seurat," p. 108.)

31. These are "Les Impressionnistes," *La Vogue*, June 13–20, 1886, pp. 261–275 (reprinted with minor changes in *Les Impressionnistes en 1886*, Paris, 1886, pp. 9–26), the technical aspects of which were checked by Pissarro, and about which Seurat wrote: "I always consider Fénéon's brochure as the exposition of my ideas on painting." (letter from Seurat to Signac, August 26, 1888, published in Rewald, *Seurat*, Paris, 1948, p. 115); "Le Néo-impressionnisme," *L'Art moderne*, May 1, 1887, pp. 138–140; and "Signac," *Les Hommes d'aujourd'hui*, VIII, 373 [1890], no pagination. About the last-mentioned article, Seurat wrote to Maurice Beaubourg (August 28, 1890): "There you will find the technique of *optical mixture* described perfectly from a scientific point of view." Also, in a letter to Fénéon (June 20, 1890), versions "A," "B," and "C," the artist pointed out that, except for one or two insignificant details, this article accurately described him (Seurat) and his vision, though without mentioning him by name.

32. Fénéon, "Le Néo-impressionnisme," *L'Art moderne*, May 1, 1887, p. 139. A very close correspondence exists between a large part of Fénéon's account of Seurat's procedures and Rood's coverage of the same subject; the American scientist wrote the following about the effects of lighting on a colored surface: "The resultant tint of the surface will depend on three circumstances: first, on the colour which it assumes owing to the presence of white light — that is to say, which it has owing to its natural or, as artists call it, "local colour"; secondly, on the colour communicated to it by that portion of the coloured light which is reflected unaltered from its surface; and to these there must be added, thirdly, the effects produced by the coloured light which penetrates below the surface, and is reflected after undergoing a certain amount of absorption." (Rood, *Text-Book of Color*, pp. 149–150.)

33. Hennequin, *loc. cit.*
34. Rood, *Text-Book of Color*, p. 278. These quotations were taken from p. 221 and 218–219 of Ruskin's *Elements of Drawing* (London, 1857). In an authoritative article on the theory of chromo-luminarism, Alphonse Germain concisely summarized these very passages as a means of demonstrating Ruskin's significance for the Neo-Impressionists ("Théorie chromo-luminariste," *La Plume*, September 1, 1891, p. 286).
35. Fénéon, "Les Impressionnistes," p. 271.
36. Fénéon, "Signac" [p. 1].
37. Letter from Seurat to Beaubourg, August 28, 1890.
38. Fénéon, "Signac" [p. 1].
39. *Ibid.*
40. Chevreul, *The Principles of Harmony and Contrast of Colours*, p. 123.
41. *Ibid.*, p. 8.
42. Fénéon, "Les Impressionnistes," p. 271.
43. *Ibid.*
44. Fénéon, "Signac" [p. 1].
45. *Ibid.*
46. Fénéon, "Les Impressionnistes," pp. 271–272.
47. Rood, *Text-Book*, pp. 148–149.
48. Fénéon, "Les Impressionnistes," p. 272.
49. For an account of these experiments, see Rood, *Text-Book*, pp. 146–149.
50. *Ibid.*, p. 147.
51. Letter from Seurat to Beaubourg, August 28, 1890.
52. Rood, *Text-Book*, p. 207.
53. *Ibid.*
54. Fénéon, "Les Impressionnistes," pp. 273–274.
55. As far as this writer knows, no French translation of Dove's *Darstellung der Farbenlehre und optische Studien* (Berlin, 1853) was made during Seurat's lifetime.
56. Rood, *Text-Book*, p. 280.
57. Fénéon, "Les Impressionnistes," p. 273.
58. The *croqueton* that reveals the use of small dots in its execution is *Étude pour la composition complète de "La Grande Jatte"* (D.-R. 137).
59. Blanc, *The Grammar of Painting and Engraving*, p. 164.
60. Rood, *Text-Book*, pp. 139–140.
61. Hennequin, *loc. cit.*
62. Rood, *Text-Book*, p. 140.
63. The reports of Seurat's interest in Murillo's work come from Gustave Kahn, "Seurat," p. 108, and "Au Temps du pointillisme," p. 15.

64. Seurat's conception of the surface of *La Grande Jatte* and later paintings as an abstract screen composed of tiny molecular units that transmit colored light has obvious analogies with the primitive color photographs of his day. Could he have been influenced by them? We have no concrete evidence to indicate that he studied color photography, but because of the similarities between this medium and his painting technique, the possibility of influence should at least be considered. The process of three-color photography was invented in France by Louis Ducos du Hauron (1837–1920) and Charles Cros (1842–1888); basing their technique partly on the researches of James Clerk Maxwell, they discovered the solution to the problem independently of each other in 1869. Their method was derived from the premise that all visible colors could be reproduced by various combinations (either additive or subtractive) of three primary colors. Thus, when separate photographic records corresponding to these colors were projected on a screen or superimposed, the original hues of the subject would be reconstituted. Seurat could have seen such photographs as early as 1878 at the Exposition Universelle Internationale in Paris. There Ducos du Hauron exhibited a dozen three-color prints, along with some three-color separation negatives. Furthermore, in the 1880's Charles Cros, who was also a poet, was in close touch with Félix Fénéon, Charles Henry, and their circle. We cannot be certain that Cros personally influenced Seurat, but there is a very strong possibility that they exchanged ideas at the gatherings of the Symbolist literary group.

65. Seurat's palette is preserved in the collection of Mme. Ginette Signac. Although I have studied it personally, I was unable to obtain permission to photograph it in color and thus it cannot be reproduced here. The arrangement of pigments on Seurat's palette went through several stages of evolution; the palette in Mme. Signac's collection probably reflects his later concepts of color. For a description of an earlier palette arrangement, see Coquiot, *Seurat*, p. 40. Cf. also my "Notes on Seurat's Palette," *The Burlington Magazine*, CI, May, 1959, pp. 192–193.

66. Fénéon, "Exposition des Artistes-Indépendants," *L'Art moderne*, October 27, 1889, p. 339.

67. Cf. Rood, *Text-Book*, pp. 179–180, and Chevreul, *Principles of Harmony and Contrast*, pp. 57–58.

68. Zunbul-Zadé quoted in *The Intimate Journals of Paul Gauguin*, p. 32.

69. Seurat wrote to Fénéon: "I abandoned earth colors from [18]82 to 1884." (Unpublished letter [June 20, 1890], version "C," collection of César de Hauke.)

70. Signac, *Delacroix au néo-impressionnisme*, pp. 84–85.

71. Unpublished letter from Signac to Amédée Ozenfant, dated March 5, 1935 (Collection of Amédée Ozenfant, Cannes). Additional information about the technique of preserving the purity of color may be found in an unpublished letter from Signac to Arsène Alexandre, dated May 13, 1902, in the Museum of Modern Art, New York. Here Signac explained that if the Neo-Impressionists wish to produce a sensation of violet, they put down on the canvas a touch of violet (which exists on their palette), not a touch of red beside a touch of blue. Also, it was permissible to add small quantities of red or blue to this violet. But, he declared that mixtures of complementaries should be avoided because they produce muddy tones. Complementaries, however, could be set down side by side on the canvas: the result, according to Signac, would be a fine and luminous optical gray.

72. Signac, *Delacroix au néo-impressionnisme*, pp. 73–74.

73. Unpublished letter from Signac to Ozenfant, March 5, 1935.

74. Rood, *Text-Book*, p. 292.

75. Letter from Seurat to Beaubourg, August 28, 1890.

76. Chevreul, *Principles of Harmony and Contrast*, pp. 69–70.

77. *Gazette des beaux-arts*, XXXIX, April, 1952, p. 304.

78. Couture, *Conversations on Art Methods*, p. 160.

79. Fénéon, "Le Néo-impressionnisme," *L'Art moderne*, May 1, 1887, p. 139.

80. Fénéon, "Signac" [p. 2].

81. Fénéon, "L'Impressionnisme aux Tuileries," *L'Art moderne*, September 19, 1886, p. 300.

82. Fénéon, "Le Néo-impressionnisme," *L'Art moderne*, May 1, 1887, p. 139.

83. Fénéon, "Signac" [p. 2].

84. Fénéon, "Le Néo-impressionnisme," *L'Art moderne*, May 1, 1887, p. 139.

85. Fénéon, "Signac" [p. 1].

86. George Moore, *Modern Painting*, London, n.d., pp. 89–90.

87. Fénéon, "L'Impressionnisme aux Tuileries," p. 300.

88. These are "L'Impressionnisme aux Tuileries," *L'Art moderne*, September 19, 1886, pp. 300–302, and "Le Néo-impressionnisme," *L'Art moderne*, May 1, 1887, pp. 138–140.

89. Fénéon, "Les Impressionnistes," p. 271.

90. *Ibid.*, p. 275; "L'Impressionnisme aux Tuileries," p. 392; "Le Néo-impressionnisme," *L'Art moderne*, May 1, 1887, p. 138; and *Les Impressionnistes en 1886*, p. 43.

91. Fénéon, "L'Impressionnisme aux Tuileries," p. 302.

92. Letter from Signac to Paul Alexis, February 6, 1888, published in *Le Cri du peuple*, February 9, 1888.

93. Letter from Camille Pissarro to Lucien Pissarro, May 15, 1887 (published in Camille Pissarro, *Letters to his Son Lucien*, p. 110).

94. Fénéon, "L'Impressionnisme aux Tuileries," p. 302.

95. Henry van de Velde, "Notes sur l'art — 'Chahut,'" *La Wallonie*, V, 1890, p. 122.

96. Fénéon, "L'Impressionnisme aux Tuileries," p. 301.

97. Often considered a preparatory study, the small version of *Les Poseuses* was identified as a small replica of the large canvas by Fénéon in the catalogue he prepared for the Seurat exhibition held at the Bernheim-Jeune Galleries in 1908–1909.

98. Fénéon, "Le Néo-impressionnisme," *L'Art moderne*, May 1, 1887, p. 139.

99. J. K. Huysmans, "Chronique d'art — Les Indépendants," *La Revue indépendante*, April 1887, p. 54.

100. Fénéon, "Le Néo-impressionnisme," *L'Art moderne*, May 1, 1887, p. 139.

101. Hennequin, "Notes d'art — L'Exposition des Artistes Indépendants," p. 581.

102. George Moore, *Modern Painting*, p. 94.

103. In his *Recent Ideals of American Art* (New York, c. 1890, p. 160), George W. Sheldon reported the results of an interview with Camille Pissarro, in which the following instructions about viewing distance were given: "A painting should be seen, as Nature is seen, at a distance sufficient to allow its colors to blend; or, generally speaking, at a distance as long as three times its diagonal." While Sheldon believed that he was recounting the tenets of Impressionism — and indeed he had received information from one of the former practitioners of that style — at the time of the interview Pissarro had been influenced heavily by the Neo-Impressionists and was undoubtedly echoing their theories, not those of the original Impressionist group. We thus have one piece of fairly reliable evidence concerning the viewing distance advocated by the Neo-Impressionists. Significantly, the distance of five to seven feet that the present writer recommends for viewing the small version of *Les Poseuses*, which is based on actual experience and trial and error, is confirmed by Pissarro's instructions: the length of the diagonal of *Les Poseuses* (small version) is 24.5 inches; when multiplied by three the result is 6.12 feet.

104. Rood. *Text-Book*, p. 280.

105. An excellent discussion of the phenomenon of lustre in painting appears in Roland Rood, *Color and Light in Painting*, pp. 118–143.

4

SEURAT'S THEORIES OF EXPRESSION, THEIR
SOURCES AND APPLICATION (1887–1891)

1. Gustave Kahn, "Seurat," p. 108.
2. T. de Wyzewa, "Georges Seurat," *L'Art dans les deux mondes*, April 18, 1891, p. 263.
3. Letter from Seurat to Fénéon (June 20, 1890), version "B."
4. "Introduction à une esthétique scientifique," *La Revue contemporaine*, August 1885, pp. 441–469.
5. Fénéon, "L'Impressionnisme aux Tuileries," p. 302.
6. The full title of this elephant folio by Henry is: *Cercle chromatique de M. Charles Henry présentant tous les compléments et toutes les harmonies de couleurs avec une introduction sur la théorie générale de la dynamogénie autrement dit du contraste, du rythme et de la mesure.*
7. Fénéon, "Le Néo-impressionnisme," *L'Art moderne*, May 1, 1887, p. 140.
8. Fénéon, "Le Néo-impressionnisme," *L'Art moderne*, April 15, 1888, p. 122.
9. Herbert, "Seurat in Chicago and New York," *The Burlington Magazine*, C, May, 1958, p. 152. The drawing is in the collection of Mme. Ginette Signac.
10. Gustave Kahn, "Peinture: Exposition des Indépendants," *La Revue indépendante*, April, 1888, p. 160.
11. Fénéon, "5e Exposition de la Société des Artistes Indépendants," *La Vogue*, September, 1889 (reprinted in *L'Art moderne*, October 27, 1889, p. 339).
12. Fénéon, "Certains," *Art et critique*, December 14, 1889, p. 454.
13. Georges Lecomte, "Société des Artistes Indépendants," *L'Art moderne*, March 30, 1890, pp. 100–101. Although Seurat illustrated his letter to Beaubourg of August 20, 1890, with three-pronged diagrams (Figure 58, page 204), an unpublished draft of the theory that appears in that letter (collection of Mme. Ginette Signac) is also illustrated with "V"-shaped angular diagrams, as described by Lecomte.
14. Kahn, "Seurat," p. 109.
15. Letter from Seurat to Fénéon (June 24, 1890), published in de Hauke, *op. cit.*, I, p. xxiii.
16. Jules Christophe, "Georges Seurat," *Les Hommes d'aujourd'hui*, VIII, 368, no pagination [p. 3]. This article is undated; Dorra and Rewald have dated it about March–April, 1890 (*op. cit.*, p. 294).

17. Letter from Seurat to Fénéon (June 24, 1890), published in de Hauke, *op. cit.*, I, p. xxiii.

18. Gustave Coquiot, *Georges Seurat*, Paris, 1924, pp. 232–233, and *Des Peintres maudits*, Paris, 1924, p. 132; Walter Pach published an English translation of the letter in *Georges Seurat*, New York, 1923, pp. 24–25.

19. A photograph of this letter was reproduced by Rey, *La Renaissance du sentiment classique*, opp. p. 132.

20. Émile Verhaeren, "Georges Seurat," *La Société nouvelle*, April 1891, p. 434.

21. Kahn, "Seurat," p. 109.

22. For Henry's biography see *Cahiers de l'étoile*, no. 13, January–February, 1930 (a special issue including twenty-two articles on his life and work); Francis Warrain, *L'Oeuvre psychobiophysique de Charles Henry*, Paris, 1931, pp. 9–19; and Jacques Boyer, "Nécrologie: Charles Henry," *Revue générale des sciences pures et appliquées*, XXXVIII, January 15, 1927, pp. 1–2. For an analysis of Henry's research and an evaluation of his contribution to scientific thought, see Warrain, *op. cit.*, and C. Andry-Bourgeois, *L'Oeuvre de Charles Henry et le problème de la survie*, Paris, 1931.

23. Henry's relationship to the Symbolist literary group has been discussed by Rewald in *Post-Impressionism — from Van Gogh to Gauguin*; Warren Ramsey in *Jules Laforgue and the Ironic Inheritance*, New York, 1953; Marie-Jeanne Durry in *Jules Laforgue*, Paris, n.d.; and Sven Lövgren, *The Genesis of Modernism*. Henry is also known to have influenced the Symbolist poets' theories of expression (see Gustave Kahn, "Réponse aux symbolistes," *L'Événement*, September 28, 1886).

24. Signac described his collaboration with Henry as follows: "Around 1890 I was his obedient collaborator. After my day of painting, I worked on his *Rapporteur esthétique* and *Cercle chromatique* for him, analyzing or calculating lengths, rhythms, hues, and harmonies." (*Cahiers de l'étoile*, January–February, 1930, p. 72.) Cf. also Signac's letter to Van Gogh (letter 584a) published in *The Complete Letters of Vincent Van Gogh*, III, Greenwich (Conn.), n.d. [1960], p. 153.

25. A valuable account of the relationship between Henry, Pissarro, and Seurat, including reference to one of Henry's demonstrations, was published by Pissarro's friend and biographer Georges Lecomte: "Even if Camille Pissarro did have a few chances to meet Charles Henry, whose accounts of his work during this period were neither very clear nor very exciting, perhaps it was above all Georges Seurat, who, having frequented Charles Henry's 'school,' knew how to speak to

Camille Pissarro in a language both persuasive and accessible for a painter little acquainted with mathematics and chemical formulae. Henry addressed the painters with chalk in hand and at the blackboard spoke about art with them. I still remember a fuliginous conversation of that kind, at the end of which Henry was squatting in front of an immense blackboard, which he had covered from top to bottom and from East to Far-West with equations and formulae during the course of this bizarre esthetic chat. These scholarly demonstrations about the nature of light — which certainly could have used some of it — were to leave the outsider Pissarro untouched, that artist in love with truth and poetry, that sincere and profoundly moved interpreter of his sensations. But the serious and patient Seurat, whose youthful fervor was fired by these theories to the point of listening to them tirelessly, clarified them in a more lucid painterly language so that Camille Pissarro could in turn become permeated with them." (*Camille Pissarro*, Paris, 1922, p. 75.)

26. Gustave Kahn, for example, wrote "that he became familiar with Charles Henry's precise works on scientific esthetics, and notably the *Cercle chromatique*, with its preface going beyond the question of color alone in order to examine more thoroughly the phenomena of line." ("Seurat," p. 109.) While Kahn stressed the importance of the *Cercle chromatique* for Seurat, Alphonse Germain mentioned the *Rapporteur esthétique* as being one of his sources: "Somewhat later, Seurat and Signac, very much taken by the *Rapporteur esthétique* by Charles Henry, added to the contrasts of color — in order to reinforce the sensations — the contrast of linear directions." ("Théorie chromo-luminariste," p. 285.)

27. Henry, "Introduction à une esthétique scientifique," p. 441.

28. *Ibid.*, p. 442.

29. *Ibid.*, p. 445.

30. *Ibid.*, p. 447.

31. *Ibid.*

32. *Ibid.*

33. *Ibid.*

34. *Ibid.*, pp. 451–452.

35. The writer wishes to acknowledge the assistance of Dr. Richard E. Quandt, Professor of Mathematical Economics, Princeton University, in checking the mathematical calculations derived from Henry's theories.

36. Henry, "Introduction à une esthétique scientifique," p. 454.

37. *Ibid.*

38. *Ibid.*, pp. 455–456.

39. Henry, *Cercle chromatique*, Paris, 1889, p. 23.
40. Henry, "Introduction à une esthétique scientifique," p. 457.
41. More detailed suggestions about the construction of this circle were given by Henry in his *Harmonies de formes et de couleurs*, Paris, 1891, p. 40: "To obtain pleasing juxtaposition of colors, I cut out small apertures in this screen, which is exactly equal in size to the chromatic circle; those which are situated on the circumference present more or less refrangible hues, and those situated on the radius present tones that are more or less cleansed of white and more or less reduced in black. Since these apertures are no larger than three millimeters, on the average, they present colors which appear to be of uniform hue and value because of the mixture. All these apertures, situated at an equal distance from the center and separated one from the other by a section of the circumference whose reciprocal is a rhythmic number, present colors whose juxtaposition is pleasing to the eye; all the other apertures present displeasing juxtapositions." In his diary, Signac referred to the public's need for a simple chromatic circle, which, in general purpose and construction, corresponds very closely to Henry's ideas: "[At the sight of some ugly houses] . . . This again gives me the wish to publish a small device — a chromatic circle with a screen — giving the two, three, or four tones and tints which go well together and harmonize with one another. It would render the greatest service to dressmakers, modistes, house painters, upholsterers, and would prevent them from falling into those serious errors which too frequently spoil their best creations. It would lead them toward harmony, without groping. — A small 10-line note would tell them: 'If you have a red and want to make it agree with two other tints . . . turn the disk and you will find the three tints which harmonize best.'" ("Extraits du journal inédit de Paul Signac, I, 1894–1895," pp. 167–168.)
42. There appears to be a very high degree of correspondence between Seurat's color harmonies in *La Parade*, *Le Chahut*, and *Le Cirque* and the harmonious color relationships obtained by superimposing the cardboard screen over Henry's *cercle chromatique*. In order to demonstrate these correlations conclusively, however, it would be necessary to compare Henry's circle to the original paintings, rather than to color transparencies, which the writer was unable to do.
43. From Signac, who executed the plates for Henry's *Rapporteur esthétique*, we have a firsthand account of the value of the *rapporteur* (protractor) for artists; in a letter to Vincent Van Gogh he wrote: "I seize the opportunity afforded by this hitch to carry out the blocks for a work

commissioned from me, in collaboration with Mr. Ch. Henry, by the Librairie de l'Art (perhaps you have read a number of articles by my collaborator in the *Revue Indépendante*). It is a book on the Aesthetics of Forms, for which an instrument — the aesthetic protractor [*rapporteur esthétique*] constructed by Ch. Henry — permits one to study the measurements and the angles. In this way one can see whether a form is harmonious or not. This will be of great social importance, especially with reference to industrial art. We are going to teach the workmen, apprentices, etc., to see the correctness and beauty of things, for till now they have only received aesthetic education by means of empirical formulae couched in misleading or fatuous advice. I am going to send you one of these pamphlets as soon as they have been published." (Letter 584a, *The Complete Letters of Vincent Van Gogh*, III, p. 153.)

44. Dorra and Rewald (*op. cit.*, pp. lxxii, xciv), for example, have linked Seurat's letter to Beaubourg with Henry's ideas. On the other hand, in his article "Une Source oubliée de Seurat" (*Archives de l'art français*, XXII, 1959, p. 401), André Chastel stated that "the letter to Maurice Beaubourg of August 28, 1890, proposes a systematization largely borrowed from Sutter's articles, 'Les Phénomènes de la vision' (1880)." The present writer finds it very difficult to defend such a statement in the light of evidence that relegates Sutter's influence on the Beaubourg letter to a relatively small role. The main clue to the sources upon which Seurat relied in composing this statement is found in the title of an unpublished draft for it (collection of Mme. Ginette Signac): "General practical theory proceeding from Delacroix and oriental precepts, and drawing upon the experiments of Chevreul, Rood, Helmholtz and C. Henry."

45. Henry, *Rapporteur esthétique*, p. 15.

46. Signac listed Humbert de Superville among the authors Seurat studied (*Delacroix au néo-impressionnisme*, p. 80). For a discussion of Humbert's influence on Seurat's theories, see Chastel, *op. cit.* For a detailed study of his life and work, see Cornelia Magdalena de Haas, *Humbert de Superville*, Leyden, 1941.

47. D. P. G. Humbert de Superville, *Essai sur les signes inconditionnels dans l'art*, Leyden, 1827–1832, p. 6.

48. *Ibid.*, p. 7. Humbert de Superville's diagrams of the human face (Figure 56, page 201) were popularized through Blanc's *Grammaire des arts du dessin*, p. 33, and Dr. Mathias Duval's *Précis d'anatomie*, Paris, n.d. [1881]. p. 293.

49. *Ibid.*, p. 8.

50. *Ibid.*, p. 9.
51. *Ibid.*, p. 10.
52. *Ibid.*, p. 25.
53. These are in the collection of Mme. Ginette Signac. Some of the sketches are on the same sheet as drawings for *La Parade*, and thus may be dated tentatively in 1887–1888. Among this group of documents are diagrams Seurat drew on the basis of such configurations as Figures 55 and 61 (pages 201 and 208, respectively).
54. Signac, *Delacroix au néo-impressionnisme*, p. 80.
55. *Ibid.*, p. 25.
56. Sutter, "Les Phénomènes de la vision," *L'Art*, XX, 1880, p. 75.
57. *Ibid.*, p. 76.
58. Blanc, *Grammaire des arts du dessin*, p. 33.
59. *Ibid.*
60. Blanc, *The Grammar of Painting and Engraving*, p. 111.
61. *Ibid.*, p. 127.
62. *Ibid.*, p. 40.
63. *Ibid.*, pp. 40–44.
64. *Ibid.*, pp. 34–35.
65. The writer is indebted to Jennifer Montagu's historical account of the concept of the "modes" in her "Charles le Brun's Conférence sur l'expression générale et particulière," unpublished Ph.D. dissertation, University of London, 1959. See also Jan Bialostocki, "Das Modusproblem in den bildenden Künsten," *Zeitschrift für Kunstgeschichte*, XXIV, 2, 1961, pp. 128–141.
66. Letter published in C. Jouanny, *Correspondance de Nicolas Poussin*, Paris, 1911, pp. 372–374 (translation from Elizabeth Holt, *Literary Sources of Art History*, Princeton, 1947, p. 380). Poussin's conception of modes has been traced by Anthony Blunt to the influence of the writings of the sixteenth-century Venetian composer Gioseffo Zarlino (see Paul Alfassa, "L'Origine de la lettre de Poussin sur les modes," *Bulletin de la Société de l'Histoire de l'Art Français*, 1933, pp. 125–143).
67. See Le Brun's remarks published in *Mémoires inédits sur la vie et les ouvrages des membres de l'Académie Royale de Peinture et de Sculpture*, I, Paris, 1854, pp. 253–254; a report on the *séance* of March 1, 1870 by Guillet de Saint-Georges quoted in André Fontaine, *Conférences inédites de l'Académie Royale de Peinture et de Sculpture*, Paris, 1903, pp. 116–117. Cf. also André Félibien's preface to the *Conférences de l'Académie Royale de Peinture et de Sculpture*, Paris, 1705; Henry Testelin, *Sentimens des plus habiles peintres sur la pratique de la peinture et sculpture*, Paris, 1696, p. 20;

and Florent le Comte, *Cabinet des singularitez d'architecture, peinture, sculpture, et graveure*, Paris, 1699. (These references were cited in Montagu, *op. cit.*)

68. Sutter, *Philosophie des beaux-arts*, Paris, 1858, p. 218.

69. Signac, "Les Besoins individuels et la peinture," *Encyclopédie française*, XVI, p. 16.84–87.

70. *Ibid*.

71. H. von Helmholtz, "L'Optique et la peinture" (in E. W. von Brücke, *Principes scientifiques des beaux-arts*, Paris, 1878), pp. 207–209; Sutter, "Les Phénomènes de la vision," p. 216; Henry, *Cercle chromatique*, pp. 23–24.

72. From H. von Helmholtz, *loc. cit.*, pp. 207–208 (this translation is from Helmholtz's *Popular Lectures on Scientific Subjects*, London, 1881, p. 119). It should be pointed out that Rood did not discuss the principle of irradiation. Thus, we must turn either to Helmholtz or to Henry as the probable source for Seurat's understanding of this phenomenon.

73. Fénéon, "Signac" [p. 1].

74. It is almost certain that Seurat understood the term "irradiation" in a scientific sense, that is, as interpreted by Robert Rey, who probably obtained information about this phenomenon from Seurat's friends Signac and Cross. He discussed the application of the law of irradiation in painting as follows: "It is to be noted that within the zone of shadow, the darkest part is not to be found exactly at the limit of contrast but slightly beyond it. This is by virtue of the law of *irradiation*. The higher tone, the brighter light always drives back the darker tone, the less intense light behind the actual borders." (*La Renaissance du sentiment classique*, pp. 110–111.) Although Sutter discussed "irradiation," he used the word in a nonscientific way to refer to the effects of contrast ("Les Phénomènes de la vision," p. 216).

75. Something should be said here about Helmholtz's remarks on color in "L'Optique et la peinture," which Seurat probably knew. Undoubtedly of value to the painter were Helmholtz's observations on simultaneous contrast, in which he reviewed and amplified some of Chevreul's theories and pointed out how they could be applied in painting. Of particular interest is Helmholtz's belief that optical effects of contrast should be duplicated in the work of art: "If . . . with the pigments at his command, the artist wishes to reproduce the impression which objects give, as strikingly as possible, he must paint the contrasts which they produce. If the colours on the picture are as brilliant and luminous as in the actual objects, the contrasts in the former case would produce them-

selves as spontaneously as in the latter. Here, also, subjective phenomena of the eye must be objectively introduced into the picture, because the scale of colour and of brightness is different upon the latter" (translation from Helmholtz, *Popular Scientific Lectures*, p. 118). From this subject he passed to the matter of irradiation, which we have discussed earlier. Helmholtz also recommended two systems of harmony: like Rood, he believed that complementary pairs and triads of color were innately harmonious; and like Chevreul, he realized that analogous colors harmonized with each other. While Rood and Chevreul dealt with practical aspects of color composition and proposed general rules for harmony, Helmholtz provided a physiological and psychological basis for the approach to nature that Seurat appears to have followed. The German scientist not only examined physical phenomena carefully but also took into account the characteristics of the perceiving organism. In short, he felt that the artist should incorporate in his canvases his subjective visual reactions to nature's phenomena.

76. It is interesting to note, parenthetically, that Seurat's conclusions about the expressive value of color and line were confirmed in several experiments conducted by psychologists during this century: cf. A. T. Poffenberger and B. E. Barrows, "The Feeling Value of Lines," *Journal of Applied Psychology*, VIII, 2, 1924, pp. 187–205; Helge Lundholm, "The Affective Tone of Lines: Experimental Researches," *The Psychological Review*, XXIII, January, 1921, pp. 43–60; Newton A. Wells, "A Description of the Affective Character of the Colors of the Spectrum," *The Psychological Bulletin*, VII, June 15, 1910, pp. 181–195; Kate Hevner, "Experimental Studies of the Affective Value of Colors and Lines," *Journal of Applied Psychology*, XIX, August, 1935, pp. 385–398.

77. Fénéon, "Le Néo-impressionnisme," *L'Art moderne*, April 15, 1888, p. 122.

78. Although we referred to the small replica of *Les Poseuses* in discussing fusion and modeling, our analysis of color harmony will be based on the earlier, large version of the picture in the Barnes Foundation, Merion, Pa.

79. Arsène Alexandre, "Chroniques d'aujourd'hui: un vaillant," *Paris*, April 1, 1891.

80. About *Les Poseuses*, van de Velde wrote: "His execution became more supple, his combinations grew bold, coming closer to true light, and in place of the hieratic postures of *La Grande Jatte*, we have the moving, undulating lines, the beautiful, lithe, fleshy bodies of *Les Poseuses*. One objection [to *La Grande Jatte*] among others: a style which would im-

mobilize life, which clothed the figures with a wooden rigidity and delighted in static attitudes more puerile than synthetic, had visibly struck Seurat; and to the stiff promenaders who actually become the background of his *Poseuses*, he opposes the beautiful, moving bodies of women!" (Henry van de Velde, "Georges Seurat," *La Wallonie*, April 1891, p. 169.)

81. Thorough careful analysis of *La Parade*, Dorra (*op. cit.*, pp. xciii–xciv) has shown that the composition was based on the golden section ratio; he also demonstrated that this ratio was used as the basis of the composition of *Le Chahut* and *Le Cirque* (*op. cit.*, pp. c–ci, civ–cv).

82. Rood, *Text-book*, p. 293. Rood divided the contrast diagram (reproduced as Figure 14, page 40) into two halves by a line drawn from yellow-green to violet; the left-hand side contains the warm colors, and the right-hand side, the cool ones.

83. Signac, "Les Besoins individuels et la peinture," p. 16.84–7.

84. It is interesting to note that in one of his early oil studies for this painting, *Étude pour "Le Chahut"* (D.-R. 197; The Home House Trustees, London), Seurat planned the color harmony as a "triad" of red-orange (mixed with white), green, and ultramarine blue. However, he abandoned this traditional mode of color organization in the *Étude finale pour "Le Chahut"* (D.-R. 198, Albright Art Gallery, Buffalo) where, as in the final large canvas, a warm "dominant" prevails.

85. Henry, "Introduction à une esthétique scientifique," pp. 446–447. Similar ideas concerning the "rhythm of gesture" were communicated by Signac to George Moore who wrote: "According to Signac, the raising of the face and hands expresses joy, the depression of the face and hands denotes sadness." (*Modern Painting*, p. 94.)

86. We have discovered no documentary proof that Seurat used Henry's *rapporteur*, or protractor, in measuring the angles in *Le Chahut* and *Le Cirque*; however, as suggested in the text of this chapter, the correlations between Seurat's angular measurements and Henry's precepts are extremely close. Interestingly, in his comments on Seurat's drawing for the cover of Victor Joze's *L'Homme à femmes* (1889; D.-R. 196a) Georges Lecomte related the work to Henry's ideas: "In the background: women with simple, harmonic curves like those in nature. The gentleness of the movement of the terrain, the voluted majesty of the topographical lines — one would have thought them calculated by Charles Henry." ("La Ménagerie sociale, de M. Victor Joze — Une Couverture de M. Seurat," *Art et critique*, February 1, 1890, p. 87.) It is worth noting that Signac stated that he had followed (in paintings of 1889–1890)

"the recent discoveries of Charles Henry on the rhythms and measures of lines and colors." ("Catalogue de l'exposition des XX," *Art et critique*, February 1, 1890, p. 77.)

87. Dorra and Rewald, *Seurat*, p. c and Figure 38 (showing a grid of horizontals, verticals, and 45-degree diagonals superimposed over a photograph of *Le Chahut*).
88. Dorra and Rewald, *Seurat*, p. civ.
89. For Dorra's plate illustrating this gridwork see *ibid.*, Figure 41.
90. *Ibid.*, p. cvi.
91. Seurat seems to have had definite ideas about the nature of these changes and the amount of time he intended to devote to each phase of his "research." As his friend Teodor de Wyzewa recalled: "I did not tire of hearing him explain his researches in detail, the order which he planned to use, the number of years he expected to spend on them. Neither did he himself tire of explaining them to me." ("Georges Seurat," p. 263.)

5

## SEURAT AND SCIENCE

1. This letter was published in Dorra and Rewald, *Seurat*, pp. l–li.
2. *Loc. cit.*
3. This letter was published in Dorra and Rewald, *op. cit.*, pp. li–lii.
4. *Loc. cit.*
5. Fénéon, "L'Impressionnisme aux Tuileries," p. 302.
6. Émile Verhaeren, "Le Salon des *Vingt* à Bruxelles," *La Vie moderne*, February 26, 1887, p. 138.
7. Signac, *Delacroix au néo-impressionnisme*, pp. 120–121.
8. Kahn, "Seurat," p. 109.
9. Fénéon, "Au Pavillon de la ville de Paris," *Le Chat noir*, April 2, 1892, p. 1932.
10. Fénéon, "Paul Signac," *La Plume*, September 1, 1891, p. 299.
11. Kahn, "Seurat," pp. 108–109.
12. Verhaeren, "Georges Seurat," *La Société nouvelle*, April, 1891, p. 434.
13. *Ibid.*, p. 436.
14. De Wyzewa, "Georges Seurat," p. 263.
15. Verhaeren, *Sensations*, Paris, 1927, p. 203.
16. Letter published in Rewald, *Georges Seurat*, Paris, 1948, p. 115.
17. Sutter, "Les Phénomènes de la vision," p. 269.
18. Henry, *Rapporteur esthétique*, p. 15.

# Selected Bibliography

## BOOKS PUBLISHED BEFORE 1895

Blanc, Charles, *Artistes de mon temps*, Paris, 1876.

———, *Grammaire des arts du dessin*, Paris, 1867.

———, *The Grammar of Painting and Engraving*, trans. by Kate Newell Doggett, Chicago, 1879 (English translation of parts of the preceding).

———, *La Peinture*, Paris, 1886.

Bourgeois, Charles, *Leçons expérimentales d'optique sur la lumière et les couleurs*, Paris, 1816–1817.

———, *Manuel d'optique expérimentale, à l'usage des artistes et des physiciens*, Paris, 1821.

Bracquemond, Félix, *Du Dessin et de la couleur*, Paris, 1885.

Brücke, E. W. von, *Principes scientifiques des beaux-arts . . . suivies de l'optique et la peinture par H. Helmholtz*, Paris, 1878.

Chesneau, Ernest, *The Education of the Artist*, trans. by Clara Bell, London, 1886.

Chevreul, Michel-Eugène, *De la loi du contraste simultané des couleurs et de l'assortiment des objets colorés*, Paris, 1839.

———, *The Principles of Harmony and Contrast of Colours*, trans. by Charles Martel, London, 1872 (English translation of the preceding).

Couture, Thomas, *Méthode et entretiens d'atelier*, Paris, 1867.

———, *Conversations on Art Methods*, trans. by S. E. Stewart, New York, 1879 (English translation of the preceding).

Dove, Heinrich-Wilhelm, *Darstellung der Farbenlehre und optische Studien*, Berlin, 1853.

Fechner, Gustav Theodor, *Vorschule der Aesthetik*, Leipzig, 1876.

Fénéon, Félix, *Les Impressionnistes en 1886*, Paris, 1886.

Féré, C., *La Pathologie des émotions*, Paris, 1892.

Guillemin, Amédée, *La Lumière et les couleurs*, Paris, 1874.

Helmholtz, Hermann von, *Handbuch der physiologischen Optik*, Leipzig, 1867.

Hennequin, Émile, *La Critique scientifique*, Paris, 1888.

Henry, Charles, *Application de nouveaux instruments de précision à l'archéologie*, Paris, 1890.

Henry, Charles, *Cercle chromatique*, Paris, 1889.
———, *Harmonies de formes et de couleurs*, Paris, 1891.
———, *Rapporteur esthétique*, Paris, 1888.
Humbert de Superville, D. P. G., *Essai sur les signes inconditionnels dans l'art*, Leyden, 1827–1832.
Huysmans, J. K., *L'Art moderne*, Paris, 1883.
Leonardo da Vinci, *Traité de la peinture*, trans. by Roland Fréart de Chambray, Paris, 1651.
Lévèque, Charles, *La Science du beau*, 2 vols., Paris, 1872.
Moore, George, *Modern Painting*, London, 1893.
*Notice sur les travaux scientifiques de M. Charles Henry*, Rome, 1891.
Piron, A., *Eugène Delacroix, sa vie et ses œuvres*, Paris, 1865.
Rood, Ogden N., *Modern Chromatics* (*Students' Text-Book of Color*, New York, 1881), New York, 1879.
———, *Théorie scientifique des couleurs*, Paris, 1881 (French translation of the preceding).
Rosenstiehl, M. A., *Les premiers éléments de la science de la couleur*, Mulhouse, 1884.
Ruskin, John, *The Elements of Drawing*, London, 1856.
Sheldon, George W., *Recent Ideals of American Art*, New York, n.d. [c. 1890].
Silvestre, Théophile, *Eugène Delacroix*, Paris, 1864.
———, *Histoire des artistes vivants*, Paris, 1856.
Sully-Prudhomme, *Prose: l'expression dans les beaux-arts*, Paris, 1883.
Sutter, David, *L'Esthétique générale et appliquée*, Paris, 1865.
———, *Philosophie des beaux-arts*, Paris, 1858.
Véron, Eugène, *L'Esthétique*, 2nd ed., Paris, 1883.
Vibert, J.-G., *La Science de la peinture*, Paris, 1891.
Young, Thomas, *A Course of Lectures on Natural Philosophy and the Mechanical Arts*, I, London, 1807.
Ziegler, J., *Traité de la couleur et de la lumière*, Paris, 1852.

## BOOKS PUBLISHED AFTER 1895

Ajalbert, Jean, *Mémoires en vrac*, Paris, 1938.
Badt, Kurt, *Die Farbenlehre Van Goghs*, Köln, 1961.
Bernal, John D., *Science and Industry in the Nineteenth Century*, London, 1953.
Besson, Georges, *Paul Signac*, Paris, 1935.
———, *Paul Signac*, Paris, London, and New York, n.d.
———, *Paul Signac–Dessins*, Paris, 1950.

Boigey, Maurice, *La Science des couleurs et l'art du peintre*, Paris, 1923.

Boring, Edwin G., *History of Experimental Psychology*, 2nd ed., New York, 1950.

——, *Sensation and Perception in the History of Experimental Psychology*, New York, 1942.

Committee on Colorimetry, Optical Society of America, *The Science of Color*, New York, 1953.

*Complete Letters of Vincent Van Gogh*, 3 vols., Greenwich (Conn.), n.d. [1960].

Cooper, Douglas, *Georges Seurat: Une Baignade, Asnières*, London, n.d. [1945].

Coquiot, Gustave, *Cubistes, Futuristes, Passéistes*, Paris, 1914.

——, *Georges Seurat*, Paris, 1924.

——, *Les Indépendants, 1884–1920*, Paris, n.d.

——, *Des Peintres maudits*, Paris, 1924.

Cousturier, Lucie, *Paul Signac*, Paris, 1922.

——, *Seurat*, Paris, 1926.

*La Création de l'œuvre chez Paul Signac* (exhibition catalogue), Marlborough Fine Art, Ltd., London, April–May, 1958.

Cross, Henri-Edmond, *Carnet*, Paris, n.d.

——, *Carnet de dessins*, Paris, 1959.

Dampier, William, *A History of Science*, New York, 1938.

De Haas, Cornelia Magdalena, *David Pierre Giottino Humbert de Superville*, Leyden, 1941.

De Hauke, C. M., *Seurat et son œuvre*, 2 vols., Paris, 1961 [i.e., 1962].

Delacroix, Eugène, *Correspondance générale* (André Joubin, ed.), 5 vols., Paris, 1935.

——, *Journal* (André Joubin, ed.), 3 vols., Paris, 1932.

——, *Oeuvres littéraires*, 2 vols., Paris, 1923.

Dorra, Henri, and Rewald, John, *Seurat; l'œuvre peint; biographie et catalogue critique*, Paris, 1959.

Dumas, Horace, *La Physique des couleurs et la peinture*, Paris, 1930.

Duret, Théodore, *Histoire des peintres impressionnistes*, nouvelle édition, Paris, 1919.

Eder, Josef Marie, *History of Photography*, trans. by Edward Epstean, New York, 1945.

Evans, Ralph M., *Introduction to Color*, New York, 1948.

——, Hanson, W. T., Jr., and Brewer, W. Lyle, *Principles of Color Photography*, New York and London, 1953.

*Exposition d'œuvres de Paul Signac* (intro. by Arsène Alexandre), Paris, 1902.

Fénéon, Félix, *Oeuvres* (intro. by Jean Paulhan), Paris, 1948.

Fer, Édouard, *Solfège de la couleur*, Paris, 1954.

Friedman, Joseph S., *History of Color Photography*, Boston, 1947.

Gauss, Charles E., *The Aesthetic Theories of French Artists*, Baltimore, 1949.

Graves, Maitland, *Color Fundamentals*, New York, Toronto, and London, 1952.

*Le Groupe des XX et son temps* (exhibition catalogue), Brussels and Otterlo, 1962.

Herbert, Eugenia W., *The Artist and Social Reform*, New Haven, 1961.

Hess, Walter, *Das Problem der Farbe in den Selbstzeugnissen moderner Maler*, Munich, 1953.

———, *Die Farbe in der modernen Malerei*, Munich, 1950.

Johnson, Lee, *Delacroix*, London, 1963.

Kahn, Gustave, *Les Dessins de Seurat*, Paris, n.d. [1928].

———, *Symbolistes et décadents*, Paris, 1902.

Katz, David, *The World of Colour*, London, 1935.

Kouwer, B. J., *Colors and their Character*, The Hague, 1949.

Ladd-Franklin, Christine, *Colour and Colour Theories*, New York, 1929.

Laforgue, Jules, *Oeuvres complètes: mélanges posthumes*, Paris, 1919.

Lapparent, Paul de, *La Logique des procédés impressionnistes*, Paris, 1926.

Lecomte, Georges, *Camille Pissarro*, Paris, 1922.

Le Grand, Yves, *Optique physiologique*, 3 vols., Paris, 1946–1956.

Leonardo da Vinci, *Treatise on Painting*, trans. by A. Philip McMahon, 2 vols., Princeton, 1956.

Lövgren, Sven, *The Genesis of Modernism*, Uppsala, 1959.

Luckiesh, M., *Color and its Applications*, New York, 1921.

Maret, François [Franz van Ermengen], *Les Peintres luministes*, Brussels, 1944.

Maus, M.-O., *Trente années de lutte pour l'art, 1884–1914*, Brussels, 1926.

Meadmore, W. S., *Lucien Pissarro*, London, 1962.

Meier-Graefe, Julius, *Entwicklungsgeschichte der modernen Kunst*, Stuttgart, 1904.

———, *Der moderne Impressionismus*, Berlin, n.d.

Minnaert, M., *Light and Color in the Open Air*, trans. by H. M. Kremer-Priest, rev. ed., London, 1940.

Mirabaud, Robert, *Charles Henry et l'idéalisme scientifique*, Paris, 1926.

Mustoxidi, T. M., *Histoire de l'esthétique française*, Paris, 1920.

Natanson, Thadée, *Peints à leur tour*, Paris, 1948.

Ostwald, Wilhelm, *Color Science*, parts I and II, London, n.d.

Papanastassiou, C.-É., *Les Théories sur la nature de la lumière, de Descartes à nos jours, et l'évolution de la théorie physique*, Paris, 1935.

*Paul Signac* (introductions by Georges Besson, Paul Gay, and Félix Fénéon) (exhibition catalogue), Marlborough Fine Art, Ltd., London, March–April, 1954.

Piot, René, *Les Palettes de Delacroix*, Paris, 1931.

Pissarro, Camille, *Letters to his Son Lucien* (John Rewald, ed.), New York, 1943.

——, *Lettres à son fils Lucien* (John Rewald, ed.), Paris, 1950.

Pogu, Guy, "Sommaire de technologie divisionniste" (introduction to catalogue of Petitjean exhibition), Paris, 1955.

Pope, Arthur, *The Language of Drawing and Painting*, Cambridge (Mass.), 1949.

Previati, Gaetano, *I Principii scientifici del divisionismo*, 2nd ed., Torino, 1929.

Ramsey, Warren, *Jules Laforgue and the Ironic Inheritance*, New York, 1953.

Rewald, John, *Georges Seurat*, New York, 1943.

——, *Georges Seurat*, Paris, 1948.

——, *The History of Impressionism*, New York, 1946; revised and enlarged edition, New York, 1961.

——, *Post-Impressionism — from Van Gogh to Gauguin*, New York, 1956; 2nd ed., 1962.

Rey, Robert, *La Renaissance du sentiment classique dans la peinture française à la fin du XIXe siècle*, Paris, 1931.

Rich, Daniel C., *Seurat and the Evolution of "La Grande Jatte,"* Chicago, 1935.

—— (ed.), *Seurat: Paintings and Drawings* (exhibition catalogue), Chicago and New York, 1958.

Rookmaaker, H. R., *Synthetist Art Theories*, Amsterdam, 1959.

Seligman, Germain, *The Drawings of Georges Seurat*, New York, 1945.

*Seurat and his Friends* (intro. by John Rewald) (exhibition catalogue), Wildenstein Galleries, New York, November–December, 1953.

*Seurat et ses amis — la suite de l'impressionnisme* (exhibition catalogue), Galérie Wildenstein, Paris, December 1933–January 1934.

*Seurat — Paintings and Drawings* (exhibition catalogue), Knoedler Galleries, New York, April–May, 1949.

*P. Signac* (intro. by Jean Cassou)(exhibition catalogue), Musée National d'Art Moderne, Paris, October–December, 1951.

Signac, Paul, *D'Eugène Delacroix au néo-impressionnisme*, Paris, 1899; 4th ed., 1939.

Souriau, Paul, *L'Esthétique de la lumière*, Paris, 1913.

Southall, James P. C., *Introduction to Physiological Optics*, London, New York, and Toronto, 1937.

Tabarant, A., *Camille Pissarro*, Paris, 1924.

Tschermak-Seysenegg, Armin von, *Introduction to Physiological Optics*, trans. by Paul Boeder, Springfield (Ill.), 1952.

Van de Velde, Henry, *Geschichte meines Lebens*, München, 1962.

Venturi, Lionello, *Les Archives de l'impressionnisme*, 2 vols., Paris, 1939.

——, *Impressionists and Symbolists*, New York, 1950.

——, *History of Art Criticism*, New York, 1936.

——, and Pissarro, Ludovic Rodo, *Camille Pissarro, son art, son œuvre*, 2 vols., Paris, 1939.

Verhaeren, Émile, *Sensations*, Paris, 1927.

Vollard, Ambroise, *En Écoutant Cézanne, Degas, Renoir*, Paris, 1938.

Warrain, Francis, *L'Oeuvre psychobiophysique de Charles Henry*, Paris, 1931.

Wright, W. D., *The Measurement of Colour*, New York, 1958.

## ARTICLES PUBLISHED BEFORE 1895

Adam, Paul, "Les Artistes indépendants," *La Vogue*, September 6–13, 1886, pp. 260–267.

——, "Les Impressionnistes à l'Exposition des Indépendants," *La Vie moderne*, April 15, 1888, pp. 228–229.

——, "Peintres impressionnistes," *La Revue contemporaine*, April–May, 1886, pp. 523–551.

Ajalbert, J., "Le Salon des impressionnistes," *La Revue moderne*, June 20, 1886, pp. 385–393.

Alexandre, Arsène, "Chroniques d'aujourd'hui: un vaillant," *Paris*, April 1, 1891.

——, "Critique décadent: Les Impressionnistes en 1886," *L'Événement*, December 10, 1886, no pagination.

Antoine, Jules, "Georges Seurat," *La Revue indépendante*, April, 1891, pp. 89–93.

——, "Les Peintres néo-impressionnistes," *Art et critique*, August 9, 1890, pp. 509–510, and August 16, 1890, pp. 524–526.

Blanc, Charles, "Eugène Delacroix," *Gazette des beaux-arts*, XVI, January, 1864, pp. 5–27, and February, 1864, pp. 97–129.

Chevreul, Michel-Eugène, "Mémoire sur l'influence que deux couleurs peuvent avoir l'une sur l'autre quand on les voit simultanément," *Mémoires de l'Académie Royale des Sciences de l'Institut de France*, XI, 1832, pp. 447–520.

Christophe, Jules, "Chronique: Rue Laffitte, No. 1," *Journal des Artistes*, June 13, 1886, pp. 193–194.

————, "Dubois-Pillet," *Les Hommes d'aujourd'hui*, VIII, 370 [1890], no pagination.

————, "Les Évolutionnistes du Pavillon de la Ville de Paris," *Journal des Artistes*, April 24, 1887, pp. 122–123.

————, "Georges Seurat," *Les Hommes d'aujourd'hui*, VIII, 368 [1890], no pagination.

"Chronique scientifique," *La Cravache*, February 2, 1889, no pagination.

De la Rochefoucauld, A., "Paul Signac," *Le Cœur*, May 1893, pp. 4–5.

De Wyzewa, T., "Une Critique," *La Revue indépendante*, November–December, 1886, pp. 49–78.

————, "Georges Seurat," *L'Art dans les deux mondes*, April 18, 1891, pp. 263–264.

"Une Esthétique scientifique," *L'Art moderne*, February 10, 1889, p. 46.

Fénéon, Félix, "Au Pavillon de la ville de Paris," *Le Chat noir*, April 2, 1892, p. 1932.

————, "Autre groupe impressionniste," *La Cravache*, July 6, 1889, no pagination.

————, "Certains," *Art et critique*, December 14, 1889, pp. 453–455.

————, "Charles Vignier," *Les Hommes d'aujourd'hui*, VI, 300, no pagination.

————, "Une Esthétique scientifique," *La Cravache*, May 18, 1889, no pagination.

————, "Exposition des Artistes Indépendants à Paris," *L'Art moderne*, October 27, 1889, pp. 339–341.

————, "Feu Cros," *La Cravache*, August 18, 1888, no pagination.

————, "L'Impressionnisme aux Tuileries," *L'Art moderne*, September 19, 1886, pp. 300–302.

————, "Le Néo-impressionnisme," *L'Art moderne*, May 1, 1887, pp. 138–140.

————, "Le Néo-impressionnisme," *L'Art moderne*, April 15, 1888, pp. 121–123.

————, "Les Impressionnistes," *La Vogue*, June 13–20, 1886, pp. 261–275.

————, "Paul Signac," *La Plume*, September 1, 1891, pp. 292–299.

————, "Signac," *Les Hommes d'aujourd'hui*, VIII, 373 [1890], no pagination.

Fèvre, Henry, "L'Exposition des Impressionnistes," *La Revue de demain*, May–June, 1886, pp. 148–156.

Germain, Alphonse, "Le Chromo-luminarisme," *Essais d'art libre* (special issue), February–March, 1893, pp. 13–20.

Germain, Alphonse, "Delacroix théoricien," *Art et critique*, October 25, 1890, pp. 683–685.

———, "Les Néo-impressionnistes et leur théorie," *Art et critique*, September 15, 1889, pp. 250–252.

———, "Du Symbolisme dans la peinture," *Art et critique*, July 5, 1890, pp. 417–420.

———, "Théorie chromo-luminariste," *La Plume*, September 1, 1891, pp. 285–287.

Geffroy, Gustave, "Chronique: Pointillé-cloisonisme," *La Justice*, April 11, 1888, no pagination.

Hennequin, Émile, "Notes d'art — Exposition des Artistes Indépendants," *La Vie moderne*, September 11, 1886, pp. 581–582.

———, "Notes d'art — les impressionnistes," *La Vie moderne*, June 19, 1886, pp. 389–390.

Henry, Charles, "Cercle chromatique et sensation de couleur," *La Revue indépendante*, May, 1888, pp. 238–289.

———, "Le Contraste, le rythme, et la mesure," *Revue philosophique*, XXVIII, October, 1889, pp. 356–381.

———, "L'Esthétique des formes," *La Revue blanche*, VII, August, 1894, pp. 118–129; October, 1894, pp. 308–322; December, 1894, pp. 511–525; VIII, 1st sem., 1895, pp. 117–120.

———, "Harmonies de couleurs," *La Revue indépendante*, June, 1888, pp. 458–478.

———, "Introduction à une esthétique scientifique, *La Revue contemporaine*, August, 1885, pp. 441–469.

———, "Rapporteur esthétique et sensation de forme," *La Revue indépendante*, April, 1888, pp. 73–90.

———, "Sur la dynamogénie et l'inhibition," *Comptes rendus de l'Académie des Sciences*, CVIII, January 7, 1889, pp. 70–71.

———, "Sur un cercle chromatique, un rapporteur et un triple décimètre esthétiques," *Comptes rendus de l'Académie des Sciences*, CVIII, January 28, 1889, pp. 169–171.

Héricourt, J., "Une Théorie mathématique de l'expression: le contraste, le rythme, et la mesure, d'après les travaux de M. Charles Henry," *Revue scientifique*, XLIV, November 9, 1889, pp. 586–593.

Huysmans, J. K., "Chronique d'art — Les Indépendants," *La Revue indépendante*, April, 1887, pp. 51–57.

Kahn, Gustave, "De l'Esthétique du verre polychrome," *La Vogue*, April 18, 1886, pp. 54–65.

————, "Peinture: Exposition des Indépendants," *La Revue indépendante*, April, 1888, pp. 160–164.

————, "Seurat," *L'Art moderne*, April 5, 1891, pp. 107–110.

————, "La Vie artistique," *La Vie moderne*, April 9, 1887, pp. 229–231.

Lechalas, Georges, Review of Charles Henry, *Cercle chromatique* (Paris, 1889) and *Rapporteur esthétique* (Paris, 1889), *Revue philosophique*, XXVIII, December, 1889, pp. 635–645.

Lecomte, Georges, "Camille Pissarro," *Les Hommes d'aujourd'hui*, VIII, 366 [1890], no pagination.

————, "L'Exposition des néo-impressionnistes," *Art et critique*, March 29, 1890, pp. 203–205.

————, "Le Salon des Indépendants," *L'Art dans les deux mondes*, March 28, 1891, p. 225.

————, "Société des Artistes Indépendants," *L'Art moderne*, March 30, 1890, pp. 100–101.

Le Fustec, J., "Exposition de la Société des Artistes Indépendants," *Journal des artistes*, August 22, 1886, p. 282.

Maus, Octave, "La Recherche de la lumière dans la peinture," *Catalogue de la V<sup>e</sup> Exposition des XX*, Brussels, 1888 (also in *L'Art moderne*, June 26, 1887, pp. 201–202).

Meyerson, Émile, "Les Travaux de M. Charles Henry sur une théorie mathématique de l'expression," *Bulletin scientifique*, December 20, 1889, pp. 98–100.

Michel, Albert, "Le Néo-impressionnisme," *L'Art moderne*, March 10, 1888, pp. 83–85.

Néo [Paul Signac], "A Minuit: IV<sup>e</sup> Exposition des Artistes Indépendants" [letter from Signac to Paul Alexis], *Le Cri du peuple*, March 29, 1888, no pagination.

————, "Les XX — Lettre à Trublot" [letter from Signac to Paul Alexis], *Le Cri du peuple*, February 9, 1888, no pagination.

Rood, O. N., "Modern Optics and Painting," *The Popular Science Monthly*, XXII, February, 1874, pp. 415–421; March, 1874, pp. 572–581.

S. P. [Paul Signac], "Catalogue de l'Exposition des XX," *Art et critique*, February 1, 1890, pp. 76–78.

"Le Salon des XX — L'ancien et le nouvel impressionnisme," *L'Art moderne*, February 6, 1888, pp. 41–42.

Sutter, David, "Les Phénomènes de la vision," *L'Art*, XX, 1880, pp. 74–76, 124–128, 147–149, 195–197, 216–220, 268–269.

"La Théorie des néo-impressionnistes en 1834," *L'Art moderne*, September 2, 1888, pp. 284–285.

Thérèse [Félix Fénéon], "Une Affiche," *La Cravache*, September 15, 1888, no pagination.

"Types d'artistes," *L'Art moderne*, March 2, 1890, pp. 65–67.

Van de Velde, Henry, "Georges Seurat," *La Wallonie*, April, 1891, pp. 167–171.

———, "Notes sur l'art — 'Chahut,'" *La Wallonie*, V, 1890, pp. 122–125.

Verhaeren, Émile, "Chronique artistique — Les XX," *La Société nouvelle*, February, 1891, pp. 248–254.

———, "Le Salon des *Vingt* à Bruxelles," *La Vie moderne*, February 26, 1887, pp. 135–139.

———, "Georges Seurat," *La Société nouvelle*, April, 1891, pp. 429–438.

"Les Vingtistes parisiens," *L'Art moderne*, June 27, 1886, pp. 201–204.


ARTICLES PUBLISHED AFTER 1895

Anon. [Félix Fénéon], "Précisions concernant Seurat," *Le Bulletin de la vie artistique*, August 15, 1924, pp. 358–360.

———, "Sur Georges Seurat," *Le Bulletin de la vie artistique*, June 15, 1922, pp. 154–158.

Alexandre, Arsène, "Paul Signac — président des Indépendants," *Comoedia*, March 26, 1910, p. 3.

Besson, Georges, "Lettre à la brabançonne," *Les Arts plastiques*, no. 4, January–February, 1952, pp. 279–288.

———, "Paul Signac," *Arts de France*, no. 2, January 15, 1946, pp. 3–8.

Bonnet, Paul, "Seurat et le Néo-impressionnisme," *Le Crocodile*, October–December, 1957, pp. 6–22.

Brown, Richard F., "Impressionist Technique: Pissarro's Optical Mixture," *Magazine of Art*, XLIII, January, 1950, pp. 12–15.

Cachin-Signac, Ginette, "Documenti inediti sul'neo-impressionismo," *La Biennale di Venezia*, no. 6, October, 1951, pp. 20–23.

———, "Autour de la correspondance de Signac," *Arts*, September 7, 1951, p. 8.

*Cahiers de l'étoile*, no. 13, January–February, 1930 (special issue devoted to Charles Henry).

Chastel, André, "Une Source oubliée de Seurat," *Études et documents sur l'art français*, XXII, 1959, pp. 400–407.

———, "Seurat et Gauguin," *Art de France*, II, 1962, pp. 298–304.

Deene, J. F. van, "Georges Seurat," *Maandblad voor Beeldende Kunsten*, 8th year, no. 6, June 6, 1931, pp. 163–176.

Eglinton, Guy, "The Theory of Seurat," *International Studio*, May, 1925, pp. 113–117, and July, 1925, pp. 289–292.

Elliot, Eugene Clinton, "On the Understanding of Color in Painting," *Journal of Aesthetics and Art Criticism*, XVI, June, 1958, pp. 453–470.

Fénéon, Félix (ed.), "Notes inédites de Seurat sur Delacroix," *Le Bulletin de la vie artistique*, April 1, 1922, pp. 154–158.

Fer, Édouard, "Les Principes scientifiques du néo-impressionnisme," *Pages d'art*, December, 1917, pp. 501–512; May, 1918, pp. 181–194.

Fosca, François, "La Méthode picturale des impressionnistes et les historiens de l'art," *Werk*, no. 6, June, 1952, pp. 198–200.

Fry, Roger, "Seurat's 'La Parade,'" *The Burlington Magazine*, LV, December, 1929, pp. 289–293.

Goldwater, Robert J., "Some Aspects of the Development of Seurat's Style," *The Art Bulletin*, XXIII, June, 1941, pp. 117–130.

Guenne, Jacques, "Entretien avec Paul Signac," *L'Art vivant*, March 20, 1925, pp. 1–4.

Guilbeaux, Henri, "Paul Signac et les Indépendants," *Les Hommes du jour*, April 22, 1911, no pagination.

Habasque, Guy, "Le Contraste simultané des couleurs et son emploi en peinture depuis un siècle," in Ignace Meyerson, *Problèmes de la couleur*, Paris, 1957.

Hartridge, H., "The Visual Perception of Fine Detail," *Philosophical Transactions of the Royal Society of London*, Series B, CCXXXII, May 15, 1947, pp. 519–671.

Henry, Charles, "La Lumière, la couleur, la forme," *L'Esprit nouveau*, 1921, pp. 605–623, 729–736, 948–958, 1068–1075.

Herbert, Robert L., "Seurat and Chéret," *The Art Bulletin*, XL, June, 1958, pp. 156–158.

——, "Seurat and Émile Verhaeren — Unpublished Letters," *Gazette des beaux-arts*, LIV, December, 1959, pp. 315–328.

——, "Seurat and Puvis de Chavannes," *Yale University Art Gallery Bulletin*, XXV, October, 1959, pp. 22–29.

——, "Seurat in Chicago and New York," *The Burlington Magazine*, C, May, 1958, pp. 146–155.

Homer, William I., "Concerning Muybridge, Marey, and Seurat" (letter), *The Burlington Magazine*, CIV, September, 1962, pp. 391–392.

——, "The Literature of Art: Seurat's Paintings and Drawings," *The Burlington Magazine*, CV, June, 1963, pp. 282–284.

——, "Notes on Seurat's Palette," *The Burlington Magazine*, CI, May, 1959, pp. 192–193.

Homer, William I., Review of Henri Dorra and John Rewald, *Seurat; l'œuvre peint; biographie et catalogue critique* (Paris, 1959), *The Art Bulletin*, XLII, September, 1960, pp. 228–233.

——, "Seurat's Formative Period, 1880–1884," *The Connoisseur*, CXLII, August–September, 1958, pp. 58–62.

——, "Seurat's Port-en-Bessin," *Minneapolis Institute of Arts Bulletin*, XLVI, Summer, 1957, pp. 17–41.

Jamot, Paul, "Une Étude pour le 'Dimanche à la Grande Jatte' de Georges Seurat," *Bulletin des musées de France*, March 1930, pp. 49–52.

——, "Ernest Laurent," *Gazette des beaux-arts*, V, March, 1911, pp. 173–203.

Jourdain, François, "Paul Signac," *Art-Documents*, no. 13, October, 1951, p. 5.

Kahn, Gustave, "Au Temps du pointillisme," *Mercure de France*, April, 1924, pp. 5–22.

Keller, Henry G., and MacLeod, J. J. R., "The Application of the Physiology of Color Vision in Modern Art," *The Popular Science Monthly*, LXXXIII, November, 1913, pp. 450–465.

Lhote, André, "Composition du tableau," *Encyclopédie française*, XVI, Paris, 1935, pp. 16.30-6–16.30-9.

Lövgren, Sven, "Symbolismens genombrott i det franska 1880-talsmåleriet," *Konstrevy*, no. 3, 1956, pp. 105–107, 124.

Nicolson, Benedict, "Seurat's 'La Baignade,'" *The Burlington Magazine*, LXXIX, November, 1941, pp. 139–146.

——, "The Literature of Art: Reflections on Seurat," *The Burlington Magazine*, CIV, May, 1962, pp. 213–214.

Rewald, John (ed.), "Extraits du journal inédit de Paul Signac, I (1894–95)," *Gazette des beaux-arts*, XXXVI, July–September, 1949, pp. 97–128.

——, "Extraits du journal inédit de Paul Signac, II (1897–98)," *Gazette des beaux-arts*, XXIX, April, 1952, pp. 265–284.

——, "Extraits du journal inédit de Paul Signac, III (1898–1899)." *Gazette des beaux-arts*, XLII, July–August, 1953, pp. 27–57.

——, "Félix Fénéon," *Gazette des beaux-arts*, XXXII, July–August, 1947, pp. 45–62, and XXXIV, February, 1948, pp. 107–126.

——, "Seurat: the Meaning of the Dots," *Art News*, XLVIII, April, 1949, pp. 24–27, 61–63.

Rey, Robert, "Le Néo-impressionnisme," in *Histoire de l'art contemporain* (ed. by René Huyghe), Paris, 1935, pp. 33–35.

Roger-Marx, Claude, "Paul Signac," in *Histoire de l'art contemporain* (ed. by René Huyghe), Paris, 1935, pp. 36–38, 39–40.

Schapiro, Meyer, "New Light on Seurat," *Art News*, LVII, April, 1958, pp. 23–24, 44–45, 52.

———, "Seurat and 'La Grande Jatte,'" *The Columbia Review*, November, 1935, pp. 9–16.

Scharf, Aaron, "Painting, Photography, and the Image of Movement," *The Burlington Magazine*, CIV, May, 1962, pp. 186–195.

Signac, Paul, "Le Néo-impressionnisme — Documents," *Gazette des beaux-arts*, XI, January, 1934, pp. 49–59.

———, "Les Besoins individuels et la peinture," *Encyclopédie française*, XVI, Paris, 1935, pp. 16.84-7–16.84-10.

Venturi, Lionello, "The Art of Seurat," *Gazette des beaux-arts*, XXVI, July–December, 1944, pp. 421–430.

Webster, J. Carson, "The Technique of Impressionism: a Reappraisal," *College Art Journal*, IV, November, 1944, pp. 3–22.

Zervos, Christian, "Une Dimanche à La Grande Jatte et la technique de Seurat," *Cahiers d'art*, no. 9, 1928, pp. 361–375.

## UNPUBLISHED MATERIAL

Brown, Richard F., "The Color Technique of Camille Pissarro." Unpublished Ph.D. dissertation, Harvard University, 1952.

Calkins, Robert G., "Seurat, Van Gogh, and Gauguin." Unpublished research paper, Department of Fine Arts, Harvard University, March 20, 1962.

Jones, S. Rees, "The Hue of a Small Color Patch." Unpublished manuscript.

Martin, Elizabeth P., "The Symbolist Criticism of Painting in France: 1880–95." Unpublished Ph.D. dissertation, Bryn Mawr College, 1952.

## BIBLIOGRAPHICAL ADDENDA (1964–1970)

Argüelles, José, "Paul Signac's *Against the Enamel of a Back-ground Rhythmic with Beats and Angles, Tones and Colors, Portrait of M. Félix Fénéon in 1890, Opus 217*," *The Journal of Aesthetics and Art Criticism*, XXVIII, Fall, 1969, pp. 49–53.

Courthion, Pierre, *Georges Seurat*, New York, 1968.

Dorra, Henri, "Charles Henry's 'Scientific' Aesthetic," *Gazette des Beaux-Arts*, LXXIV, December, 1969, pp. 345–356.

Herbert Robert L., *Neo-Impressionism* (exhibition catalogue), The Solomon R. Guggenheim Museum, New York, February–April, 1968.

Perruchot, Henri, *La Vie de Seurat*, Paris, 1966.

Revel, J. F., "Charles Henry et la science des arts," *L'Oiel*, No. 119, November, 1964, pp. 21–27, 44, 58.

Signac, Paul, *D'Eugène Delacroix au néo-impressionnisme* (Françoise Cachin, ed.), Paris, 1964.

Sutter, Jean, *Les Néo-Impressionnistes*, Neuchâtel, 1970.

# Index

# Index

(Works by Seurat are indexed by title; works by other artists are listed under artist's name)

Abstract art, 251, 256
Académie des Beaux-Arts, 272
Académie Royale de Peinture et de Sculpture, 210
Achromatism, 30
Additive mixture, 8, 9, 10, 11, 38, 39, 163, 246, 261, 262, 263, 264, 275
After-image, positive, 39
Alexandre, Arsène, 219, 265, 267, 269
Aman-Jean, Edmond, 14, 264, 267, 283
Angles, rhythmical, 192, 196, 198, 226, 228, 232, 240
Angrand, Charles, 119–120, 264
Asnières, 55, 98
Atelier libre de Bin, Paris, 266
Aurier, Albert, 253
Aviat, Mme. J., 18, 99

Badt, Kurt, 5
*Baignade, Asnières, Une,* 11, 15, 19, 51, 54, 55, 60, 65–70, 73–82, 84, 87–94, 96–101, 103, 105, 106, 107, 109–111, 114, 116, 120, 122–123, 125, 128, 129, 132, 133, 134, 135, 137, 142, 153, 154, 157, 162, 236, 246, 266, 285, 287
*Baigneur assis,* 60, 62
Balla, Giacomo, 256
Barbizon, 284
Barbizon School, 15, 17, 97, 267
Basis, 240, 241
Beaubourg, Maurice, Seurat's letter to, 12, 135, 140, 156, 180, 183, 186–187, 188, 198, 199–200, 202, 210, 212, 214, 216, 219, 220, 224, 228, 234, 239, 240, 248, 299
Beaumont, Adalbert de, 77
Berès Collection, Paris, 264

Bernard, Claude, 189, 252
*Introduction a l'etude de la medecine experimentale*, 252
Bert, Paul, 189
Besson, Georges, 266, 267
Blanc, Charles, 17, 29–36, 44, 45, 47, 66, 67, 70, 72, 73, 74, 77, 80, 82, 84, 90, 93, 95, 96, 106, 107, 111, 131, 133, 134, 135, 144, 150, 198, 199, 208, 210, 211, 213, 215, 216, 243, 244, 245, 246, 247, 248, 254, 261, 268, 269, 271–272, 273, 288
*Artistes de mon temps,* 18
*Grammaire des arts du dessin,* 17, 29, 34, 35, 85, 131, 208, 209, 211, 244, 268, 269, 299
Boccioni, Umberto, 256
Bollweiler, Alsace, 188
Bonnet, Professor Paul, 267
Bourgeois, Charles, 30, 34, 216
Braque, Georges, 255
Brest, 13, 14, 17, 266
Brown, Richard F., 5–6
Brücke, Ernst Wilhelm von, 246
*Principes scientifiques des beaux-arts,* 289
Brushstroke, brushwork, Delacroix's, 48, 89, 107, 108
Impressionist, 57, 60, 70, 88, 108, 145
Monet's, 60, 89
Neo-Impressionist, 160
Pissarro's, 60, 88
pointillist, 146
Renoir's, 54, 89
Seurat's, 60, 65, 87–88, 89, 103, 107, 109, 112, 118, 122–123, 142, 144, 160, 165, 178, 252
Burty, Philippe, 270

Carracci, the, 46
*Centre, moyenne distance, "femme à la jupe rose,"* 118
Cézanne, Paul, 250, 251
*Chahut, Le,* 179, 185, 188, 205, 220, 223–224, 226, 228, 229, 230, 232, 234, 238, 239, 240, 298, 303
Chamber of Deputies, Paris, 72
*Chapeau, souliers, linge,* 101
Charlet, Delacroix's article on, 273
*Chevaux dans le fleuve,* 60, 62
*Chevreul, Michel-Eugène,* 17, 18, 20, 27–29, 31, 32, 34, 35, 36, 39, 40, 44, 66–67, 72, 73, 74, 80, 82–84, 86, 90, 93, 94, 95, 106, 107, 111, 120, 128, 129, 130, 131, 134, 135, 136, 149, 150, 153, 154, 155, 157, 162, 163, 164, 192, 194, 198, 199, 213, 215, 216, 238, 244, 245, 246, 247, 256, 261, 268, 269, 270–271, 272, 273, 275, 282–283, 288, 289, 290, 299, 301, 302
  *De la loi du contraste simultané des couleurs,* 18, 20, 36, 136, 157, 199, 244, 268, 269, 271, 272
Christophe, Jules, 185, 186, 187, 188, 234, 265
Chromatic circle, Chevreul's, 21, 192–194, 245, 284
  Henry's, 183, 194–196, 198, 217, 220, 223, 232, 298
  Rood's, 220, 261, 263
  Signac's, 298
Chromo-luminarism, 4, 11, 132, 157, 164, 175, 179, 180, 208, 236, 238, 247, 248–249, 285
*Chromomètre,* 284
*Cirque, Le,* 179, 185, 188, 205, 220, 223, 228–230, 232, 234, 238, 239, 240, 298, 303
Collège de France, Paris, 188–189, 272
Collège Rollin, Paris, 266
Color, colors, complementary, 30, 36, 39–40, 44, 48, 57, 64, 65, 72, 74, 79, 80, 82, 83, 86, 92, 93, 120, 137, 138, 144, 245, 247, 284, 293
  "dimensions" of, 6–7
  division of, 62, 70, 90, 107, 123, 132, 158, 216, 246, *see also* Tone, division of

earth, 57, 90, 91, 108, 109, 112, 122, 146, 150, 151, 284, 292
  expression through, *see* Expression, through color
  *finesse* of, 74
  harmony of, *see* Harmony of color
  mixture of, 8, 32, 36, 38, 74, 91, 103, 122, 123, 144, 150, 152, 274
  primary, *see* Primary colors
  purity of, 122, 123, 150, 152–153, 255
  spectral, 91, 152
  symbolism of, 44, 254
Color photography, 189, 262, 292
Color triangle, Rood's, 38, 263, 275
Columbia College, New York, 273
Complementary colors, *see* Colors, complementary
Composition, Seurat's, 96–97, 111, 251
Concordance of color and line, 181, 184, 204, 206, 214
Constable, John, 49, 107
Contrast, 20, 28, 35, 36, 55, 79, 85, 92, 94, 100, 106, 107, 135, 182, 215, 216, 246, 283, 297, 301
  of color, 20, 39–40, 256
  of hues, 57, 64, 79, 81, 82, 84, 86, 100, 107, 108, 109, 118, 136, 138
  of values, 20, 43, 57, 78, 79, 80, 81, 82, 85, 86, 101, 109, 118, 128–129, 136, 138
  simultaneous, *see* Simultaneous contrast
Contrast-diagram, Rood's, 39–40, 80, 86, 94, 135, 137, 154, 247, 263, 275, 303
  Seurat's copy of, 40, 86
Coquiot, Gustave, 186, 264
Corot, Jean Baptiste Camille, 17, 18, 55, 96, 99, 157, 240, 268
Correspondences, theory of, 253
Cousturier, Lucie, 264, 267
Couture, Thomas, 17, 18, 55, 73–74, 157, 199, 268, 270
  *Méthode et entretiens d'atelier,* 18, 73, 270
Cros, Charles, 189, 292
Cros, Henri, 189
Cross, Henri-Edmond, 255, 256, 301
Crotoy, Le, 188, 239
*Crotoy, après-midi, Le,* 184

*Crotoy, matin, Le,* 184
Cubist, 251, 256
Dadaists, 256
David, Jacques Louis, 97
Deductive method, 251, 252
Degas, Edgar, 54
Delacroix, Eugène, 2, 15, 17, 18, 19, 30,
    32, 33, 34–36, 48–51, 54, 57, 64,
    70, 72, 76, 77, 85, 89, 90, 91, 93,
    95, 97, 106, 107, 108, 110, 133,
    135, 145, 146, 153, 199, 206–207,
    213, 215, 216, 243, 244, 245, 247,
    254, 259, 267, 268, 269, 270, 272,
    273, 281, 284
    *Convulsionnaires de Tanger, Les,* 48
    *Cortège de l'empereur du Maroc,* 48
    *Femmes d'Alger dans leur appartement,*
      35, 50
    *Héliodore chassé du Temple,* 93
    *Lutte de Jacob et de l'ange, La,* 89
    *Scène du Massacre de Scio,* 49, 145
    Seurat's notes on, 15, 48, 73, 206
Denis, Maurice, 253
De Wyzewa, Teodor, 181–182, 242–243,
    265
*Dimanche à la Grande Jatte, Un,* 11, 98,
    105, 111, 112, 114–116, 118, 119,
    120, 123, 125, 128, 129, 130, 131–
    139, 142–144, 153–157, 159, 162,
    163–164, 167, 169, 171, 173–175,
    178, 180, 218, 219, 235–236, 246,
    250, 252, 287, 292, 302
Divisionism, 119, 169
    Italian, 255
Dominant, dominants, 181, 199, 206, 209,
    210, 214, 218, 219, 220, 223, 228,
    230, 303
Dorra, Henri, 4, 5, 123, 228, 232, 251
Dove, Heinrich-Wilhelm, 42, 114, 142–
    143, 159, 172, 216, 273
    *Darstellung der Farbenlehre und optische*
      *Studien,* 291
Drawing, role of, 99, 105, 125, 129
Dubois-Pillet, Albert, 114, 158
Durand-Ruel, 17, 130
Dürer, Albrecht, 242
Duval, Dr. Mathias, *Précis d'anatomie,* 299
*Dynamogénie,* Dynamogeny, 182, 197,
    204, 223, 226, 230

*Écho,* 101, 105
École des Beaux-Arts, Paris, 13, 14, 15,
    46, 51, 97, 242–243, 265, 266, 272,
    276, 284
École des Hautes-Études, Paris, 189
École Municipale de Dessin et de Sculp-
    ture du 10ème Arrondissement,
    Paris, 265
École Nationale Supérieure des Arts
    Décoratifs, Paris, 266
Esthetic protractor, 192, 196, 198, 226,
    232, 240, 298–299, 303
Esthetics, applied, 45
    experimental, 48, 217
    speculative, 45
*Étude finale pour la composition de "La*
    *Grande Jatte,"* 123
*Étude finale pour "Le Chahut,"* 303
*Étude finale pour "Une Baignade,"* 60, 62,
    64–65
*Étude pour la composition complète de "La*
    *Grande Jatte,"* 291
*Étude pour "Le Chahut,"* 303
Exposition Internationale, Fifth, 288
Exposition Universelle Internationale,
    Paris, 292
Expression, through color, 12, 29, 33–34,
    180, 184, 187, 190, 194, 197, 199,
    200, 202, 205, 209, 211, 213, 220,
    248
    through line, 12, 180, 184, 187, 190,
    191, 199, 200, 202, 205, 208, 209,
    211, 220, 226, 230, 248
    through value, 12, 180, 187, 209, 220,
    230
Expressionism, 256

Fauves, Les, 255
Fechner, Gustav Theodor, 191, 248
Félibien, André, 211, 212
    *Conférences,* 211
Fénéon, Félix, 5, 17, 19, 54, 68, 112, 114,
    129, 132, 133, 134, 135, 136, 137,
    139, 144, 147, 149, 157, 158, 159,
    160, 161, 162, 165, 170, 172, 173,
    174, 175, 182, 183, 184, 185, 186,
    189, 215, 217, 236, 238, 239, 260,
    264, 265, 267, 268, 269, 270, 288,
    290, 292, 294

Fénéon, Félix (*continued*)
    *Les Impressionnistes en 1886*, 162, 236,
       288
Fer, Édouard, 5, 261
Féré, Charles, 248
Fréart, Paul de, Sieur de Chantelou, 210
Fresnel, Augustin-Jean, 216
Futurism, 255–256
Futurists, Italian, 255

*Garçon assis*, 101
*Garçons se baignant*, 60
Gauguin, Paul, 130–131, 253, 289
Gauss's theory, 192, 248
Gille, Philippe, 17, 19
Gobelins, Les (tapestry workshop), Paris,
    20, 130, 270, 288
Goethe, Johann Wolfgang von, 44
Gogh, Vincent van, 5, 253–254
Golden section, 240, 248, 251, 303
Gradation, 33, 36, 40, 42, 43, 49, 55, 76–
    77, 89, 93, 106, 107, 108, 118, 133,
    135, 163, 215, 246
Grandcamp, 115, 144
Grautoff, Otto, 6
Gray, optical, *see* Optical gray
Grays, colored, 31, 48, 72, 73
Grubicy, Vittore, 255
Guenne, Jacques, 267
Guiffrey, J.-J., 270
Guillaumin, Armand, 57, 266, 286

Half-tint, 72, 281
Harmony, Seurat's definition of, 156, 199
Harmony of color, 12, 27, 49, 50, 55, 77,
    91, 93, 94, 95, 96, 106, 108, 109,
    111, 153–157, 163, 164, 190, 218,
    219, 229, 246, 247, 252, 256, 298,
    303
    Blanc's principles of, 31, 245
    Chevreul's principles of, 21, 24, 27–
       28, 31, 94, 155–156, 245
    Delacroix's principles of, 35, 245
    Helmholtz's principles of, 302
    Henry's principles of, 194, 195–196, 218
    Rood's principles of, 42, 94–95, 98,
       154, 246–247
    Sutter's principles of, 44–45
Harmony of lines, 181, 183, 190
Hauke, César de, 260, 268

Hauron, Louis Ducos du, 292
Hayet, Louis, 256
Helmholtz, Hermann von, 39, 114, 131,
    215, 216, 246, 248, 261, 262, 263,
    268, 288–290, 299, 301–302
    *Handbuch der physiologischen Optik*, 261
    "L'Optique et la peinture," 289
Hennequin, Émile, 130, 133, 145, 171
Henry, Charles, 4, 47, 181–183, 184, 185,
    188–192, 194, 195, 196, 197, 198,
    199, 200, 202, 204, 205, 209, 213,
    214, 215, 216, 217, 218, 219, 223,
    224, 226, 228, 229, 232, 234, 238–
    240, 243, 245, 247–248, 252, 253,
    275, 292, 296–297, 298, 299, 301,
    303
    *Cercle chromatique*, 182, 190, 194, 196,
       197, 214, 268, 297
    "Introduction à une esthétique scien-
       tifique," 182, 183, 189, 197, 198,
       200, 226
    *Rapporteur esthétique*, 190, 196, 197,
       214, 226, 243, 297
Herbert, Robert L., 5, 183
Hogarth, William, 191
*Homme étendu*, 103
Honfleur, 165, 236
*Honfleur, un soir, embouchure de la Seine*,
    165
Humbert de Superville, David Pierre
    Giottino, 191, 200, 202, 204, 205,
    208, 209, 211, 214, 215, 230, 248,
    268, 299
    *Essai sur les signes inconditionnels dans
       l'art*, 191, 200, 204, 208, 211, 226

Impressionism, Impressionists, 2, 6, 14,
    15, 17, 19, 51, 54, 55, 60, 62, 64,
    65, 66, 67, 70, 77, 81–82, 88, 96,
    97, 98, 100, 106, 107, 108, 110,
    111, 112, 114, 116, 120, 132, 133,
    135, 145, 146, 151, 158, 161, 162,
    163, 164, 169, 235, 236, 238, 249–
    252, 254, 266, 267, 277, 285
    characteristics of, 56–64, 278–281
Impressionist exhibition, eighth, 114, 115,
    181
*Impressionniste-luministe*, 286
Indépendants, 130
    Groupe des Artistes, 15, 266

second exhibition, 288
Société des Artistes, second exhibition, 162
Inductive method, 251, 252
Ingres, Jean-Auguste-Dominique, 13, 14, 15, 97, 242
Inhibition, 197, 204
Irradiation, 43, 135, 215, 216, 301, 302

Joze, Victor, *L'Homme à femmes*, 303

Kahn, Gustave, 54, 130, 131, 181, 182, 183, 184, 185, 187, 189, 238, 240, 241, 265
Kandinsky, Wassily, 255, 256
Keller, Henry G., 5
Klee, Paul, 256

Laboratoire de Physiologie des Sensations, Sorbonne, Paris, 189
Laforgue, Jules, 56, 189
Land, Dr. Edwin, 262–263
Laurent, Ernest, 14, 267, 283
Le Bail, Louis, 280, 281
Le Brun, Charles, 211
Lecomte, Georges, 184
Lehmann, Heinrich, 13, 14, 46, 243
Lemmen, Georges, 254
Leonardo da Vinci, 43, 55, 80, 85, 86, 106, 128, 191, 209, 242, 283
    *Traité de la peinture*, 283
    *Trattato della Pittura*, 47, 85
Lequien, Justin, 13
Lévèque, Charles, 191
Liebig, Justus, Baron von, 273
Light, color of, 24, 33, 39, 57, 60, 65–66, 67, 68, 69, 108, 110, 116, 118–119, 132, 134, 139, 142, 164, 167, 169, 220, 229, 290
    mixture of, 9, 37–39, 74, 139, 140, 145, 171, 223, 245–246, 261, 263, 274
Light impression, duration of, 140–141, 214
Louvre, Paris, 14, 145, 160
Lövgren, Sven, 275
Luce, Maximilien, 254
Lustre, 42, 142–143, 159, 172, 173, 174, 175, 179, 294
Luxembourg Palace, library, Paris, 32

MacLeod, J. J. R., 5
Magnus, Heinrich Gustav, 273
Matisse, Henri, 255
Maxwell, James Clerk, 38, 114, 130, 131, 216, 246, 262, 274, 292
Maxwell's discs, 37, 38, 39, 130, 139, 141
Measure, 182, 304
Michelangelo, 191
Mile, Dr. Jean, 37, 144, 216, 274
Mixture, optical, *see* Optical mixture
Modes, 300
    theory of, 210–212
Mondrian, Piet, 255, 256
Monet, Claude, 15, 17, 54, 56, 60, 64, 89, 107, 146, 161, 237, 266, 268, 278, 279, 280, 281
    *Chasse, La*, 145
    *Fisherman's Cottage on the Cliffs at Varengeville*, 60
    *Path in the Île St. Martin, Vétheuil*, 64
    *River Scene, Vétheuil*, 60
    *Saint-Lazare Station*, 64
Montabert, Paillot de, 211
    *Traité complet de la peinture*, 211
Moore, George, 157–158, 159, 171
    *Modern Painting*, 159
Morocco, 49
*Moyenne distance, gauche*, 118
*Moyenne distance, gauche, avec homme debout*, 118
Murillo, Bartolomé Esteban, 145, 146, 290
    *Naissance de la Vierge, La*, 145
Muséum d'Histoire Naturelle, Paris, 271

National Academy of Design, New York, 273
*Néo-impressionnisme*, origin of the term, 161–162
*Néo-impressionniste*, origin of the term, 161–162
Neo-Traditionalists, 2
Newton, Sir Isaac, 150

Optical gray, 70, 72, 73, 74, 87, 169, 282, 293
Optical mixture, 11, 28, 31, 32, 36, 49, 55, 57, 62, 69–70, 72–75, 87, 89, 90, 101, 103, 105, 106, 108, 109, 119, 122, 123, 128, 135, 139–143,

Optical mixture (*continued*)
150, 158–159, 160, 163, 165, 169,
170, 171, 172, 174, 177, 178, 179,
180, 216, 246, 290
Orientals, oriental tradition, 33, 34, 49,
77, 215, 216, 244, 245
Ostwald, Wilhelm, 6

Pach, Walter, 186
Palette, Impressionist, 91, 151, 281
Seurat's, 146–153, 259, 292
Signac's, 151, 259
spectrum, 151, 153, 281
*Parade de Cirque, La*, 164, 175, 177–179,
183, 188, 219–220, 223, 229, 240,
246, 298, 300, 303
*Peinture optique*, 19, 123, 268, 286
Pellizza da Volpedo, Giuseppe, 255
Petitjean, Hippolyte, 254, 256
Piron, A., *Eugène Delacroix, sa vie et ses
oeuvres*, 270
Pissarro, Camille, 5, 15, 17, 54, 56, 60,
88, 107, 114, 130, 132, 158, 161,
184, 190, 237, 254, 266, 268, 279,
280, 286, 288, 289, 294, 296–297
*Paysannes au repos*, 60
Pissarro, Lucien, 114, 158, 161, 275
Pointillism, 87, 90, 145, 160, 264
Pointillist technique, 32, 42, 55, 103, 141,
145, 165
Pope, Arthur, 6–8
Port-en-Bessin, 266
*Poseuses, Les*, 164–165, 178, 183, 188,
217–219, 229, 232, 246, 250, 302–
303
*Poseuses, Les* (small version), 165, 167–
175, 294
Poussin, Nicolas, 210, 212, 242, 300
Previati, Gaetano, 5, 255
Primary colors, 8–10, 29–30, 262, 263,
275
Prismatic spectrum, 147
Puvis de Chavannes, Pierre, 17, 97, 110, 212
*Pauvre pêcheur, Le*, 212, 268

Quandt, Dr. Richard E., 297

Rameau, Jean Philippe, 191
Reaction, Reactions, 120, 134–135, 137,
138, 139, 142, 215, 229

Reflections, 60, 68–69, 70, 132, 135, 164
Renoir, Pierre-Auguste, 15, 17, 54, 56,
70, 82, 89, 107, 161, 266, 278–279
*Boating Party at Châtou*, 70
*Mme. Charpentier and her Children*, 54,
277
*Rocky Crags, L'Estaque*, 60
Rewald, John, 5, 268, 275
Rey, Robert, 4, 5, 264, 276, 301
Rhythm, 182, 304
Rhythm of gesture, 303
Richter, George M., 6
Rochefoucauld, Antoine de la, 267
Roger-Marx, Claude, 54, 267
Rood, Ogden N., 17, 18–19, 36–40, 42–
43, 66, 67–68, 72, 73, 74–75, 77,
82, 86, 90, 94–95, 96, 98, 99, 100,
106, 111, 114, 118, 120, 130, 131,
133, 134, 136, 139, 140–141, 143,
145, 147, 149, 150, 153, 154, 162,
163, 164, 171, 174, 175, 182, 198,
214, 215, 216, 218, 219, 237, 238,
245, 246–247, 248, 261, 268, 273–
274, 275, 288, 290, 299, 301, 302
*Modern Chromatics*, 19, 36
*Students' Text-Book of Color*, 19, 36,
107, 111, 139, 141, 216, 246, 290
*Théorie scientifique des couleurs*, 18, 130,
133, 216, 246, 247
Rood, Roland, 5
Rubens, Peter Paul, 33, 273
Ruskin, John, 42, 130, 131, 133, 144, 145,
163, 215, 273
*Elements of Drawing*, 130, 133, 145
Russolo, Luigi, 256
Rysselberghe, Théo van, 254

Saint-Sulpice (Paris), Chapelle des Saints-
Anges (Delacroix frescoes), 15,
50–51, 72, 76, 80, 89, 90, 93, 108,
281–282, 290
Salon, 15, 91, 97, 267
of 1879, 277
of 1884, 15
Schapiro, Meyer, 56
Science, art and, 12, 46, 235, 237, *et
passim*
Chevreul's, 111
Rood's, 111

Seurat's, 3, 12, 109, 216, 234, 235–236, 237–239, 241, 243, 244–249
*Section de gauche, groupement de personnages,* 118, 119
Segantini, Giovanni, 255
Senate, Paris, 72
Sérusier, Paul, 253
  *ABC de la peinture,* 253
Seurat, Georges, biography, 13–17, *et passim*
  letter to Maurice Beaubourg, *see* Beaubourg, Maurice, Seurat's letter to
Severini, Gino, 256
Shadow, color of, 57, 60, 66, 67, 70, 73, 80, 108, 110, 116, 122, 134, 135, 139, 167, 170, 177, 215, 220, 223
Sheldon, George W., 294
Signac, Mme. Ginette, 259, 275, 289, 292, 295, 299, 300
Signac, Paul, 1–3, 4, 15, 35, 48–51, 57, 68, 72, 73, 82, 89, 90, 93, 114, 119, 130, 135, 145, 151, 152, 158, 161, 171, 182, 184, 190, 206, 212, 223, 236, 238, 254, 255, 256, 259, 264, 265, 267, 268, 269–270, 286, 288, 289, 296, 298, 301, 303
  *Apprêteuse et garnisseuse (modes), rue du Caire,* 286–287
  biography, 266–267
  *D'Eugène Delacroix au néo-impressionnisme,* 1–3, 36, 48, 255
  diary, 2, 259
  *Gazomètres, Clichy, Les,* 287
  *Passage du Puits-Bertin, Clichy,* 287
Simultaneous contrast, 105, 120, 125, 134, 136, 138, 163, 282, 301
  of color, 20, 27, 30, 82
  of hues, 49
  of values, 20, 83
Sisley, Alfred, 17, 56, 161, 279
Solar spectrum, hues of, 57, 90, 109, 150
Sorbonne, Paris, 188, 189
Subtractive mixture, 8–9, 38, 69, 73, 88, 122, 140, 142, 246, 261–262
Sully-Prudhomme, René François Armand, 191
Suresnes, 285
Surrealists, 256

Sutter, David, 17, 18, 43–47, 106, 107, 135, 199, 207–208, 211, 214, 215, 216, 248, 261, 268, 275–276, 299
  *L'Esthétique générale et appliquée,* 276
  "Les Phénomènes de la vision," 18, 43, 45, 47, 85, 207, 212, 268, 299
  *Philosophie des beaux-arts,* 212, 276
Sutter, Dr. Jean, 266
Symbolism, Symbolists (literary), 253, 288, 292, 296
Symbolism, Symbolists (pictorial), 2, 249, 253, 254

Taine, Hippolyte, 191
Tintoretto (Jacopo Robusti), 273
Tone, division of, 161, 178, 184
*Trois femmes,* 125, 128
Troy University, New York, 273
Turner, Joseph Mallord William, 107, 273

Vauquelin, Louis Nicolas, 270
Velde, Henry van de, 164, 219
Venturi, Lionello, 56
Verhaeren, Émile, 187, 237, 238, 241, 242, 265
Veronese, Paolo, 33, 74, 80, 107, 290
  *Il Calvario,* 80
*Vêtements,* 60
*Vieille femme et nourrice,* 125, 128
Viewing distance, 142, 143, 159–160, 169, 170, 172–175, 177, 179, 294
*Vue du fond avec quelques personnages,* 120, 122–123
*Vue générale, avec groupement de personnages,* 118, 119

Webster, J. Carson, 5, 62
White and black, role of, 95–96
Wundt, Wilhelm, 191, 248

Young, Thomas, 261, 262, 263

Zarlino, Gioseffo, 210
  *Istitutioni Harmoniche,* 210
Ziegler, J., *Traité de la couleur et de la lumière,* 272
Zunbul-Zadé, Vehbi Mohamed, 130–131, 150, 289